"See you at the house."

"See you at the house."

The stories
BOB BENSON
used to tell.

Selected & Edited By
R. Benson

A Solitude & Celebration Press Book
Published By
Generoux
Nashville, Tennessee

First printing November 1986.
Printed in the United States of America

Library of Congress Cataloging in Publication Data
Benson, Bob
  "See you at the house."
  1. Christian life — Nazarene authors. 2. Benson, Bob. I. Title.

ISBN 084-9906-199

This is a first edition.
Distributed to the trade by Word Books, Waco, Texas.

The stories in this book are my father's.
The editor's only claim is
that he loved them and the storyteller
as well as he knew how.

So the stories themselves,
as with each time they were told,
are again dedicated
to Peggy and the five children.
The ones who were fortunate enough
to have grown up together and loved each other,
and put the laughter within the walls
of the places the storyteller first called home.
The storyteller himself would
certainly have chosen to do the same.

Whatever is in these pages
that is fairly an editor's to dedicate
is dedicated to the youngest Robert Green Benson.
The first, but not the last,
of the children who will hear these stories
and know the love they represent.
My house will always be your house.
Until we see Poppa and the Father
at the House.
May you find your own story
and tell it to your children as well.

About The Author.

Bob Benson was born in Nashville, Tennessee in 1930, the son of a religious music publisher, the grandson of a charter member of the Church of the Nazarene. He was educated, for the most part, at Nazarene schools, including the Nazarene Theological Seminary in Kansas City. He was an ordained minister in the church and held pastorates in Florida, Missouri, California, and Tennessee.

In the early sixties, he returned to Nashville and joined his father in the family publishing business. Over the next twenty years, he became one of the Christian world's leading publishing executives. His efforts at The John T. Benson Publishing Company were characterized by a deep sensitivity for the quality of the published product and a pronounced emphasis on the quality of the ministry of the product itself.

Along the way, he came to be highly sought after as a speaker for retreats, conferences, and college campuses because of his warmth, his dry wit, and his keen insight. His unique ability to see the deep spiritual truths in the everyday occurrences of life earned him a place in the hearts of the thousands of people who heard him speak all over the country. As his reputation as a speaker grew, he began to write, publishing six books and a monthly newsletter over the course of his career.

In the late seventies, a sense of calling to spend his days speaking and writing on a full-time basis led him to resign from the publishing company. For a little more than six years, he traveled and wrote.

For many of the country's Christian artists and writers, as well as for pastors and lay leaders everywhere, Bob Benson was a friend, counselor, sounding board, chaplain, fellow pilgrim, and comrade-in-arms in the struggle to punch as many holes in the darkness as they could. He laughed with, created with, argued with, prayed with, corresponded with, and retreated with enough of them to earn a place that few others will ever acheive.

In March, 1986, he finally lost one last battle to cancer, which he had fought valiantly for more than a dozen years. He, of course, would say that he won the war.

Other Books By Bob Benson

Laughter In The Walls
Come Share The Being
Something's Going On Here
In Quest Of The Shared Life
He Speaks Softly
Disciplines For The Inner Life
(With Michael W. Benson)

Table Of Contents.

Introduction.

Everyone, or so it seemed, kept saying the same two things to me after my dad died in the spring.

"I was sure sorry to hear about Bob ..." they would begin. And they were. He had been a friend and brother and leader and borderline guru to a great number of folks.

And then they would say, "I remember the first time I heard him and he told that story about ..."

Most of them had a favorite or two and would spend the next few minutes retelling it in their own way. We almost always ended up laughing our way through our tears or crying our way through our laughter as we remembered the story together.

Whatever else he was—writer, publisher, minister, speaker, churchman, father, husband—he was a storyteller. It was his stories, the way that he told them, and the truth that they revealed, that drew people to him.

What you hold in your hands now is a collection of his best ones.

Some of them are stories that were first whispered to sleeping infants who didn't even know that Poppa was in the room. Some came from times around a noisy family table, the kind you have in a house with five children where the only real rule at mealtime is that everyone has to keep one foot on the floor at all times. A lot of them featured family and friends in the "starring" roles; he used to say with pride that most of what he learned, he learned at home.

Some of them were first told on a telephone from somewhere far away when he would say, " Have you got a second, I gotta tell you what I saw today. It was the neatest thing." I heard a lot of them that way for the first time myself and I know that I wasn't the only one. Some of them were told first in a Sunday School class, where he practiced his stuff on college kids to see if it would hold water out there in the "real" world. Still others just popped into his head, usually when he was speaking somewhere and looking for a closing piece that would help to make a moment happen for those who came to hear him.

Some of them were "stolen" from somebody. He was a serious book-lover and note-taker and was forever quoting someone that most of us had never heard of. He used to have a "three-quote" rule. The first three times that you used someone else's story, you had to give them credit, after that the story was public domain. Since most of us who have known him have stolen his stuff pretty regularly, it has all probably evened out over the years.

Some of them were first told on stages in big halls or big churches in front of hundreds or even thousands of people. Others were shared at close range on a retreat in some state park or district campground where the few who were gathered were close enough to borrow a handkerchief from him when they needed to and they often did.

Sooner or later, all of them—borrowed, stolen, observed, lived out, found, or written — showed up somewhere.

For this collection, some of them were taken from tapes of his sermons or from the books that he wrote or from the newsletter that he published after he left the music company to speak and write full-time. A lot of them are "classic Bob Benson," a term that others applied to them after he had left town and gone to an airport someplace to try and get home to his garden before the weeds took it over. A few of them are new, unheard but by his closest friends.

Nearly all of them are about simple things. The kind of things that you and I see all the time and don't notice as being particularly significant, much less full of deep spiritual truth. But he did. And that was his great gift.

They are grouped together in a way that hopefully lets you see how one thing led to another in his life. I think he would think it's the right thing to do, since he was a believer in the processes of life, in the idea that things lead from one to another until the common threads are bound up together to make a whole.

The first group is about growing up and about his first steps in the life of faith. The second is about the things that he believed about God. His perception of God as Father is critical to understanding the things he said about discipleship, which is the next group. The section that follows is about families and kids and such, and the one that is next is about the church. He carried a burden and a love for both of his "families" that members of either family will find impossible to replace at worst and difficult to go on without at best. The last section is about the last things. A story must have an ending and his has a good one.

As you read along, you'll learn some things about his story. But that is only part of the point and not the biggest part, at that. He didn't tell many stories on himself where he was the hero.

More importantly, I think you will learn some things about your own story. At least that has been true for those of us who heard him and read his work.

There is one Bob Benson story here that you won't find anywhere else. He never had a chance to tell it. That's because it is one he and I whispered back and forth to each other in the spring on one of the last times that I saw him. He might not have ever gotten around to telling it anyway, since he was the hero in it.

Last year, just after Christmas, well before any of us (except perhaps he himself) knew just how ill he was becoming, the family trooped their way up to the Smokies for a belated Christmas vacation together. My dad was always a big vacation planner, usually figuring out a plan that involved several cars and numerous stops for meals and neat little places to stay. Some of our best memeories of "home" didn't take place at home at all, they happened on some beach or in some city far away or beside an interstate highway when we all got so tickled at each other we could hardly stand it. And so we all looked forward to the trip.

He told me later that it really wasn't one of his better outings as a leader. He was tired and anxious about a week-long speaking engagement that was coming up a few days after the trip and he never did seem to get into the spirit of the trip at all. Until we started for the Chimney Tops.

The Chimneys is a peak just outside Gatlinburg that is the first mountain of any sort that I ever remember climbing with dad. It was one of the few, too, since his idea of woodsy was planting a row of something real close to a fence and mine is playing a couple of sets of tennis with a wooden racquet. Dad, my brother Mike, our good friend Bob MacKenzie, and I had climbed the Chimneys together once when I was about twelve.

Since then, I've gone back to the Smokies a lot just to climb the Chimneys. It has always been a special place to me and often in my life I went back there when I was tired or discouraged just to climb up on that rock at the top and feel the wind and think. It turned out that my sister Leigh had been there, too, for the same reasons.

So Dad and Leigh and I set out to climb the Chimneys together. Actually, more climbers than that started out with us. In my enthusiasm, I thought it would be great if Mom, my aunt Bo, my wife Jetta, and Jetta Elizabeth, our one-year-old beginning climber, went, too. Troopers though they were, there was a little more ice and snow still up there than they needed and they headed back. And rightly so. I am still willing to forgive them for muttering under their breath at me on the way down, if they are willing to forgive me for getting them into such a mess in the first place.

But Leigh and Dad and I pressed on. And to be honest it was a struggle for Dad. People with asthma don't always make good climbers and Dad wasn't very strong to boot and so it took us a while in the snow and ice. But we made it.

We didn't stay up there very long, since we had taken most of the afternoon light coming up and we were afraid to let it get too dark before we started back down. But there was time for an apple or two and a candy bar that we had saved for the occasion and so we sat for a few minutes together. Nobody said much, we all just kept grinning at each other. And we snapped what was left of a roll of film that I had, just in case we needed proof later on that we hadn't bailed out along the way.

The next day, we all kind of packed up in a hurry and headed our various ways and a few weeks later, the next time I saw my dad, he had spoken for what was to be the last time and he was about to check into the hospital for what was to be the last time.

I took the pictures we had shot up on the mountain to show dad one night not long after the doctors had gathered us all together to tell us that he wouldn't be coming home to us again. The doctors saw the pictures, too, and couldn't believe that he had even tried the climb much less finished it. I wasn't surprised much. He spent most of his life climbing up one mountain or another—illness, discouragement, rejection slips, business problems, and the stuff that goes with being a parent to five kids.

I could have told the doctors that my dad was always funny like that, he just thought mountains were for climbing. He also thought songs were for singing and hands were for holding and people were for loving and stories were for telling and life was for living. He may not have been here long but he didn't miss much.

I really brought him the pictures because I wanted to be sure that he saw the ones of his granddaughter (and *my* daughter) on her first climb. In a decidedly uncharacteristic move, he kept looking at the ones of himself up on the very top of Chimney Tops. And I watched him while he watched those pictures as though he could still feel the wind on his face and the sweat in his shirt and the mud on his hands and the pain in his chest from the climb.

After a while, he laid his head back on the pillow and held my hand and whispered, "I'm so glad that I climbed that mountain. I'm so glad I made it to the top. It doesn't matter what it cost me. I did make it to the top, didn't I?"

Yeah, Dad, you made it to the top. Again. Get some rest, have another apple or two, and we'll see you at the house.

R. Benson
Hermitage, Tennessee
1 October 1986

Looking For The Threads.

I used to think,
loving life so greatly,
that to die would be like
leaving the party before the end.

But now I know
that the party is really happening
somewhere else.
That the light and the music
escaping in snatches,
to make the pulse beat faster
and the tempo quicken,
comes from another place.

And I know, too,
that when I get there,
the music and the love and the praise
will belong to him
and the music will never end.

Looking For The Threads.

Several months ago, I moved my office across Nashville from Madison to Brentwood. It shortened a journey of some forty miles round trip to one of just over three. Since that move, I have made one more which established my office upstairs in the back of our home. And that turned a three mile trip into a stroll down the hall.

Leaving Madison was kind of a final break with the side of town in which I had lived most of my life. When I was growing up in east Nashville, Madison was just a wide place in the road with a few stores and a theater that showed westerns on Saturday afternoons. However, the five or six mile journey out there held all kinds of adventure, especially if you were riding on your bicycle. Maybe it was partly because I wasn't really supposed to ride my bike on Gallatin Pike anyway.

So it was with some sadness that I drove the rental truck filled with my books, shelves, antique tables, pictures, and John F. Lawhon couch and chair away from the Madison building. But I was looking forward to getting all my stuff set up in my new office, or "office suite" as the landlord had called it when I had inquired about renting it.

I have always loved an office. In our first pastorate after seminary, I could hardly wait to get my office fixed up. However, since the new congregation in Modesto, California, did not have its own building, we had to rent a place to worship. Initially we met in the front of a former feedstore and later on in a community clubhouse. Since neither had office space for a young parson I divided our part of the garage with refrigerator crates to have a place to get up and go to in the mornings. The garage for the duplex had already been divided once and a rising young foot doctor made plaster molds of his patient's feet in the other side of it. It was hot and dusty in the summer and cold and clammy in the winter, but I steadfastly maintained office hours (although it never seemed quite fitting that a fiery young prophet should be preparing his messages in a Kelvinator crate).

So in Brentwood I fell joyfully to the task of unpacking my books and arranging and rearranging the furniture as Patrick (my youngest son) and Patrick (one of his biggest friends) hauled it all up the hall and into my new quarters. I am one of those people who actually likes to shift furniture around. I came by this quite honestly because my mother was and is a confirmed furniture mover. She belongs to the school that holds that furniture was made to be moved and, furthermore, that there is no way of knowing how the piano will look over by the other wall until you move it over there and see. Fortunately, my wife Peggy is a rearranger also. And at the times when it seems as if our lives are sinking slowly away into the doldrums we will often begin our escape by moving the living room furniture around.

When the furniture was all in and the books were back on the shelves it was time to hang my pictures and stuff on the walls. This is a project in itself because over the years I have accumulated an amazing array of things to hang around me.

It is almost as if when we did not know quite what to do with something we just had it framed and put in on the wall somewhere. There are pictures, macrames, paintings, plaques, certificates, diplomas, logos, poems, mottos, awards, cartoons, and a brass plate proclaiming "Confessions Held 5:00 to 7:00 Daily." And now all of these items were clamoring to be displayed in a manner befitting their importance.

The pictures are the easiest to hang because for the most part they aren't of me except in a group or on a team. They are of family and friends at various stages and ages. Then I always hestitate a little with the diplomas and the degrees. They seem a trifle ostentatious, to say the least. Usually, though, my need to appear important overcomes my need to be humble and I mix them in as unobtrusively as I can here and there. As E. B. White has correctly observed, the plaques and trophies give you the most trouble.

In my more reflective moments, I am aware that it is probably a little much for some group or organization to have publicly proclaimed, much less to have engraved in bronze, that I was or am or will be "an outstanding Christian leader" or some other phrase equally heartwarming to me. But they do have a nice ring to them. Since they are impressive metal plaques mounted on rich mahogany-finished bases, it seems a shame to throw them away. And anyway, somebody else said all those things. I just am not sure I ought to keep on posting them since I am so thoroughly familiar with the facts.

When I get all my stuff up, I am home. For they are all mine — collected, framed, bought, received — and they are the things that make a place mine whether it is a refrigerator crate or an "office suite." They are a sort of a running account of the places I have been, the things I have done, the people I have loved, and the gifts from people who have said they loved me.

Somehow all of this, my office and the things occupying its walls, not to mention my heart and all that its surfaces are covered with, came to mind recently as I was reading. And I was reminded that there is an all-pervading purpose around which we may cluster all that we do and say and try to accomplish. I cannot think of anything more frightening about life than to have lived it without any real reason. Certainly I am not alone in wondering about how to find true meaning.

It seems to me that it is possible to find the central thread around which each of our lives is woven. In fact, I believe the longer I live the more it seems that all the places that I have been were indeed heading in one direction.

Even places that at one time looked like detours at best, or dead-end roads at their worst, appear now to have moved me along to where I am.

I Don't Know About My Wellnesses, Either.

My mother, who brought up five children, recently wrote in her memoirs that I was "the only baby she raised who had none of the normal baby ailments." She reported that I "ate what I was fed, digested it, slept well, and was generally happy and a delight." Someone has since pointed out that I was either resting up to be sick from then on, or else I was playing some kind of monstrous trick on my parents, not to mention myself. My dad, who is the family historian, recently said that as far as he was able to determine, I was certainly among the leading contenders for being the sickest of the clan in at least seven or eight generations.

By the time I was four, my brother John was beginning to bring home from school all the common childhood illnesses. In one year alone he spread measles, chicken pox, and mumps through our household. Early on I showed a marked talent for getting sick as soon as the two of them, John and the disease, came in the door. Generally, I was not one to mess around with a mild case either.

When I was six years old or so I came down with severe asthma. This new ability to develop my own diseases marked a turning point in my life. No longer would I have to wait for someone to bring them to me. Ever since that time I have shown a remarkable propensity to come up with illnesses and maladies that are new to the family.

Bronchial asthma is among the most serious of childhood diseases and afflictions. It is baffling and capricious and unlike other illnesses such as scarlet fever or getting your tonsils taken out. You do not just get over it. One never seems to know when another attack is to be forthcoming.

For reasons unknown, asthma is usually a disease of the night, often occurring in the wee hours of the morning. It begins with a tightening of the chest and a dry cough. Breathing becomes more and more difficult until one is panting for air. In fact, the Greek word for asthma is "panting." This is accompanied by a deep wheezing and one is forced to sit up in bed, battling, struggling, fighting for breath with elbows propped on knees, shoulders hunched, and head thrown back literally gasping for air. It is a terrifying experience for a small boy and I suspect it must have been equally terrifying for my young parents.

Mom and Dad would come to me in the middle of the night with the usual treatments. There was the Asthma Nefrin nebulizer with the squeeze bulb that was good at dropping off and rolling under the bed. And there was a greenish powder called Asthmador which you burned in a jar lid so you could inhale the smoke. I would pile it up like a tiny mountain and light it in one spot and watch the flaming sparks spread like a forest fire until it was blackened all over. Hopefully, the rising smoke allowed me enough breath to lie down again and go back to sleep. Asthmador also came in cigarettes and as a mixture for pipe smoking but, of course, I only read about these forms of evil on the side of can.

On cold winter nights when an attack would come and I would be unable to breathe lying down, Dad would build a fire in the fireplace and tuck the covers around me in his big, easy chair. Mom would read to me until I would finally fall asleep again. Sometimes, if the nebulizer or the smoke wouldn't work, they would bundle me up and take me over to Dr. Elliott's house on Eastdale Avenue for a shot of adrenaline.

Between attacks there were trips to all kinds of doctors and specialists with numerous tests to try to determine what was the cause. It was apparent that the fall of the year was the most difficult season for me and that ragweed and other things in the air would give me attacks. I spent many weeks out of school and the home-bound teacher would come to me. Sometimes my mother would take me to North Carolina to see if the mountain air would help. Sometimes we would go to Florida or the Alabama coast to see if the sea air was any freer of the pollens that provoked the attacks. But usually something—dust, pollen, damp night air, changes in temperature, cat fur, dog hair, feather pillows, being at home, being away from home, or some culprit unknown to me—managed to continue to disrupt my life by provoking asthma to "attack" me.

Even when I was feeling well enough to go to school, there were many notes sent along to everybody about how to "take care of Bob." Of course, I was told always to keep my head covered, my sweater on, and my feet dry. Once I remember it started snowing one afternoon while we were in school. The class could hardly wait for the bell to ring so we could get out into the big, moist snowflakes that were already beginning to cover the ground. There was a knock on the seventh grade classroom door and I saw a mother's hand pass a pair of galoshes through the crack in the doorway to the teacher. Being especially susceptible to such protection, I remember thinking how embarrassed some poor kid was going to be. And I can remember even clearer the feeling when Mrs. McDaniel turned to the class and said, "Bob Benson, come get your galoshes."

As you might well imagine, as a father now, I have a much deeper appreciation for my parents' investment in midnight vigils and trips to anywhere there might be help and galoshes when it began to snow during the school day.

I don't always know what to say about my illnesses. As much of the time as we can at our house, we try to laugh about them. Just the other morning Peg remarked that she had a cold and I responded, "I do, too." She accused me of trying to have everything she did. So we decided to divide the diseases. She would have all the minor ones and I would have all the major stuff—the things that really bring out people's sympathy and flowers and cookies and cards. In the case of a brand new disease, I am to get the first option until we find out whether it is going to be major or not.

But then again, I don't know what to say about my wellnesses, either. As surely as I do not understand why I so often have been the one to get sick, neither do I understand why I am the one who has so often gotten well from so many things. But I do believe that something has grown out of both experiences over the years that has enriched the soil into which my faith has sunk its roots.

There was some kind of lesson learned, however faint it might have been when

I was younger. Maybe it was about vulnerability. To be sure, there were mornings when it was nice in a way to be staying home as John and Laura were getting ready for school. But there were other times when I could not help but wonder why I wasn't as sturdy as Bill Hunt or Roland Downing or Mack Parsons who always seemed ready to play in the woods and along in the creek that flowed through our back yard.

Early on, there was a dimly increasing awareness that all was not as it was purported to be. That even though it seemed that most of life's lessons had to do with oneself—self-control, self-development, self-assertiveness, self-preservation—maybe there was something truer to be learned. Life was simple on the surface. One only had to learn to talk, walk, dress, read, write, add, subtract, multiply, divide, ride a bicycle, drive a car, and acquaint oneself with some important, but never again to be used, facts such as Boise is the capital of Idaho and water is one part hydrogen and two parts oxygen. One had to learn to make choices and to make waves and to make a living and then came the rewards—self-confidence, self-support, self-reliance, completeness.

It is a strong theory but it doesn't always test out well when as a kid you wake up in the middle of the night unable to catch your breath. Or later on, in a sort of a mid-life course correction, when a doctor tells you this particular lump is malignant and must be removed. One does not particularly become a theologian at seven (or at forty-two, either) but there has always seemed to be the sound of other meanings coming forth from somewhere back there—a sound that quietly but firmly pointed out that faith would have to find its refuge outside of self. That sound gently but resolutely confirmed that there was One who could gather up the circumstances of our days and use them to his purposes and to our good.

It is partially, at least, from this perspective of illness and wellness that I so strongly see and believe that one can come to know that God is infinitely willing and abundantly able to bring good out of the processes of our lives. Perhaps this is also where I have begun to learn to hear the calling voice of God in the happenings and events of life.

The Cool, Clear Water At Ruskin Cave.

When I was of junior high school age, there was a group of us at the church who had driven several men and women out of the Sunday School teaching profession. One by one, licking their wounds, they had gladly retreated to the peace and quiet of the couples' class.

We met in an old attic classroom that was furnished with seats taken from Nashville's newly defunct street car system. The backs of the seats still moved like they did when the car came to the end of the line. The motorman switched seats, attached the rear power pole, and moved to the other end of the car to make it the front. As soon as the teacher of the junior high class walked to the front of the room, we promptly reversed the seats and left him at the rear of the coach. Finally, my Dad was appointed teacher of the class. That act in itself took care of the behavior of one class member. He promptly went to work on the others.

He suggested that one weekend we go to Ruskin Cave in West Tennessee to camp out. There were some old buildings there which were left over from the days when a college was located there. Dad had attended the school for a year or so and he was anxious to get close to us by taking us through the cave and swimming in Yellow Creek.

The closer the time for us to take the trip came, the less Dad relished going off by himself with that crowd of boys. He invited some of the couples in the church and prevailed on Mom to go along to cook. He persuaded the pastor to come and speak. Ruskin Cave Camp Meeting was born. That camp meeting was only held for a few years but there are some great memories from those days in a lot of people's hearts.

The old hotel, itself an ancient repository of memories, was dilapidated and without furniture or indoor plumbing. Stoves and refrigerators and beds and about everything else had to be hauled down there for the camp. It must have been a tremendous amount of trouble for Dad, and for Mom as well, who was chief cook and bottlewasher. But it wasn't any trouble for me! We held the services in the cave. It was "air conditioned" before anyone knew what air conditioning was.

Over thirty years ago a close friend of mine, Don Irwin, was speaking in the afternoon service. I went forward and knelt in the straw at an old rough bench and dedicated my life to the Lord and to whatever he wanted me to do.

Just outside the cave there was a fountain that just bubbled up all the time with cold, clear water coming out from under that Tennessee limestone hillside. I'm certain that on that hot, dusty August afternoon I got a drink as I went into service and another when I came out. Over the span of those years some wonderful things have happened to me. I have also had some moments of abject discouragement. But the vow I made that afternoon has been lifelong.

In my office I have a collection of Bibles and Testaments on the bottom shelf of my bookcase. All of them together, from the Thompson Chain Reference Edition of the King James Version, through the Phillips, the Revised Standard Version, the New English Bible, and the New International Version, mark my sporadic journeys with the Word for nearly forty years. One of the volumes, now tattered age, is a Precious Promise Testament of the King James Authorized Version with the words of Jesus in red.

I used it in my younger days when I was a new convert and later when I became a student preacher. My first sermon was preached from that little Precious Promise Testament. In its flyleaf, there is a calendar marking some events that occurred in my teenage years. Each was an event that had deep significance in my life.

7/15/46 saved *Tennesse District Camp Meeting*
8/28/46 sanctified *Ruskin Camp Meeting*
8/24/47 called to preach *Ruskin Camp Meeting*
8/26/48 first sermon *Ruskin Camp Meeting*

Each of those notations marks a time at which I heard God speaking to me. I must confess that on each occasion whatever he said came in such a quiet, gentle way that I did not then, and perhaps still don't, fully understand. I only know that they were turning points for me.

On the evening first noted in mid-July of 1946, I do not recall anything that would have even remotely warned me I was going to round a corner that would send me in one direction, however fitfully, for the rest of my life. In all likelihood on that summer night in 1946, Gene Williams, Bill Anderson and I went out to the Trevecca campus to the Tennessee District Campmeeting in the absence of something better to do. It may have been that my Dad, who was the song leader for the meeting, had offered to let us take him home after the service and use the Dodge afterward if we would go and sing in the choir. He had a little Chinese proverb that he often quoted, to me in particular, "No singee, no ridee." But I am quite sure that I didn't join the crowd in the tent pitched on the basketball court next to old Hardy Hall that night with express purpose of "getting saved."

To my recollection, I had never gone forward or made any kind of profession of faith previous to that evening. To this day I cannot remember having even thought about it until the invitation was given that night. Gene had "gotten religion" a Sunday night or so before, and when they sang the invitation song, he asked Bill and me if we would like to go to the altar. I remember he said we could all go down together. The three of us went forward that night for prayer.

I don't recall much about kneeling there with the altar workers who alternated between telling the penitents to "let go" and to "hold on." I don't remember what I prayed and I can't tell you any answers that I heard coming back to me either. For that matter, I couldn't tell you precisely what I heard God say to me at any of the other times that are duly noted in my Precious Promise Testament. And it is certain that the outline for that first sermon has been long forgotten by both the speaker and the hearers. But I do know it was on those occasions I first began to recognize the calling voice of God in such a way that I responded and obeyed.

I don't believe that God suddenly decided that he would speak to me in the summer of my sixteenth year. Rather, long before that night when I "went forward," in ways I cannot even remember and in processes I could not see or even suspect, he had been standing at the door of my heart and knocking so that I might hear and obey his voice.

I have come to know that those brief encounters in the life of a teenager were only the beginnings of his message to me. Those experiences, as important as they were in the directing of my life, were more like the start of a dialogue. It was not as if he had now told me what I needed to know and then just hung up the phone on me. He was not finished with his call for me, he was just beginning. And he still does not seem to be through telling me what he would have me know and do and be.

Looking back across the nearly forty years that have passed since I first responded to the voice I heard, I am aware of coming to places in my life which I never could have imagined. His providences and purposes have steadfastly moved and worked in and around the circumstances of my life. My choices and commitments, sometimes faithful and true, sometimes hazy and weak, have also been ways that his words have been relayed to me. Even now his calling to me is being reshaped and refined. It is as fresh and new as the morning.

My son Tom asked us one night if it is true that God always wants you to do "what you don't want to do the most." I suppose everyone wonders at times if his ways are good ways. Is he really like a shepherd who "leads beside the still waters" or is he some arbitrary crank who has this uncanny way of making pianists play left guard and fullbacks cut paperdolls?

A couple of months ago I was speaking at a retreat in West Tennessee. Tom, Patrick and I took the pickup truck and our Hondas. The retreat site was only about twenty miles from Ruskin, so after the Saturday morning service we drove over to see the old camp meeting site. We walked over the grounds and got a drink from the fountain which was still bubbling forth as crystal clear as ever.

We went into the cave and I showed them how we had set up the chairs and benches to make a place for the services. I pointed out the spot where the choir had stood as Dad led the singing. I showed them the place where I knelt when I made that vow. I told them, as best I could, that just as surely as that fountain still gave forth clear, pure water, his grace and goodness flooded and filled my being that morning just as it had so many years before.

We put on our helmets and rode away. As we did, I was praying that I had answered a little bit of Tom's question. Thirty years—and if it had changed at all it only tasted better.

My Heart Is Hooked On Words.

I was in the sixth grade when I began my first serious writing project. It was a novel set in Canada, and it was as colorful as a red Mountie uniform against the driven snow. My friend, Jimmy Bateman, was my editor-typist.

Jimmy was a seventh grader, but he was old for his age. He was the only kid I knew who had his own typewriter. His hideout was a cabin across the road from his house. The cabin was a half-mile or so away if you went around Brush Hill and down Cedarwood. But I could be there in a couple of minutes by crossing the creek behind our house and following the path through the woods.

In writing my novel I made a concerted effort toward genuine authenticity. I took the names of the characters for my story straight from the Canadian map in the geography book. It was the name of the hero which first became the problem. Jimmy laughed so heartily when he saw it that the book died just as it was beginning to pick up momentum on page four.

I still think "Rupert St. John" is not such a bad name for a Canadian hero. But Jimmy succeeded in driving a promising young writer from the profession. So I was well into my thirties before I really discovered the joy and reward of committing one's thoughts and conclusions to paper.

My interest in putting things in writing was a gift to me from both my parents. I have kept the letters my mother wrote to us when we were away in school and then later in the pastorate. They were usually typed in triplicate. One copy would go to my sister, Laura, who lived in Ohio; another copy to Carolyn, my sister in college in Kentucky; and the third, to Peg and me.

Each of us has claimed that someone else always got the original and we got the carbon. But carbon or not, these letters were a breath of home. Mom's humor, wisdom, and love were captured in her easy, free-flowing style. The words seemed to have tumbled from her typewriter and from her heart.

Pop, my father, on the other hand, is a "working" writer. He edits and reedits and reedits some more. He condenses and lengthens, though usually it is the latter. The process continues until he is satisfied that his words and sentences adequately convey his thoughts and thoroughly describe all the details.

Pop is the historian of the family. Each member of the family has been given a "Benson Book." The 10″ x 16″ leatherette volume is bound so that it can be added to regularly. It contains articles, family charts, and a history of the Benson bunch dating back as far as 1796 when they crossed the mountains from North Carolina to Tennessee.

But the "Benson Book" is far more than a record of the past. It is also a commentary on our present. Pop is a chronicler of our trips and celebrations. He spends hours carefully recording these events and sending along new pages for our books.

My own adventures as a "published" writer began inconspicuously enough. My friend, Walt Moore, editor of our local church paper, asked me to do some writing for *The Nazarene Weekly*. His column, "Around the Corner," is so consistently good from week to week that I really didn't want to be in print alongside it. Finally, I did begin to do some little free verse essays about my my life and my family.He ran them under the title, "Lines To Live By." *The Weekly* was the first place I saw anything of my own in print. And it awakened the long-dormant desire of a would-have-been novelist.

I submitted a few of my early essays to a publisher or two and received encouragement from some and rejection slips from others. One editor sent me two rejection slips at once. He enclosed a note advising me that one was for the present manuscript and the other was for my next effort. But, eventually, these essays grew into a book and were published under the title *Laughter In The Walls*.

A second book grew out of my studies for the college class at the church and our discussions on Sunday mornings. During this time I began to travel and speak some on weekends at retreats and conferences and I gathered my thoughts for another year or two and in time they, too, became a book.

In one way I am always ready to write another book. I make it a habit to jot down words, phrases, and thoughts—the things I have heard or read or which come to me from time to time. Sometimes I scribble them down in church and sometimes while I'm traveling and almost anywhere in-between. I'm not always prepared for this spontaneous note-taking and so I use whatever is at hand—ticket envelope, calling card (mine or yours), laundry claim stub, boarding pass, or paper napkin.

I stuff this assortment of memos and notes in my coat pockets. At the end of the day, or at least before sending the suit to the cleaners, I will lay them on top of the counter in the bathroom. When Peg cleans, she puts my "research" into the top right-hand drawer, which she has reserved for this very purpose.

When the drawer is full, she will transfer the contents to a storage file that looks remarkably like a grocery bag. When I have accumulated about three bags full, I begin to think that it is time to write again.

And so, a bag at a time, I have come to be a purveyor of words, a dealer in ideas and phrases. I am a speaker and a writer, a user of words, a bearer of truth. Words are the tools of my chosen craft and trade—or maybe the tools of the craft that has chosen me.

I go from town to town searching for people to hear my words. Each evening they come—kindly, expectant, appreciative groups—to listen to this merchandiser of words. There is one problem that often occurs. It is that the crowds are too small. Now I don't mean that I have to have big audiences. I'm willing to run my words through their paces practically anywhere. That's not it. It is just that bigger audiences are safer. In a small group, you see, there is time to learn about the hurts and hopes that go along with the names. And in small groups I become more and more aware of how deep the need is for my words to be true.

I cannot just express my opinions or share a collection of jokes and stories. So I find myself carefully going over my words in my room before I speak in the hope they will deserve being heard. Sometimes my words have needed to carry comfort and assurance and guidance to an eight-year-old boy whose mother just up and left the weekend before with another man. Sometimes they need to be said to a dedicated young lady who desperately wants to serve people but who is out of work. Once they were to a young professional whose wife died of cancer a few days before he was licensed to practice. There are times when I do not seem to have as many words at my command as I would like to have.

I am a writer of words, too—an author of published works, if you please. Being a lover of books, I was overjoyed one afternoon to see in the block next to where I was staying a three-story building that was labeled, THE BOOK EXCHANGE—THE SOUTH'S GREATEST BOOKSTORE. As soon as I could, I made my way into its shelf-lined innards. I don't believe I have ever seen as many books for sale in one place in my life. I was almost mesmerized there were so many! There were new ones, old ones, used ones, discontinued ones, culls, cutouts, and seconds on what must have been very conceivable subject from every conceivable viewpoint.

"So you want to be a writer," I mumbled to myself. "And just where in this vast graveyard of author's aspirations would you like for the remainder editions of your words to be placed? On the second floor in the section marked Divinity Suitdents? Or maybe down below in one of the many rooms through which the general reader can browse for bargains? Or to save the embarrassment of seeing the $7.95 crossed out on the dust jackets of your learned tomes and 75 cents penciled in, you prefer to continue to buy them all yourself and keep force-feeding them to your garage until somehow it finally regurgitates them all?"

A dealer in words? Why not automobiles, or lamps, or trees, or bedsheets, or anything but words?

Because my heart is hooked on words.

I Likes To Be Chose.

"You did not choose me. I chose you." (John 15:15.)

I have come to the place where I dread to travel. When I know that I am going to be leaving home on Friday morning, I start getting homesick on Wednesday. On Thursday night Peg always asks if I am going to pack my suitcase before I go to bed. But just in case the thing is cancelled and I will not have to go, I wait until I get up on Friday to pack.

And Peggy will say to me, "Why are you going?"

"Well, I told them that I would come, so I guess I will."

"Why did you tell them that you would come?"

"Because I was chosen."

In recent days it seems so very obvious that not only have I been chosen, but also protected and spared. We were playing the little "Why are you going?" game one night not too long ago, and Peggy said, "You have to go."

"Why do I have to go?"

"You were chosen."

Now I know that I am an improbable choice. You certainly cannot tell why I was chosen by observing me. And if you use me as an example, it will be clear that the process by which God chooses men cannot be understood by looking at the *choosee.*

In the first place, I have consistently managed to be smaller than my contemporaries. One hundred forty-five pounds or so looks as if it is going to be it. And it is stretched over a frame that seems to be going from five-foot-ten and three-quarters back to five-foot ten. I did get up to one hundred sixty-three pounds once. But I looked like a squirrel with acorns in its jaws. After my recent illness, Tom looked at my legs as I came out of the shower and called me Olive Oyl. In heaven, if I could be about six-foot-two and weigh around two hundred thirty-five, I would be willing to let someone else have my wings and I'd probably throw in my harp to boot.

I was always a frail kid. I can remember when we used to go out to recess in grammar school. The two biggest and strongest kids in the class were always made captains of the softball teams. Usually they made themselves pitchers of the teams first, and then they picked the rest. One by one each kid was chosen—for athletic prowess, for friendship, for size—until everybody was on a team. Well, almost everybody.

"The game can't start until someone takes Bob," the teacher would insist.

And one of the captains would kick the dust and say in disgust, "We'll take him."

And I was usually sent to play behind the right fielder. I don't think I came up to bat until I was in the eighth grade. I wasn't too surprised to strike out then.

So, I likes to be *chose.*

In addition to not being very big, I have a very, very soft speaking voice. And a most disconcerting habit of lowering my voice even further when I get to something that I really want to emphasize. People often come up when I finish speaking and say to me, "I couldn't hear more than about half of what you said tonight."

"If you tell me the half you heard, I'll tell you the other half again," is my reply, and it usually turns out they can't even remember the half they heard.

I think of Moses who, incidentally, probably did talk loud. He was instructed by God to turn aside and see the burning bush. God did not tell him to scream and jump over the bush. He told him to take off his shoes because he was on holy ground. Holy ground makes me quieter than ever.

It is fun to observe people when I am first introduced and begin to speak. It seems that they are saying to themselves, "Well, I can hardly hear him, so I will try to read his lips." And then they notice that I do not move my lips very much, either. When you don't talk any louder than I do, you don't have to move your mouth very much. The words just sort of sneak out. My speech teacher told me that I had lazy lips.

Further, I am a shy person who does not initate conversations with strangers. I am not even noted for talking to those I do know. If you rode from here to Tallahassee beside me on a bus, I probably would not say much more than "Good morning" unless you happened to be sitting on my hat. To say the very least, I am not noted as a brilliant conversationalist.

If you add it all up, and it doesn't take long, I'm not the most impressive speaker you've ever seen. The other day somebody was saying, "Where is the speaker?" I didn't mind that too much because it was before the service. It happened again a little bit later and this time it was more humbling. Because this time I had just finished speaking.

And when you think of a rather shy little man with a quiet voice and lazy lips climbing on a plane to travel across the country to get up in front of a group of total strangers to talk to them, it does seem far-fetched.

So, I understand easily why it appears that I am both an implausible and illogical choice. I can only say that if it seems that way to those who know only a little about me, think how much more it is to me knowing all that I know about me. Fortunately my being chosen does not grow out of me, I am just a *choosee*.

The answer must be found in the heart of the *Chooser*. It was not something in me that made him call me. It was something in him. It began in his love for me. And that is why these words of Jesus have such a lovely sound, "You did not choose me. I chose you."

It was not that I came upon Jesus Christ and, when I saw him, something within me ran out to meet him and, holding on to him, begged him to lift me out of myself and make me the person of my dreams. It was that he came upon me. His heart rushed out to me. He held on to me. He said he would make me the person that I wanted to be. He saw me. He loved me and chose me. I didn't find him. He found me.

I heard a story the other day about being chosen. Someone asked another person if he would help him out on a project. He responded yes.

"I think it is only fair that I tell you that you were my second choice," replied the first, maybe with more honesty than was called for.

"Well, that's all right," the willing worker said, "but just out of curiosity, who was your first choice?"

"Anybody," was the reply.

But I wasn't chosen as a replacement for someone who didn't want to serve. I wasn't asked to play in the field someone was already covering. He saw me, he called me, he selected me, he picked me, he singled me out, he decided on me, he opted for me, he fixed upon me, he determined in favor of me, he preferred me, he espoused me. *He chose me.*

He did not refuse me, he did not reject me, he did not repudiate me, he did not spurn me, he did not dismiss me, he did not exclude me. He did not ignore, disregard, cast away, throw aside, or leave me out. *He chose me.*

It was not obligatory, mandatory, required, called for, deserved, necessary, imperative, compulsory, or forced. *He just chose me.*

It was his open, voluntary, willful, selective, deliberate, intentional choice. *He chose me.*

Out of his devotion, fondness, adoration, tenderness, affection, attachment, emotion, sympathy, empathy, and love, *he just chose me.*

And that has made all the difference in my life.

Non-Answer Answers.

There was a time when we won all our wars.

And there was a time when we came home proudly because we won them for the right reasons. Some where along the way, in a restaurant or at a peace conference, someone took away our white hat. They may have taken it inadvertently, but it is gone.

Drugs were once just a problem on some university campus a thousand miles away. We thought someone in charge ought to do something about it. Somehow, now the Board of Education can't seem to solve that same problem in the grammar school we pass on our way to work each weekday.

Divorce used to be "out there" in society. Oh, we all had an uncle who was divorced. But he was never really part of the family, so divorce was actually "out there." But somehow it has slipped "in here." "In here" in our churches and "in here" in our homes.

Just about the time we felt that we were getting a reasonable grip on the answers to life, someone began to come up with a whole new list of questions.

Suddenly we have become very interested in answers. We want to learn how to be total women or our own best friend or better managers or more fulfilled or less empty or something. Almost anyone or any book that comes along and remotely suggests that we can find out how is going to have a wide reception these days.

The answers can come in a variety of ways.

There are the *answer answers*. They come in three or four steps. We are told that there are certain basic steps to a particular goal. One must first do A, then B, and finally, C. If this is done in proper order, then D always happens. If we persist in attempting to stumble from B to A and then to C, well, sorry, but D will elude you.

Taken in exact order, however, the steps always work. Jump hurdle number one. Stride briskly forward and jump number two. Move straight ahead over number three. You will arrive precisely in the place you intended to go. No backing up three spaces. No going directly to jail. No paying rent on Park Place. No lost luggage and no late arrivals. Do it right the first time and you will always get there. There are a lot of people who live like that.

But there are some of us who have this strange bent of mind which leads us to doubt that many things "always happen." We prefer to get our help more on a *non-answer answer* basis. We want to hear from someone who admits that he is a fellow struggler. We listen more attentively to someone who is actually plodding along beside us. Since we have not established many absolutes or automatics, we are uneasy when the *answer answer* people shout back to us about how easily they outdistanced us.

We *non-answer answer* people like to hear someone who tells how he crawled under the first hurdle, admits that he was helped over the second by a compassionate friend, and frankly confesses that he fell over the third one. That account sounds more realistic. It certainly seems more likely the way life comes to us.

All of this brings me to an irreverent thought—which I am sure I should be squelching instead of committing to paper. If there are three basic Biblical steps to success in specific areas of life, I am a bit puzzled about the reason God chose to put one of them on page 272 of the Bible, one on page 312, and the last on page 104. That just seems like a funny way to list a set of absolutes.

I think there are two very heartening things about our day. First, we are all admitting we need some answers. That in itself is encouraging.

We are asking. We are seeking. We are knocking. Because of our training or background or personality or a combination of these and other things, we ask in different ways. But we are asking.

But it also is true that just as surely as we are looking in different ways, answers are coming to us in a diversity which reflects the mystery of God himself. The wonderful thing is that he is making certain that we are receiving and that we are finding and that doors are being opened to us.

I have found that searching for answers is almost as much fun as knowing them. Well, almost.

"If You Had More Time, Bob."

"If you had more time, Bob, we could be together more."

"Well, yes, Lord, we could. But I'm president of the company—a ministry-oriented company. And I have a big family. I travel and speak a lot on weekends for you. The company is growing and needs much attention from me. These are not easy days in which to live, much less make a company grow. I'm having a hard time keeping it all together."

"I know, I'm not trying to crowd you. And I'm not trying to add to your burdens. I do not want to make it harder for you. I was just reminding you that if you had more time, we could be together more."

For as long as I can remember I have sought the good and the sunshine in life's moments and have found the enjoyment which they brought. Even though I cannot always explain or reflect the depth of my feelings, they are there.

Recently, the kids and I took Peggy out for dinner to celebrate Mother's Day. We were all dressed up. Tom and Patrick and I were in coats and ties; Leigh and her mother were in lovely summer dresses. It was a fine restaurant with linen and silver and china and crystal and fresh flowers on the tables. The courses were served and in-between we had time to laugh and talk and listen to the background music being played softly on the piano. It was a lovely evening for me and I used a phrase to describe my feelings for them: "I'm keyed," meaning only to say how proud I was of all of them and how much it meant to me to be with them. But the words, *I'm keyed,* are words the boys use when they are talking about winning ball games or band contests, connoting excitement and laughter. And when they looked at me sitting at the head of the table quietly and with as much dignity as I could muster, they all burst into laughter. In the candlelight they could not see the tears in my eyes. I did not seem to be able to look keyed but I was keyed that night.

Thus, a part of my appreciation for the good which moments bring has come from awareness and recognition. But it has also come from a corresponding sadness which arises from their passing. When something that can never quite be reenacted, even as ordinary an event as a Mother's Day meal, comes to an end (and all moments are that way), I feel a pensiveness within. This pensiveness gives my life a quality that might be best described as bittersweet. And those moments take on double meaning and richness—because they are here now and because they will not always be.

I can remember these mixed feelings from very early in my life. My dad was always a trip-planner and there were vacations in the summers to places like Carolina, Florida, and once as far as Yellowstone National Park. But none of them hold the place in my memory of the fity-or-so-mile trips down to Ruskin Cave combination church retreat and camp meeting for the last ten days of August.

I have no happier boyhood memories than those of Ruskin. Drinking at the fountain, bathing in the creek, playing volleyball, listening to Brother Raymond, and kneeling in the straw around the altar—all flood my mind with joyful recollection.

But I also remember the last Monday mornings, usually falling on Labor Day. Our family and a few others stayed to help pack up the gear for another year. I would walk across the now-silent grounds, past the empty sidewalks and ball-fields. No screams of delight and shock were heard from divers plunging into the cold, clear swimming hole. Chairs were folded and the straw was swept up. The cave auditorium yawned still and quiet. Even then, in my early teens, I somehow knew that moments come and then they go and one is left rejoicing and wondering. Rejoicing in what had been and wondering if he had heard all the music there was to hear and should he have joined in the singing.

But moments are not so important to young men, for they also hear voices that tell them there is always time. They are told, and they tell themselves, that any-thing which they miss now can be seen or enjoyed later when it comes again. I don't have to tell you when I was born because only an older man would write—*Moments come and moments go, but they are never repeated.*

And so it was to this part of me his words, "If you had more time we could be together more," began coming and calling to what might be. But it was not only his voice I heard. The call came not from one, but from all the places of my life.

Nearly thirty-four years before, I had heard him say, "Follow me." Even then the words were not written in the sky. But I had started out, as best I knew, to live in answer to their claim on me. They had taken me to college and to seminary and into the pastorate. There had been little groups of people in tiny churches in Tennessee and in Missouri while I was in school and then California and Florida when I had graduated. My inability to shepherd those churches into growth finally brought me to discouragement and resignation. Peg and I had two little boys by then and we put all our stuff in a trailer and headed home to Nashville.

Twenty years had sped by. My dad had made a place for me in the family music business. In those early days there were only five of us in one office, but the busi-ness had grown and expanded far beyond everyone's fondest dreams and expecta-tions. Meanwhile, Peg and I had built a house by the lake, and three more children had come into the family.

For a long time after we returned to Nashville, I thought the business was only temporary for me and that the call would come and we would again go to pastor. But the phone had not rung and over the years other ways to follow him had seemed to open up through the company and in the church where we had been reared.

The very busyness of the present was gently reminding me of this. By all odds my life was like that of any other business person caught in a struggle to reach the top and to remain there, or to acknowledge and accept the fact that he'll never be there. Though we may have the youth and strength to accomplish many things, we do not have the time. A business is a jealous mistress, demanding every wak-ing hour. And even if at last she does decide to let you go home, it is with a brief-case jammed with papers and a mind overflowing with concerns.

The busyness of the present was also saying to me, "If you had more time there are walks to take, people to know, poems to write, things to be, and truths to learn. If you only had more time..."

The stepping stones that lead through the jumbled maze of my life—the people I have met, the things that have happened to me, the events that have occurred around me, and the roads that I have both taken and not taken—all lead in the same direction. And these rites of passage or rituals of transformation are becoming more readily visible to me.

There was a time when I could not see some of them for the tears. Sometimes I was so filled with impatience and frustration I refused even to look. It seemed to me that more than one thing was leading me away from the pathway which I thought I had been chosen to follow. It was easy for me to use such labels as *interruption, detour, setback, tragedy, misfortune,* and *unfair.* But when I look back now at the pathway which brought me here, everything seems to have served a common purpose. And in its way, whether by resistance or by aid and comfort, it has led me to this present place. And while there are places to which I would not choose to return, there isn't anywhere I wish I had not gone. For each of them brought something to me which has become a part of what I bring to today.

Indeed, it is true that the deepest and most precious truths that are mine to enjoy and express have often come to me on the wings of things I did not choose. One of the deepest lessons we learned as a family came tagging along with a very serious illness.

And that illness just came upon us. A routine test brought the word *cancer* into the vocabulary of our immediate family. With it came all the fear and uncertainty that word has the power to evoke. But it also brought a genesis of closeness which we had not known before. It turned our focus to the deepest values in life and in each other.

I began this book in our old house by the lake and as I was writing these lines, Tom and Patrick were coming down the driveway from school. I raised the window to wave to them from my study over the carport. They shouted back to me and started across to the house. Leigh had just come in from college for the weekend and she ran out of the house to meet them. As I watched from above, they ran into each other's arms under the basketball goal. It was a lovely scene for a father to remember. Our acquaintance with the specter of separation brought new meanings to our reunions.

And this inner realization that there was a thread that bound my life into a whole was also saying to me, "If you had more time..." This increasing certainty that my life is headed somewhere was calling me into the presence of the One who both knows and controls its direction.

There is one other significant place from which the voice was speaking to me in addition to the busyness of the present and stepping stones of the past. Gradually it came to be decision time.

Leigh said it for me.

She hadn't been sixteen very long when she announced to the family that she was going steady. Well, she told her mother and the rest of us found out. She had been dating this guy for a little while, but now it was official. She had the class ring with all the tape to prove it.

What a fine romance!

Leigh was happy because she had a boyfriend. Peg was happy because he was a courteous, fine-looking boy with good manners, who spent part of each visit to our house showering his attention on Leigh's mother.

And I was happy, too, because he lived fifty miles away and could only come to see Leigh once a week. Phone calls were long distance, so even they were few and short. What a fine romance. It was all a dad could hope for if his only daughter insisted on having a boyfriend.

She was happy. He was happy. Peg was happy and I was happy. Everybody was happy. Everybody except one football player who had been in school with Leigh since they were in fifth grade.

He had been there the first day she had worn her braces to school. He had been there many, many months later when they were gone and she had a set of lovely, straight teeth behind her smile. He had been there the first morning she had worn her glasses and also the day she had put them aside for contacts. He had watched as her mother finally gave up on the short, easy-to-fix hairdo and as Leigh's face was framed by long tresses that spilled over her shoulders. For some reason, *he* was not happy.

"What a waste, Leigh. You are just too young to go steady," said the football player. "It's all right to date that old boy once a week, but there are six other nights. To sit home all week. What a waste! You are just too young to go steady."

Sooner or later Leigh and the tall, dark, and largely absent boyfriend did decide to stop going steady and be "just friends." As soon as the football player heard this news, he asked her for a date. On the first date he asked her to go out the next night. On the second night he said to her, "Will you go steady with me?"

"No," she replied.

"Be *my* steady girlfriend," he urged.

"I can't be yours. I just got myself back."

Leave it to your children to put big, complicated things into short, simple words. What I had to do was to "get myself back."

So, a few days after my forty-ninth birthday, I was up early and seated in my big, brown, tweed, swivel chair. My thoughts were about as scattered as the books and papers in front of me on the antique walnut table that served as my desk. It was a time for thinking and reflection on this last long holiday weekend before the summer ended. And I welcomed the peace and quiet of my study.

Slowly I had been becoming more and more aware of the inner continuity of my life, of its movement and flow, and of the almost imperceptible signs of changes in direction. But changes and decisions do not come easily to me.

The years had brought peace and prosperity to us. There had been some illness and some darkness, too, which gave us some appreciation of the sunshine. They had also brought an accumulation of responsibilities and pressures that now seemed to fill my every waking hour with activity and concern.

And out of all the past and the present, I seemed to be hearing a familiar voice saying words that I had heard before. They were calling for a new commitment to an old invitation. The words were *"Follow me."*

Two words that are simple enough to be understood and obeyed in an instant but also words that are so rich and deep that one may easily spend his whole life with them as his guide and never know all their significance. And these were the words that were coming to me on that end-of-a-summer morning. All about me, almost within my vision, were the things I knew best and loved most. I picked up my pen and a pad and began to write — to myself, to my family, and to him.

"... I believe I must turn a corner. This day I am going to write the letter that starts the process of problem-solving — extricating, admitting defeat, winning, losing, or whatever is involved. I pray that it will be in an honest desire to let the deepest messages of my life be that I live my life with an 'open hand.' For I hear the words of Jesus, "What does all that matter to you? Follow me."

I do not want to try to overdramatize my decision. I know that resigning from a publishing company is a long way from nailing theses on the door at Wittenburg. But it was a turning point for me. It was an acknowledgement, an affirmation that more than anything else I wanted to answer the call of that old invitation.

I wish now that I had written a book or two that afternoon. What I was going to do is probably more impressive than what I've done. But it was to be a fresh start for me. And I believe that at least part of the great beauty hidden in the words, *follow me*, is the insight that every day, every hour, and every moment provides a chance to begin again. And most of us have a deep need to find the way and the place to start over.

In the intervening months I have found that I have followed the pathway with broken and uneven steps. There have been warm, happy days and there have been unvolunteered for weeks in the hospital. There have been mornings in the study when ideas and insights came to me in my own words and I was so moved by them I could hardly scribble them down. And I have also written down words that were so dull and dry and devoid of ideas that they seemed to blow off the page before I could get to the end of the sentence.

There have been the beginnings of a new richness in our family relationships that the simpler, slower pace has brought, although even before the letter my family surrounded me with love and support. Still, at times, my quest has come so close to selfishness that Peg kindly but aptly remarked, "It is hard to live with a saint." And the earnestness in her voice, lightly disguised with humor, made me know she was not talking to one.

Life has come along with its usual mixture of the good and the bad and the monotonous. As usual, I am not sure that I even knew which was which at the time. But I have reaffirmed some things that I have known for a long time but tend to forget.

One of those is that the quest, the quest for a share life with him, is just what the word implies. It is always a quest. The shared life is not a destination, it is a journey. It is not an arrival, it is a departure.

"What Are You Trying To Say?"

I'm sure she meant something different.

Her question went deeper than just what we were talking about at the moment. I was familiar with her question. I think I see it all the time on people's faces when I'm speaking. She asked me point-blank, "What is it that you are trying to say?"

The query came at the end of an interview for a radio program. I'm not always as excited about being interviewed as I might be. Maybe it is because I am basically a private person. But partly it is because it always seems to me that the questions are rather mundane and so I end up giving what seems to me mundane answers. Thus neither one of appears as witty and intelligent as we both undoubtedly must be.

This interviewer was good at her job, though, and I was stimulated both by the perceptiveness of her inquiries and the depth and brilliance of my responses. I was almost disappointed when she indicated that there was only this one final question she wanted to ask before turning off the tape machine. "What is it that you are trying to say?"

I don't think I had ever tried to answer this question in a brief sentence or two. Or even in a paragraph. I must have thought of it before because lurking somewhere in the back of my mind there was an answer. Apparently it had just been waiting for an invitation to come out. Especially for all those folks out in radioland. So out it came. I don't know who was the most surprised when it did, the interviewer or the interviewee. But in just seven concise, well-chosen words I gave my response.

It was a sort of mission statement for me. Now I would remind you that a mission statement is not as easy to come by as you might imagine. Once I spent the better part of a night with the senior management staff of the music company trying to put into words how we felt the mission of the business could best be defined. Such a statement, when properly worded and authentic, can help direct a company into future endeavors, as well as help indicate some areas from which time and capital should be withdrawn.

So here I suddenly was with my mission statement expressing the fundamental, underlying truth of all I want to do and to be. I wonder if you, given the challenge, could tell the rest of us the one thing that you would like us to remember about your life?

When I realize now that I can express in as few as seven words the deep foundational truth of my life, I wonder what I am doing writing another book. Why don't I just put out a new bumper sticker or get the government to issue a new postage stamp with my message emblazoned on it? When I tell people in the first service of a retreat or conference that I can express all I really need to say to them in a single sentence, I can almost hear them thinking, "Well, why don't you just go ahead and say it and get it over with and then we can go out and play golf or go shopping?" I usually tease them for a little while but in the end I always tell them.

The truth is, though, when I get ready to say the seven words I always seem to feel the need to digress and first tell everyone what those seven words have come to mean to me and how they have changed my life. Then I get to telling stories I have heard or read about other people who have come to believe the same things and it takes me awhile to say my seven words. In fact, I can usually use about as much time as the listeners will allow.

Even at the risk of your reading them and putting the book back on the counter, I am going to go ahead and tell you my seven words. Because if you begin to truly believe them, I will have said enough to you anyway. My words are: *God has something to say to you!*

Of course, I am hoping that you realize that these seven words are much more profound than they first appear to be. And I am hoping that you will want to discover what else I have to say about them. I do have lots to say and many stories to tell. But all the things I believe begin here. Nothing is more important to me than believing that God is a God who speaks to us. If you will read on, then I will tell you how I have come to believe this so strongly and what I think it can mean to you, and to me.

The Things I Believe.

The Things I Believe

I've lain in the grass on a soft spring morning
with life chirping and buzzing about me
and these were the things
I said to the buttercups and the crocuses
and sang to the robins.
I've walked into a dimly-lit room at night
illuminated only by the rays of a Donald Duck night light
and these were the things
I whispered over the sleeping forms
of my little boys.
I was out to the edge for a moment once—
out where they say you have something
we don't have a cure for—
and faced with the separation from loved ones,
with uncompleted tasks and unfulfilled dreams
these were the things that brought me
warm hope and comfort.
These are the things that I believe about God.

I'm more than just toenails and whiskers and elbows
and a social security number

way down deep inside these things pull me together
and make me a "me."
I am the measure of the truth that I have adopted
and I have believed these things
until there is no distance between me and them.
One by one, I have stripped away doubts
and questions
until I have possessed these truths
and they have possessed me.

And if you could put your ear
up tight against my heart
when trials and darkness have stilled me to a whisper
or if you were there when joy burst forth
in such a loud song that you had to back away—
these are the things that you would hear
from my voice and
from my very being.
These are the things that are really me,
they are the things that I believe about God.

Center Court.

I know that it's not quite "cricket" to respond in a book to thoughts shared in an intense, private conversation. But maybe if the friend remains anonymous (and maybe if it is apparent that his question really belongs to all of us), I will be forgiven. I am just commiting to paper the things that I have been thinking and the things I wish I had thought to say at the time.

We were at a retreat surrounded by songs, scripture study, affirmation, and prayer, things that were laden with meaning for many of us there. But my friend was not feeling very religous and none of the things that were moving and touching the rest of us were making him feel anything at all. He confided that this frightened him.

I hastened to say that straw and altars and retreats and campmeeting singing had been a part of some of our lives for a long, long time. Meanings had accumulated around them for us until they are almost sacraments to us. But I could remember kneeling in the straw at an altar just like the one at which we were bowed. I had been sixteen at the time and I had stood up and gone out into the darkness dry-eyed and somewhat bewildered. But the decision I had made changed my life from that night forward.

Then came his wistful words that carried with them the longing to be aware of the presence of Christ, to know him in some deep way. "I just wish I could play tennis with him some afternoon," said my friend.

It's an old, old idea to think that it would be a lot easier to believe in God if you could see him. How do you explain that a God you cannot see is more real than one of whom you can take a picture? And how do you tell someone about a voice that cannot be audibly heard, yet conveys more truth and meaning than all the sounds that crash in on us all the time?

How does one explain the simple but astonishing claim, "I know whom I have believed and am persuaded that he is able to keep that which I have committed unto him until that day"? How does one go about proving the reality of the kingdom?

Maybe it would help to begin with our definition of what *real* is.

Real has come to mean something we can see, or touch, drive, eat, listen to, or wear. So we think that tennis is real. There is a racquet that we can hold, a ball we can hit (or miss), sounds we can hear, lines we can contest, courts we can mark off to run, stumble, or fall on, and rules we can print and read and jump up and down and scream over. (You have correctly observed that I have been watching John McEnroe.) Tennis matches can be watched and played and won and lost. So it must be a real game. But we have to be careful about our standards for real.

To believe that the invisible intangibles are really the enduring essentials is not the way we ordinarily think about things. It is a dramatic reversal to try and comprehend that if we can wear it, drive it, dance to it, drink it, touch it, count it, draw interest on it, live in it, or have it appraised, it is not essential. It will not endure.

To begin to recognize that the intangible world is indeed the deepest reality, one must begin to remember that values, honesty, faith, love, trust, hope, dignity, purpose, character (none of which can ever be seen with our eyes or held in our hands) are the real realities of our lives. Their true realness can be seen in their power to mold us when they are embraced. And it may be seen just as surely from the emptiness that results when we disdain them.

Maybe we need to know, too, that the reality of the kingdom is a discipline that can be learned. One must submit to its demands.

Tennis takes a racquet, a ball, shoes, a court, some skills, some energy, some aching muscles, some winning, some losing, and some recovery shots for match point after four hours in the afternoon sun. One doesn't get a racquet for his birthday and enter the U.S. Open. To get to know God also requires some time, some listening, some quiet, some discipline, some desire, however faltering our ways of hearing may seem to be at first.

The longing in our hearts is already the faint perception of the voice of God calling us. We could begin to acknowledge him even if it were only to ask him for some little thing that only he could give, some direction, some sense of purpose or inner help by which only we would know something had been accomplished. Maybe a simple "answer-me-if-you-are-there" kind of prayer is what we need to pray.

So I guess I really want to answer the longing, haunting questions of my friend. Is there anybody on the other side of the net? Will the ball come bouncing back to me if I smash it across the net? If I throw prayers into the sky, will words come raining down around me?

With all my heart, I want to tell him that it is his serve. Go ahead and hit the ball. The silence will speak to you. The unseen will appear. The untouchable will grip you. The hidden will become visible. The unreachable can be reached.

God has something to say to you and you can hear him if you listen.

He Speaks To Us.

And he opened his mouth and taught them... (Matthew 5:2)

These eight words come to us as one of the most profound announcements that we will ever hear. There is not a greater revelation that this. He talks to us. He will teach us.

And since it has become known that God is a God who talks, it is easy to put words in his mouth.

I spent the other day with David and Dana Blue. They had just returned from singing up in Canada and only had a day or so in town before heading out again to Ohio to lead the music in a campmeeting. Dave was telling me a story they had heard recently in a campmeeting.

One of the speakers had brought along his four-year-old grandson. One evening the little boy had misbehaved nearly the entire time his grandfather was preaching. The next morning at the breakfast table the grandfather was telling how he had handled the situation when they had gotten back to the cottage.

"I don't know what your mother and daddy would do about this, but I will tell you what I am going to do. You go into the bedroom and I do not want you to come out until you have talked to God about your conduct and until he has talked to you about it. Do you understand?"

"Yessir," was the tearful reply, and he made his way into the bedroom.

After awhile the granddad began to think that perhaps he had been a bit hard on his grandson and he went into the bedroom and asked, "Have you told God about it?"

"Yes, sir," the answer came out between the sniffles.

"And has he talked to you?"

"Yes, sir," was again the sorrowful answer.

"Well, what did he say to you?"

"God told me you aren't even saved!"

This reminded me of a story I've heard Joy MacKenzie tell about being raised in a rather strict parsonage. I never met her father but I did become well acquainted with her mother. And knowing her it was not hard to believe that she was a dedicated minister's wife who sought to make the preacher's kids living examples of the claims of the gospel.

The children were not allowed to go to the movies and the reason given probably still has a lot of validity even today. One was not to use their money to support Hollywood and its warped values and loose morals. Growing up in a small town, it was often hard for the "P.K.'s" to explain to their friends the logic and implications of such a stand.

One day Paul, Joy's younger brother, heard that free tickets to the latest Walt Disney picture were being given away at the grocery store. Very soon he and all his friends had availed themselves of the unexpected largess. Paul ran triumphantly into the house proclaiming at the top of his voice, "Mother, Mother, I can go to the movies! And I won't be supporting them with my money, either. The ticket is free. They gave it to me at the store."

His mother, momentarily taken back by this seemingly unassailable logic, decided to spiritualize the matter. "Paul, you go upstairs and pray about this. You ask Jesus what he would have you do about this free pass to the picture show."

Joy, listening from the kitchen, was immediately sure that her mother had painted herself into a corner. For implied in her mother's instructions, at least to Paul, was that if it was all right with Jesus, it was all right with her.

Paul climbed the steps three at a time and it hardly took him a second to storm the portals of heaven and receive the answer to his prayer. Bounding back down the stairs he announced the happy news. "He said I could go! He said I could go!"

It didn't take his Mom much longer to see there were only two possible anwers, either Paul had misunderstood what Jesus had said or else Jesus was wrong this time. And you can believe that she concluded the fault to Paul. "What were his exact words to you?" was the question she pointedly asked him. And Paul knew he had been flanked.

"She won't let me go. She won't let me go." Not "he" won't let me go but "she" won't let me go, he told his friends.

God talks to us. His words may be misinterpreted and they often have been. They may be misunderstood and many times they are. They may be misapplied and it is almost certain that they will be. But still he talks to us.

But it is precisely this weakness of words and their inability to carry the same idea to everyone all the time that brings the deep meaning to this introductory line to the Sermon. For God to frame his will and intentions with the fraility of words should cause us to pause. Words that could be misinterpreted and worse still, ignored. Words that could be redirected and changed by inflection and emphasis every time they were quoted. Bolts of lightning, maybe. Crashes of thunder, yes. Winds of the tornado, better still; but words, hardly seem enough.

Underlying this willingness to use the ways of men, there must be his serene confidence that he knew he would ultimately be able to make himself known and understood by men.

And so these words have a far deeper meaning than the simple relating of a fact about another preacher speaking again. For this is God. Embedded in these words is the wonder that God would have something to say to us. And that from deep within him comes all he has been wanting to say to us.

You'll have to forgive me, but I can hear more than just teaching from that afternoon so long ago when a young preacher sat down and when he was ready, began to teach. I hear the deep longings of God, bottled up as it were, within his heart for the centuries, now bursing forth.

He is not a mute God. He is not a God whose ways are to remain unfathomable to us. We are not to forever spend our days wondering what he is thinking and what he wants from us. He is a God who talks to us.

Parental Math.

Nearly a week ago Peg and I
had a very hard week.

Wednesday night —
Mike slept downstairs in his room
where children belong
and we slept upstairs in ours
where moms and dads belong.
Thursday night —
we were 350 miles away and he was
in Ramada 325 and we were in 323
in connecting rooms and we left the door open
and talked and laughed together.
Friday night —
700 miles from home and
he was in 247 and we were in 239
but it was just down the balcony
and somehow we seemed together.
Saturday night —
he was in the freshman dorm
and we were still in 239.
Sunday night —
we were home and he was
700 miles away in Chapman 309.

Now we have been through this before
Robert had gone away to college
and we had gathered ourselves together
until we had gotten over it —
mainly because he is married now
and he only lives ten miles away
and comes to visit often.
So we thought we knew
how to handle separation pretty well
but we came away so lonely and blue.

Oh, our hearts are filled with pride
at a fine young man
and our minds are filled with memories
from tricycles to commencements
but deep down inside somewhere

The Things I Believe.

we just ached with loneliness and pain.

Somebody said you still have three at home.
Three fine kids and there is
still plenty of noise—
plenty of ballgames to go to—
plenty of responsibilities—
plenty of laughter—
plenty of everything
except Mike.
And in parental math
five minus one
just doesn't equal plenty.

And I was thinking about God.
He sure has plenty of children—
plenty of artists—
plenty of singers—
and carpenters—
and candlestick makers—
and preachers—
plenty of everybody
except you.
And all of them together
can never take your place.
And there will always be
an empty spot in his heart—
and a vacant chair at his table
when you're not home.

And if once in awhile
it seems as if he's crowding you a bit—
try to forgive him.
It may be one of those nights
when he misses you so much
he can hardly stand it.

The Scarecrow.

Looking out the window of my study, I can see in my own backyard a parable that speaks to me about life. Sitting dejectedly in the corner by the garden compost pile is my scarecrow. He is tattered and faded, evidence of his summers of defending our garden from the birds. He used to spend winter in the shed, but last fall he somehow just didn't get put away. He stayed on the fence until about February, when a windstorm blew him off and into the cornstalks.

When spring came, I dragged him into a corner of the yard and there he would have stayed, if not for Jason. Jason Runyan and his sister, Lauren, had come to spend a couple of nights with us while their parents took the church youth group on a trip to Canada. Jason had a great time fighting with this ex-protector of the harvest. He punched him and jumped on him and finally left him to die out beyond the back sidewalk. After Jason and Lauren had gone home, I rescued the vanquished warrior from the field of battle and carried him back to the house.

He really deserved a little better treatment. Leigh and I made him one spring. He was a genuine, life-sized, fully dressed (from straw hat to shoes) scarecrow. I did the body work. With a 'skin' of fence wire stretched over a 'skeleton' of tomato stake sticks, and some padding here and there made out of some plastic dry-cleaning bags he was ready for clothes. Leigh made the head out of a pillowcase and painted on a handsome face. He was a scarecrow of above average intelligence, too, because we used the *Wall Street Journal* for brains. He was a worthy addition to our garden and had done his job well.

The way his arm used to swing in the breeze that first summer made him look almost alive. He was so lifelike that people who passed by would often wave to him thinking it was me sitting on the garden fence. Once when Mike was home for a visit, he opened the door to the shed and almost jumped out of his skin when he saw the scarecrow. Even lying out in the yard, where one of Jason's solid left hooks had knocked him, he looked so real that Peggy thought I had collapsed on the way to the house.

But, of course, he was never alive and never will be. He couldn't ever get off the fence on his own and take a walk or do a dance in the morning sunlight. He couldn't ever sing a song, or write a poem, or pull a weed, or plant a row, or take a bite out of one of those Tennessee tomatoes.

My scarecrow has the form but there isn't any substance. No life is there. He is a ragged reminder that we, too, need to have the touch of Christ to become alive. Without him we are like scarecrows watching over the little patches of ground which have been entrusted to us — sitting on our fences, never knowing what makes beans sprout and corn grow and birds fly and rabbits eat lettuce.

Without him we would think that the sun rises and sets somewhere around our own little fence corners — never really laughing, never really caring, never really alive.

The Box Is Too Small.

All that came to be was alive with his life. (John 1:4)

You see a lot of funny bumper stickers these days, like the one on the back of the big truck, "If you can't stop, smile as you go under." I'm not sure about the one that says, "Your God may be dead but mine is alive and well." Now I think that you believe, don't you, that the "God is dead" crowd seems to be dying out, but I sometimes believe that we fail to act as if God is really life.
I don't only believe that God is alive—I don't even think he is sick.

They say when you get older there is less and less room in your medicine chest. And Peg and I, for varying reasons and ailments, take an assortment of pills each night. Generally the last thing we do at night before we go to bed is to meet at the sink for our nightly ritual of pill rolling. Now she has some big ones that are prettier than mine, but I take more than she does so I think it about evens out. The other night, just for fun, I said, "Let's take all the pills we have in the house and line them up and close our eyes and have mystery pill time and we'll just bless some unknown organ in our body."

I know that saying that God isn't even sick is not exactly an earth-shaking statement but somehow it means a lot to me. I don't think God takes pills for headaches or tranquilizers because he can't cope. And I mean it when I say he is alive and well and at work in his world.

Now I'm fairly sure that we all believe that but if you really want to practicalize it a little, we don't act very much like we believe it. In fact, we act like he's sort of sickly and we had better take good care of him.

It's almost like we've put him in a box and keep him down at the front of the church and say, "Do you want to come down and see God?"

Oh, of course, we'll punch some holes in the lid so he can get some air, but not big enough holes so that he can get out. And the people come down and they say, "Yeah, take the lid off, let me see him." Oh, no, if we did that, he might get out there in the world he created and get stomped or trampled. We'd better keep him in the box here on the altar. I secretly suspect that he'll be alright and that he is out there at work in a thousand ways we never suspect.

We just seem to have trouble looking at all of life like it cames from him. We have this way of categorizing everything—it's us "over here" with God's life and then it's just them "over there." It's like we're the good guys and they are the bad guys, like we have on the white hats and they have on the black hats. (I can just imagine myself in a big white hat, about a ten-gallon hat on on a two-quart head.) And we say, "We're the ones, we're the church, we're the good guys with the white hats, and God's over here with us."

And then we say, "They're the bad guys and everybody knows that God doesn't have anything to do with the bad guys." Why can't we see that "all that came to be was alive with his life." And that God is out there just working away with the good guys and the bad guys. The good guys who want to be good and the good guys who want to be bad and the bad guys who want to be bad and the bad guys who want to be good and all the in-betweens.

In fact, when Christ was on earth, the big problem to the White Hat Society was that they couldn't keep him away from the bad guys. He just wouldn't put on the white hat and stay where he belonged. He was always out there with the bad guys, just like he loved them and cared for them and wanted to eat supper with them.

In my Sunday School class I like to ask trick questions, questions when I know the only answer and everyone else's answer is wrong. That's my favorite kind of question beause I look so intelligent when I come out with the answer. Being college kids, one of them is usually a step or two ahead of me and aces me out. One of my better efforts in this category of questions was, "What are some of the gospel songs of the last five or ten years that you think have really been a blessing?" And they answered with songs like *He Touched Me, Fill My Cup, Lord,* and *How Great thou Art.* They never seem to name any of the songs that we publish.

Then very quietly and profoundly I say, "Why didn't anyone say *He Ain't Heavy, He's My Brother?*"

"That's not a gospel song!"

You mean it is not gospel to say that you love your brother so much that when you have to carry him, you don't even notice his weight and that you love him so much that you're never, never embarrassed because he is a cripple? Are you saying that's not what Christ was talking about?

I'm not saying we ought to include it in the next hymnal or even that we ought to sing it next Sunday morning in the service. But when the answer is that's not a gospel song because one of us white hats didn't write it, that it was written by one of the black hats, I always think of the verse, "all that came to be was alive with his life."

I think God is alive in his world and I wonder how many times he wants to talk to us and how much he wants to show us and how much he'd teach us in a day's time if we believed that he was as alive on Monday as he is on Sunday. I want to see what he is doing and hear what he has to say. If we are going to share in his life, we are going to have to begin to sense about him that he is life and that his life is everywhere. It is in the music and the heartbeat and the throb and pulse of the world that he made.

I was up for a kind of three-day vacation with Peg a couple of years ago and we were out on Nantucket which is about thirty miles off the coast of Cape Cod. My wife is a serious shopper and, even though I am not a shopper, since we were on vacation, in the interest of fellowship and harmony, we were shopping. And they had a lot of souvenir shops that we went through in a hurry. It had once been the whaling capital of the world and they had everything in the shape of a whale—ash trays, posters, wall-plaques, glasses, jars, bottles, watches, charms, bracelets. Whatever you needed, they had one in the shape of a whale marked SOUVENIR OF NANTUCKET on the front and MADE IN JAPAN on the back.

But there was one lovely place we went, a gift shop called the Cross-Eyed Dove. And when we walked in, we knew that this was not just a souvenir shop. Whoever owned this shop had bought and displayed everything with care and love. In the pottery and the sculptures and the paintings and the macrames, there were lovely textures and shapes and colors and sizes and beauty. And you instantly knew that here was someone who had taste and a love for beauty. Fortunately for me, everything there wasn't Peggy's taste.

The owner's name was Robin and we became acquainted with her. She had worked around the corner in the "whale store" when the opportunity had presented itself to open her own shop. She told her previous employers that she was going to fill her shop with things she loved. And they told her that she would starve to death. "Buy the things you like and put them in your house. But for the store, buy all the silly, dumb things tourists will buy and sell them to them and then go home to the things that you love." But that wasn't what Robin wanted to do and she didn't.

On our last day there, we were waiting on the ferry and Robin came along from lunch. And we were visiting for the last time. "Tell me again what you do," she said.

"I'm in the religious publishing business."

"I don't believe much in religion."

"Is that right?"

"Yes, I don't think I believe in God."

"Well, I think you do."

"No, I don't."

"But I think that you do."

"Well, why do you say that?"

"Well, maybe you don't believe in God in a personal sense, but you like so many of the things that he does. You know, all the colors and shapes and textures and fibers and wood and clay—all the things you love—come from his hand, for all that came to be was alive with his life. And you may not call on his name yet, but you'd really like him because you already like so many things about him."

We were back up there the next summer and were going up the street to her shop when we met her. "Do you remember us?"

"Sure, you're the Bensons, and you're the one who tried to convert me."

"No, I was the one who was trying to tell you that you were already partly converted."

Am I trying to say to you that Robin could accept Christ because she likes pottery or that there is another way to the Father except through Christ? No, I know about redemption and forgiveness and the cross and the blood and confession and profession. But are you trying to say to me that God is not alive and speaking to Robin in a hundred different ways?

Sometimes, the box is just too small.

It Is A Me-Book, Too.

Recently in Nashville, a group of minister-marchers protested against the new paraphrase of the Scriptures called The Living Bible. The polite name for them is "ultra-conservative," a term which can also be roughly translated "red neck." Now you generally protest in Nashville in one of two places — the State Capitol or the Baptist Book Store. Since there were no Living Bibles on sale at the Capitol, the logical place seemed to be the Baptist Book Store. And so they came, and they marched.

Now I don't doubt for an instant the sincerity of what they were trying to do. But I am convinced that if nobody ever goes down on Broad Street at the corner of Tenth across from the old Union Station and marches in front of the Baptist Book Store, God is, and will be, speaking to people through his Word. No group of translators or scholars can lock God out of his own Word. He is alive and he speaks through his book.

The fact that we in the church treat God as if he were a wheelchair patient is utterly surprising. For instance, some people feel that God must be carefully protected and explained or he will not have enough life to make himself heard.

I certainly believe that as earlier and earlier manuscripts are found, men should carefully and diligently study and research to make every attempt to discover as nearly as possible the exact things that God was saying through these men who wrote the Holy Bible. I am somewhere between amused and irked at all the people who feel that only through their eternal vigilance will God be able to speak through the Bible. If they are not careful, some group of translators will silence God forever.

This is the God-book. It is the speaking word of God and his ability to speak through it does not depend on minister-marchers, or involved hassles between various groups of fundamentalists on tenses and Greek and Hebrew words, or on English words whose meanings have changed through history. It is the living, healing, moving, probing, convicting, speaking Word. And he has been, and he is, and he always will be heard through it, for it is filled with his life. It is the Living Word of God. It is the God-book.

But I am also convinced that his life makes it a "me-book".

Out on the West Coast there is a company that has devised a very ingenious scheme for personalizing children's books. I'm sure the color illustrations throughout the book are printed in large mass runs for economy's sake. Then, on the basis of information the buyer sends along with the order, each book is run through a computer. Such questions as the child's name, age, birthday, street address, friends, dog or cat's name, and other assorted tidbits are put on the order blank. When the book is printed by the computer, each book is a story with the child as the chief character.

Last Christmas my mother had ordered one of these books for our youngest son, Patrick. You can hardly imagine his surprise and delight when he pulled it out from under the tree and unwrapped it and began to read, "Once upon a time in a place called Hendersonville, there lived a little boy named Patrick Benson. Now Patrick wasn't just an ordinary little boy. This is a story about one of his adventures. It's the story of the day that Patrick met a giraffe..."

Over seventy times Patrick and his street and his friends were named and when he got better acquainted with the giraffe it even had the same birthday and its name was "Kcirtap," which if you didn't notice is Patrick spelled backwards.

Do you think Patrick likes that book? It is one of his favorite and most important books because to him it is a "me-book." And I suspect we are all that way. We like stories about ourselves.

And this living book of God is about us. Read it — the King James, the Revised Standard Version, the New English Bible, the Living Bible, in the Greek or Hebrew, or any one of a dozen other translations, and you will find that he will be saying things to you that guide and comfort and bless and heal and answer the deep questions of your life.

We are in that book. It is a "me-book" and a "you-book." We all have taken our turn at saying, "There is no room in the inn," and we all know what it is like to sadly reverse our paths like the rich, young ruler. We all know what it is to say, "I do not know him," or to leave unsaid, "Yes, I am a follower of his." We all have bravely said in stirring faith, "Thou art the Christ, the Son of the Living God," and we all have felt or said, "Unless I touch the prints of his hands."

It is not just a book written a long time ago about some people who lived way back then. It is about us. It is not just a book about a few men to whom he said, "Lo, I will never leave you." It is to us as well that these words still speak. It was not only their sorrow he promised to turn into joy, but he was saying to us just as surely as if he were looking us in the face that the thing that seems like sorrow to us today, he would have us writing poems and singing songs about tomorrow or next week. These things were said to us and for us and about us in this living book of God.

Now, we all believe that, don't we? I haven't written anything that we wouldn't all nod our heads in agreement on, have I? Then why don't, or why can't, we act like this is the Living Word. Why do we say, "I try to read the Bible, but it just is dull, monotonous, and routine?"

Maybe it is because we haven't realized that it is a "me-book."

And that he was not only speaking to Paul on the Damascus Road, but he was just as surely speaking to Patrick on Bayshore Drive.

Home-Home

"Apart from me...nothing." (John 15:5)

For several years, Peggy and I casually looked for a place around Middle Tennessee or Kentucky that we could use for small retreats. It had to be reasonably close to home and big enough to divide into sleeping spaces. To be honest with you, we found a place and then later discovered maybe we didn't need it as badly as we had thought we did. But that is another story.

The place we found is a lovely log house up near Russellville, Kentucky. Russellville has its own claim to history. The oldest bank up there is the first bank that Jesse James ever held up. I tried to get a little money out of that bank myself, but it always seemed that the banker had the gun.

Anyway, when we were looking at the house, we wanted the kids to like it. Tom and Patrick showed some enthusiasm and probably would have been willing to move up there. Leigh's a sentimental girl, though, and she didn't even want to look at some place that might even remotely compete for the name "home." She was plenty happy right where she was.

Finally, I got her to ride up there with me and look at the house. I pointed out the great stone fireplaces, one of which was in what could have been her room, and the beauty of the logs. We walked through the wooded acreage and I finally asked her, "Do you like it at all?"

"It's okay."

"Well, would you come up here with us if it was ours?"

"I guess so," was her begrudging answer.

We were quiet a minute and then she said to me, "Just as long as we all realize that when it is time to go home, we go to our *"home-home."*

And I understood what she was feeling so deeply.

I think her words *home-home* tell us a little of what Jesus was meaning when he said, "...apart from me...nothing." He wants to be our *home-home.*

Not our summer place, not our vacation retreat, not somewhere we go from time to time, but the place we are when we want to be *home-home.*

He is saying that we will never be at home until we are at home in him. For there is no life apart from the source of life and he is the source. When he says "apart from me," he is not just talking about what we do. He is asking us where we live.

The Life Of Life.

"Apart from me...nothing." (John 15:5)

Last Christmas was one of the brightest, happiest times I can remember. My heart is still filled with such delightful memories that I am smiling just thinking about it.

We had just moved into a new house. Well, it was new to us anyway. After twenty years in your other place, you wonder whether you will ever be able to feel you are at home in the new one.

Our old house had grown with the family over the years. Robert and Mike and I had remodeled the garage into a recreation room. Later, with the help of a real carpenter, we had added a dining room, primarily to display some stained-glass windows we found in a junk shop. The kitchen had been enlarged and a sunny plant room attached. Finally, a guest house with a place for a study for me was added until we sprawled across the hillside overlooking Old Hickory Lake. Now we had decided to move south, closer to town. We wondered, though, if we could ever find a place we would learn to love as well as our lakeside home.

When we drove by and saw the "For Sale" sign in the yard, we knew this faded brown New England saltbox with the yellow door was for us. With some paint and wallpaper, it has become an almost perfect setting for Peg's antiques and primitives.

Sometimes, it seems like we've been moving to Birmingham twenty miles at a time because this was really our second move within the year. Rather, it was Peg's second move. I was in the hospital when the time came to leave the other house. So Peg and the kids moved. But when I got out, I found them. She can't get away from me. I've told her if she ever decides to leave me she should pack my bags, too, because I am going with her.

The people from the church had helped pack, move, and put everything away again in the condominium where we were going to live until we could decide where to settle more permanently. At least they helped her put away all you could squeeze from eleven rooms and a guest house into a three-bedroom condominium. We had a lot of stuff stored in friends' attics and basements all over town. One of the reasons it was so good to get in the new house was to unpack things that we hadn't seen in months. It was like a housewarming shower all over again.

One of the things that we unpacked was the manger scene. The figures are wooden carvings and they are complete, even down to two, tiny sleeping roosters. On vacations over the years, I have collected stones and pieces of driftwood from hikes and woods and walks on beaches to make the stall and the manger and the background. So setting up the creche is my job. When I first started, Peg thought it would be better if I did it in the playroom. But I have gotten so good at it that this year she let me put it in the living room on her new wicker coffee table top. It was one of my better efforts, if I say so myself. And it seemed to speak to all of us anytime we went into the living room. A couple of nights we sat in front of the manger and listened to "The Messiah." Once in awhile I think we ought to set it up in June.

And all of the children were going to be here in our new home for Christmas. Nothing can make a father of five any happier than to have them all home at once. Especially with the bonus of daughters-in-law and a grandson. Leigh had gotten home early in December. She had been there to help pick out the tree and to help her mother decorate the house and hang the wreaths on the doors. Tom and Patrick had given up their rooms to their older, married brothers and moved in on Leigh's sofa.

For once I had done my shopping early, but on Christmas Eve morning, Leigh and I made one last desperate trip just for old times' sake. When we got home at noon, the aroma of the turkey baking in the oven wafted through the house. I puttered around the house but I was really keeping an eye on the driveway for the maroon VW convertible that was bringing Mike and Gwen home to us from Kansas City, where he is in his seminary program. The school where Gwen teaches music didn't get out until the afternoon of the twenty-third, and they were driving halfway that night and the rest of the way on Christmas Eve.

Late in the afternoon Robert and Jetta were going to fly in from Chicago. He was planning to leave his marketing agency office a little early in time to pick Jetta up at the hospital where she is a medical technologist. And they would catch the plane that would bring them home to us.

After dinner we were all going to an eleven o'clock Christmas Eve candlelight service. The pastor and his family were out of town and I had been asked to be in charge. Mike was going to read the Scripture and some of my favorite friends were singing. All of my family would be seated in the first pew, and I knew I would be having the happy privilege of seeing their faces bathed in brightness as they each lit a Christmas candle.

Need I tell you that my heart was so full of happy anticipation and mingled memories that my feet were barely touching the floor?

Then, as if I didn't have enough to be happy about, a few days before, I had received some fine news from the surgeon. "No surgery in January." You don't know what this means to a coward. I had been too sick during the surgery back in the spring for them to complete what they had started out to do. Now he told me that a procedure was being perfected that might enable them to correct what they had begun. Not only was the surgery not going to be completed in January, but I could wait, and then maybe, the whole procedure could be reversed.

So as Christmas came to our house, I felt most wonderfully blest. Good health, good news, a large, loving family, a new home and lots of friends to share it.

But it was not Christmas because the recent days had brought us to a new home. It was Christmas because Jesus brings us life. Not everybody had a new home. A young couple in our church, Rick and Jeanie, came home a few days before Christmas to find their apartment in flames and everything they owned gone.

It was not Christmas because all of the kids had come home. It was Christmas because Jesus has come. Not everybody had their loved ones with them. The only sad part about Christmas this year was that Mom and Dad were far away in Florida where he was recuperating from a painful illness. It was the first time in years we had not all gone over to their house for Christmas morning breakfast, including freshly-squeezed orange juice and homemade biscuits.

And it was not Christmas because I had good news from the doctor. It was Christmas because Jesus was born. Not everybody had good news from the doctor. Back in the summer when I was in the hospital for a short second trip, a friend of ours was also admitted. She was on the floor above me. In the spring she had received the same grim diagnosis the doctor had given me. We knew the whole family well. When I directed a teen group in our church, her kids, Ronnie and Becky, were in it. I learned to love them both. I had gone to school with her husband, Paul. She was buried a few days before Christmas.

Still, it was Christmas at the Langfords'; it was Christmas at the folks' in Fort Myers; it was Christmas at the Shields'. It was Christmas because Jesus is born. There is no Christmas without him. All the rest is just tinsel on the tree.

And the same is true with all of the rituals and all the events of our lives: Thanksgivings, birthdays, commencements, funerals, weddings, and all the others are tied just as inexorably to him. He is the very center of all the days of our lives. These words Jesus uses are pointed, but they are true: "Apart from me...nothing."

He is not saying that he is the life of the Christian, although that is true. He is not saying that he is the life of the church, although he is.

He is saying that he is the Life of life.

Mums Have A Secret.

There is a wide interest these days in plants and many books have been written about the green thumb. I even saw a self-help book for people with purple thumbs. People may need the book but I doubt that the flowers do.

A few years ago I was in Alabama sharing in a spring retreat with the young adults of a Baptist church. On Saturday afternoon we had some free time. One of the couples at the retreat was in the wholesale flower business. They invited me over to see their greenhouses.

Peg and I love flowers. We have green thumbs—pale green, maybe, but green. I like the warm, moist smell of a greenhouse. In fact, I like everything about a greenhouse.

As we toured the greenhouses, John told me about the various plants and flowers. There must have been a dozen buildings filled with plants that were blooming or about to bloom.

The last hothouse that we went to was filled with pots of chrysanthemums that were just beginning to bloom. Before long they would be loading them for the trip to markets in Nashville, where they would be sold for Mother's Day.

My first thought was that I hated to break the news to John and Brenda. But I know that in the southeast, mums don't bloom in the spring. They bloom in the fall. You know that. Everybody knows that. They certainly should have known.

Being an honest man—one who refuses to be confused by the facts—I told them that greenhouse of blooming chrysanthemums just couldn't be, because mums bloom in the fall.

"Let me tell you a secret," John said. "Mums bloom best when the days grow shorter. That's how they know that the time is right. About the last of August or early in September they seem to punch each other and say, 'Hey, Henrietta, it's time to bloom. The days are getting shorter.'

"When we want mums for spring sale we plant them early. They need to be covered with blooms when we take them to market. When it is just about time to ship them we go around every afternoon and pull the shades down."

I can just see the poor misguided mums saying to each other, "I can't believe the year has gone by so fast. But the days are getting shorter, Henrietta, and it's time to get on with it."

Now I don't exactly know what to think of someone who makes his living tricking chrysanthemums. But I do know that mums have a secret. They don't have a school for blooming or a manual. They just know it's time.

Don't you wish you had the confidence to believe that when your time comes you will just *know* and you will burst forth in blossom? Wouldn't you like to think that the psalmist was talking about you when he wrote, "He shall be like a tree that brings forth his fruit in his season?"

Mums have a secret.

The Image Of God.

Think of what you were when you were called. (I Corinthians 1:26)

Early last spring I was planting my garden. It was late on a Thursday evening and I was leaving the next morning for ten days of travel and speaking, so I was hurrying to finish before the darkness came. I had run out of sticks to mark the rows and was about to go to the kindling box in the garage and get some more so the beds would be neatly marked and labeled.

Then I suddenly wondered why I needed the labels anyway. By the time I would get back, the plants would be up and I could see where they were growing. From experience, I knew that the rabbits knew which kind of vegetables that they liked. And I sure knew that I knew peas from spinach. And the seeds sure knew what they were. Who needed labels?

So I just covered the seeds with the cool, moist earth and gently patted the beds and said, "Go ahead and sprout. You know what you are. I'll see you in a few days when I get back." And they did, and I did.

I am not sure exactly what all I think we mean when we say that we are made in the image of God. But part of it, I believe, is that the calling voice of God is sounding out in the caves and caverns deep beneath the soil of our souls. And it is by obeying this call we learn who we truly are and what we can become.

So if I do not seem to hear him speak from the outside, and if there does not seem to be any message from the sky, then I must listen to the voice that is within me. For that voice, too, is the purposeful, calling voice of God to us.

Not many of us have enough confidence in ourselves to listen to the whispering voice that comes from within. Most of the time, we do not even hear it. But it doesn't matter because we wouldn't trust it. We cannot believe that this inner voice is capable of leading us due north.

We seek advice from friends and professionals, disc jockeys and Dear Abbys. We put out a fleece. We flip coins. We take aptitude tests. We do everything but believe that we could possibly have the answers deep within.

The message of Paul in this place is that the calling indeed comes in the lives of the unlikely and the "foolish." You think you are unlikely; well you're not. You have difficulty believing that God could do great things in you; well, he wouldn't.

Now if God can take a tiny seed and, in the process of giving it his life, endow it with a knowledge of what it is supposed to be; if he can give it the purpose and strength and fruitfulness to not only accomplish it all, but to perpetuate itself as well; and if he can give it an inner calendar to tell it when all of this is supposed to be done, why is it so hard to believe he has done the same in *our* hearts?

Since he has done this for tomatoes and thistles and beans and dandelions, it shouldn't stretch our credibility so much to believe that his image in us, the image inherent in the life he gives to each of us, is calling us to *be*.

The trick is to hear the voice, to believe it, and to trust it.

The Golden Urn.

The secret is this: Christ in you, the hope of glory to come. He it is whom we proclaim. (Colossians 1:27&28)

At times there is a distinct advantage to being a slow reader. If you were just reading the "important" words you would be seeing "Christ", "hope", "glory", "he" and "proclaim." But bumping along from word to word, I dropped into the hole between "Christ" and "hope" and fell on two tremendous words: "in you."

Where is the secret? Where can you go to find it? Is it bigger than a breadbox? Tell me, where is it hidden? In you and in me. In common, ordinary, everyday folks like us.

Had I been God, I don't think I would have done that. I don't think that I would have put the secret in us. I'm certain there are some of you who couldn't be trusted with such important matters. Of course, I trust me and I know that you would certainly do the same. After all, I am a published author. But there are really some strange folks around. I am trying not to think of anyone in particular, but I don't believe I would have included everyone.

Some people don't know how to keep a secret. Peg thinks a secret is something that you tell one person at a time. That's not the worst of it. Some people can't even tell a secret. I heard of a lady who was passing on some very interesting and sensitive news to another lady. The listener was quite intrigued and wanted to know more. "I can't tell you any more," the first lady replied. "I've already told you more than I heard."

Some of us are just not too great at keeping secrets. We don't really lie. We're just like my son, Tom—we remember big. But, despite all our inadequacies, we are the hiding places for the ultimate secret of the universe.

Could I use a word here about God that doesn't quite seem to fit, and yet it does? Would you let me say we have a "cool" God? Not "cool" like in cold or indifferent, but "cool" like he is confident in the way things are going to turn out.

I'm not so certain that all of his confidence was placed in us. I am certain that he was sure about the secret. He took the truth and put it within us. He had such confidence in the truth that he thought it would all end like he wanted it to. Most of us would have taken some kind of precaution to make sure it went the way we meant for it to go, wouldn't we?

Sometimes in my imagination I wonder what would have happened if he had appointed a committee from my church board to pick a place for the secret. I can just hear someone saying, "Let's get a great big golden urn and engrave the secret on it. Then if anyone wanted to read it, we'll all know right where it is. If we engrave an urn, no one can tamper with the wording. Since God speaks English, we'll putteth it in a beautiful old English script, something likened unto the King James version."

I have observed the human predicament for a while, and I think I know what would have happened.

Seven or eight blocks from our old office, there is a huge building complex. It is the headquarters of the Baptist Sunday School Board. These buildings, along with one other over on James Robertson Parkway, are the headquarters for most of the departments which serve over twelve million Southern Baptists. With that many of them around I want to be careful what I say.

The buildings cover areas of several blocks and are joined by walkways over the streets. There are entrances on Ninth Avenue, Tenth Avenue, Broad Street, Church Street, and probably some others I don't know about. Security must be a problem.

If you wish to see someone in the headquarters complex, you have to state your business, and whom you wish to see, in the lobby before they will give you a badge to proceed. Then they will call ahead and warn them that you are on your way. If they are that protective of my good friend, Bill Reynolds, can you imagine what they might do if they had "the secret" in a big, golden urn in some room high atop the eighth floor?

"Good morning. My name is Bob Benson and I want to go up and see the urn and read the secret."

"That's fine, Mr. 'Vinson'. Could I see your card?"

Since I travel a lot I have all kinds of cards. I pull out my wallet and show them that I am in the Number One Club. I have found that this means I am usually about third in line and O.J. Simpson is gone before I even get to the counter. I also have an Inner Circle card which assures me of a hotel room with a window that overlooks the kitchen vents.

But they say to me: "Mr Vinson, we mean your Southern Baptist card."

"No, it's 'Benson', B-E-N-S-O-N. I am not a Southern Baptist. You see, I am a Nazarene. I wanted to read the 'secret' so I came to see the urn."

"You don't understand, Mr. 'Vincent'. We don't just show that to anyone. The only possible time you might get a glimpse of it would be when we are moving it to Ridgecrest or Glorietta for one of our solemn assemblies. Even then it is quite heavily guarded."

Suppose that, faced with such a situation, I got together with a few of my most trusted friends at church. One night we disguised ourselves to look like Southern Baptists. You know, white shoes and all. We broke into the Ninth Avenue entrance of Southern Baptist Headquarters and ripped off the urn. We rushed to Kansas City to put it where it belonged in the first place. If it were at our headquarters, we could decide whether we thought Southern Baptists ought to see it or not.

While we were going through St. Louis, a group of Lutherans who had dressed up like Nazarenes—black socks and everything—crowded us off the road and, before we could resist, had just plain "stolen" the urn from us rightful owners.

I don't know how the word spread so quickly, but before they could get across the city someone from the headquarters of the United Pentecostal Church got a group together and instructed them to be very quiet. Everyone had to promise not to raise their hands in the air. In fact, it would be easier if they all kept them in their pockets unless they were actually driving the getaway bus or carrying the urn.

To tell you the truth, I don't know where the urn is now. Sooner or later it will turn up, I guess. Someone will put it in a tower and build a fence around it and keep other people from seeing it. The tower will become a shrine and people will sell tickets to it. You will be able to buy color slides or little gold towers at the concession stand. Somebody will put an "I've been to the tower" sign on your bumper in the parking lot.

Other people will build motels and wax museums and hamburger stands. You can spend your entire vacation right there. Of course, there will be tours so that you can ride by the tower like you can ride by Johnny Cash's house. But you still will not know the secret because nobody will let you see the urn.

Maybe the committee would think that everyone should hear the secret. "Obviously they can't all read it for themselves but we can carry it to them. Let's engrave it on a bronze tablet and we'll go all over the country and have big rallies and read the secret to them.

"Great! We can sing and praise the Lord."

"We can all raise both hands while we sing."

At this point a great amount of discussion would take place within the committee. Some would feel it would be better to raise only one hand. Still others would be sure it would be much more dignified to just sing without raising your hands at all.

The "two-handers" quote from the Psalms about raising your hands to the Lord. "See, it's plural," they insist. The "one-handers" check into the Hebrew meaning of the words and argue very persuasively that when everybody raised one hand it would be plural collectively and this was the proper interpretation of the passage.

Finally, the matter of the order or "ardor" of the service surrounding the reading of the secret would be referred back to a sub-committee and the tour is delayed. For a while at least, the rallies won't be held and you won't be able to hear the "secret."

Some members of the committee don't even know yet — God told everybody. It is not somewhere you can't afford to go. It is not guarded by someone who won't let you see it. It is not the prized possession of some group or committee who will only give you access to the secret if you look, act, and dress in a certain way.

The secret is in you.

Some Of Us Are Peanut Butter Jars.

During the year when I was a senior in college, I started a church in the north-east area of Nashville. I was there largely as a result of someone else's vision and I really wasn't very effective.

We took some walls out of a big house to make a chapel. Peg and I later moved into the back three rooms for the first "home" of our married life. I was young and grew discouraged easily. The people I called on were not particularly interested in coming over to help me. This lack of interest is no reflection on the church, later on I was equally inept at selling Fuller brushes door-to-door.

Just down the street from the church was a lovely, old Victorian house. It was the home of a long-time friend of my folks. She was elderly and alone and was always glad to see the young parson knock on her door. I was young and alone and I was always glad to see a sympathetic friend. Besides that, I liked the tea and cookies.

One afternoon, shortly after Peg and I were married, Mrs. Payne gave me four lovely crystal glasses. They were even lovelier because she told me that they were the only four remaining of the crystal she received for her own wedding some sixty years earlier. They were thin, beautifully shaped and delicately etched. We still have them at our house.

We decided not to use Mrs. Payne's crystal. As a matter of fact, we decided not to use ours either. We're saving it for "good," whenever that comes. If using crystal is the basis for judging our married life, we haven't had much "good." Of all the things that were given to us some twenty-five years ago, the crystal is probably the least used. The toaster and the mixer have long since bitten the dust. We could use another linen shower. But the crystal is still there. We just use everyday glasses like you do.

I don't know why, but I like for glasses to match. They're not too expensive, so when I buy Christmas gifts I usually end up with a set of glasses. The last thing I do on Christmas Eve, after Peg has gone to bed and after the bikes are put together, is to take all the old glasses out and stand the new ones in neat, orderly rows.

After a few weeks, the same thing always begins to happen. Someone will empty the peanut butter jar. Someone else will stick it in the dishwasher. Someone else will put the jar on the shelf. At last, it shows up on the dinner table. There it is, thick and ugly, with part of the label still attached. There is no delicate etching. It doesn't match. It's just a big, old ex-peanut butter jar.

We all know that there are some people who seem to have all the natural graces. They know just what to say and when to say it. They move through life with ease and are like a benediction wherever they go. They are like Mrs. Payne's crystal glasses. Some folks are like that. They are better by nature than others are by grace.

Now, I hate to bring this up. Maybe I don't even need to. I'll just mention it. We all know some folks who are like peanut butter jars. You know, part of the label is hanging on. There's not much grace and beauty about them. They are always blurting out the wrong thing at the wrong time. You would think that by the law of averages they would accidentally say the right thing once in a while. They are the people who say, "I've always liked that blue dress on you," or "I like that suit better than the ones they're wearing these days."

"You are vessels unto honor," Paul writes. The variety of vessels proves that it is not that we are goblets or peanut butter jars or root beer mugs that matters. The difference proves that the power does not come from us. The power is God's alone.

We are not great because of what we are. We are great because of what we contain. He has made you a "depository of truth." The secret is this: Christ *in you*.

I know that there are some conceited people around. You run into them on occasion and usually come away wondering what it is they find to be so exciting about themselves. But for every one of the conceited people I meet, I encounter a dozen in whom I sense a deep feeling of failure and inadequacy. I wonder if the conceited folk aren't about the same as the rest of us. They are just so busy bragging that we don't notice that they are bleeding, too.

It is here in the midst of a world of fragmented, inadequate, misguided, striving people that I want to remind you again of those two little words about the secret: *in you*. As you look at yourself and others through these two words you begin to see a dignity and worth. He put the secret *in you*. You're something else!

You. You with the big nose. You with freckles. You with two left feet. You with the bald head. You with the sagging waistline. He put the secret *in you* and, because he did, you have an inherent greatness about you.

I heard my friend Grady Nutt say something along this line. I'm not certain that he said it first, but then, I'm not certain that his real name is Nutt, either. No matter who said it first, it is true: *God don't make no junk.*

God in his wisdom decided that urns, tablets, monuments and shrines were not fit dwelling places for the truth. He did not choose marble, granite, mahogany, or gold. The secret was to be indelibly engraved in the recesses of your heart. The secret brings an inestimable value to you.

What he thinks of you is a reason for you to celebrate. I mean, here *is* something to celebrate.

I have often thought that we are limited in the number of ways in which we can express our wonder and joy during church or retreats or even privately. I remember the enthusiasm of my kids as they roll down a grassy slope or jump into a pile of leaves that I am raking. I see our puppy running circles in the yard for no apparent reason except the happiness of being alive or the pleasure of feeling the wind in her face.

We ought to have a balloon filled with helium to let go of. We need a hat to throw in the air. We need a whistle to whistle or a horn to blow. Some of us are too old to roll down a hill. We would break something if we leaped into a pile of leaves. But couldn't we run around the block or throw a stone or puff a dandelion? What can we do when we want to celebrate our "me-ness"?

Don't just sit there! Do something! Sing, celebrate, rejoice, hope, jump, run, cry, believe, embrace a friend, hug your kid, kiss your spouse, clap your hands. Whatever, whenever, however — somehow celebrate yourself and the fact that he placed the secret within you. Whether you are a peanut-butter jar or something else altogether.

Because he does.

It Will Work In Your Life.

Therefore live your lives in union with Him. (Colossians 2:6)

Have you ever bought a lawnmower? The salesman shows you how easily it will start. With just one tug of the cord he starts it right up without so much as a sputter. It always starts with the first yank in the store where there is no grass, no mosquitos, no bugs, no sweat.

But come home some Friday afternoon to mow the grass in a hurry so that you can go fishing on Saturday. You pull and you yank. The mower is just not interested. You discuss the situation with the mower in simple, direct, positive statements that it can understand. Finally, you discover that even a gentle kick won't work. The fact that the mower worked in the store doesn't mean much if it won't work in your yard.

In my slow way of reading, I have come across a word which is having a richer and richer meaning to me. A speed reader who reads Paul's words is going to see "live," "life," "union," "him." A plodder like me is going to see the "your."

The teachings of Jesus are not some abstract philosophy. They are carved into the struggles and burdens and triumphs and failures of life. That is the place where his life is to be manifested.

It's good for God to have all that power and holiness and majesty and grace. It makes you want to bow down and worship him. But if all this life and power won't work in the context of your life, then it really doesn't mean much to you, does it?

Jesus brought the sanctity to life. God decided that men just weren't understanding what he was trying to tell them. He had rolled back the waters. He had sent tablets of stone and bread from heaven. The prophets had preached. People had won battles which had looked like certain defeats. But they just weren't catching on. So Jesus came.

It would seem that Jesus would have built an elaborate palace somewhere. There could have been some ticket-tour system so that you could finally get in to see what was going on with God. You would sit for a few moments on a satin pillow in his presence. You would be served some hot grapes. He would be wearing his royal purple robe. Of course, you could not ask any questions or talk. Before you could recover from the awe that filled you, some minor official would give you a souvenir map of the palace and some cheap rings with a royal insignia on them to take to your kids. The next thing you know you would be back on the street trying to cope with life.

When God wanted to show his deepest feelings about us, he sent his Son. And he didn't send him to live in a castle. He demonstrated God's love in the midst of life at its best and life at its worst. He came into the world in such a way as to say, "I am one of you." Why else would he be born in a manger? It was to say to us that we were never to be surprised at where he turned up. Once and for all he was saying, "I am here to be involved in life."

He entered into life wholeheartedly. He identified with it. He put himself within the limits of life and made no claims of immunity. He joined in exploring its possibilities. He suffered and worked at it. He addressed himself to the ills of society. He pleaded for the poor and defended those who were attacked. He entered into the disappointments and struggles that are the daily occurrences of every man's life. He embraced the world as his own. He came into the sweat, dust and tears of life.

Jesus was a holy man. But I think we often think it was because he withdrew from life. There were times when he had to be alone with the Father. But I am beginning to believe that his holiness did not come because he withdrew from life; he was holy because he entered into life at every level.

Some people imagine a Jesus who, when confronted with sorrow or sickness, slipped into a phone booth and took off his glasses and put on his God suit. It helps me more to know that he didn't have some sort of spiritual overdrive that lifted him out of the context of life. He hung in there and wept and bled and talked and healed. He was not less involved with life than we are. He was infinitely more caught up in it.

As I go to work each morning, I come up the hill to where I-65 and I-24 merge. As you top the hill, you can see the skyline of Nashville in the distance. It is nearly always interesting to see. Sometimes it is sparkling in the morning sunlight and sometimes it is shrouded in fog. As all the lanes come together everyone is jockeying for position. I'm trying to stay in the outside lane as long as I can because it is faster. Finally I have to get over in the right lane to catch I-265 around to the office. Other people are trying to do just the opposite. Frankly, I hardly ever pray over the city.

One morning Jesus came riding over the hill from Bethany and looked down on the city of Jerusalem. It was a city that had great meaning to him. It was a city in which he had preached and healed. It was the city in which he was to die. As he saw the city in the morning mist, his eyes filled with tears and he prayed. "Jerusalem, Jerusalem, how often I would have gathered you to myself, like a mother hen gathers her chicks, but you would not."

Now I ask you, who is the most involved in life? Me, blowing and honking and changing lanes, or Jesus, weeping and praying over the city? Jesus loved life and people and flowers and causes and was more aware of them than we are. In that very sacrament of humanity, his dignity and likeness to his father was magnified. In the process of revealing God to us, he also demonstrates that humanity is possible and desirable.

So the great challenge is for you to live your life in union with him. The union is here. This is the place. You are the one. The union will manifest itself in the everyday noise and the crowded streets of your life. You can be what you are. You can think what you think. You can have your temper. You can have your will. You can have your emotions. He will bring his life as the union. It is in that life together that you are gently transformed and remade.

You do not have to struggle up to where he is. It is not a question of your achieving enough to merit an audience with him on a day when he has time. He is not saying to you, "Fill out an application and leave it with the angel in charge of personnel. It won't be necessary for you to call us. We'll call you if there is an opening."

Jesus came to say, "It will work in your yard."

Three Times A Day.

Someone came to me the other day
and they were just loaded down
with guilt and hurt and shame.
Tearfully they confessed a wrong
that had long lay dormant.
And what made it even worse was the
confession had only come after discovery.
The deed and the shame of discovery
before they had confessed themselves
seemed to only double the pain.
There it was now—in the open,
like a giant black spot or smudge
on the pages of their life
and it seemed to cast a cloud
over all the bright, good things
that were really characteristic of them.
And it seemed that we were especially close
because they were pushed to a real deep level
in their life
and I, too, was having a chance to reveal how I felt.
We weren't talking about ball scores or weather,
we were talking about issues that were large
and deep and real.
I was trying to figure out a way to keep them
from feeling such guilt and shame
and how to believe again in themselves
and most of all in God's forgiveness.
And so I asked them,
"Do you have any idea how often
that could happen in your life
before God gave up on you?"
"No."
"Do you know what it would take
to make him cease to dream and hope
for you?"
"No, I guess I don't."
"Do you know how many times you would
have to do that before he even considered
changing his feelings about you?"
"No."
"About three times a day for the rest of your life."

What Makes Jesus Smile?

"I have spoken thus to you, so that my joy may be in you, and your joy complete."
(John 15:11.)

One of the young men who worked with us at the company was Phil Johnson. Phil is a talented songwriter, producer, artist, musician, husband, and father, and a warm Christian. One of his songs is called "When I Say Jesus." It expresses an inspirational thought about what the name of Jesus means to us and what that name has the power to do for us.

One afternoon I was talking to him a bit about the song and he told me that he wanted to write another song with a parallel truth, but he was afraid no one would understand it. I asked him what he would name the song. "When I Say Phil," was his reply.

I'm not sure we would understand it. Or even believe it if we did.

It is easy for us to know the wealth of meaning and grace that comes to us when we say his name—Jesus. What a flood of memories and recollections is opened up at the thought of his name. It doesn't take long to look back across your life and think of all the various times and places you have breathed that precious name. At first it was only in the hard places—when your ma died, when the baby was sick, or when you lost your job. Gradually, though, he became interwoven into the celebrations and the good times as well, and his name began to be the invocation and the benediction of all your days.

It isn't hard to sing Phil's song and know what happens in you and to you when you say Jesus. But can you believe that he speaks your name with the same depth and feeling that you speak his? Can you realize that he, too, looks back across the years to the day he chose you and rejoices in what you have come to mean to him as you have walked together?

It isn't strange to associate the word "joy" with Jesus, for it's a quality that just seems to be inherent in his mission and message from the Father. He brings joy, he gives joy, he radiates joy, he bestows joy on all those who trust him and walk in his ways. These are his ways, and we sing and say and celebrate them. We know he makes our heart glad.

But in the setting of the last hours with his disciples, around the table where they have gathered for their last meal together, Jesus is telling them how much they mean to him. He is saying these things to them so that their joy may be full and so that he may have joy in theirs. They are his joy.

Here in this upper room, he speaks about the thing that makes his heart glad. All the while we have been content to accept joy as something we receive from him. Now we hear him saying that joy is something that comes to *him* because of *us*.

What is it that makes him joyful in this hour of separation? As he looks back across the long years of preparation and the short years of public ministry, what is it that makes him smile? As he looks now across the few short hours to his death, what is is that makes him conclude that his has been a useful, worthwhile, joyful life?

It was his *joy* in his men, given to him by the Father. There wasn't anything else, they were all he had. But they were enough, they were his joy.

My son, Tom, is an avid student of expressions, mannerisms, voice inflections, and all of the other things that makes each one of us unique. As a result, he can mimic almost anyone he has been around. And as soon as he goes into one of his impressions, you realize that, although you hadn't noticed it before, that is just exactly the way that person is.

The other night at the supper table he was giving us a little rundown on the faculty at school. Some of them were people that I hadn't met. But later when I did, I knew them. Patrick goes to the same school and he knew them and nearly doubled over with laughter watching Tom do his impressions.

Tom stopped his stories to say that he loved to see Patrick laugh. When we asked him why, he gave us a description and a demonstration of Patrick's face as it moves from seriousness to mirth.

"First, his eyes brighten and his eyebrows widen and then his nostrils quiver and his mouth begins to spread upward and outward at the corners until he passes the point of no return and laughs without control."

We really have no way of knowing what Jesus actually looked like. The only way we can envision him physically is from one of the various paintings that have been rendered of him. Even then, whether it be youthful, sad, vigorous, solemn, or happy, it is only the artist's conception of Jesus. Probably none of them are just like him. The famous picture of The Last Supper didn't happen just like it appears on the canvas. It looks posed to me, like the artist told everyone who wanted to be in the picture to get on one side of the table.

Still, it helps to see a face. And when you are praying and looking up to him or when you feel him looking down on you, he very likely appears to you much like your favorite picture of him.

Can you close your eyes and visualize his face? Now, speak his name and listen as he says yours back to you. And as he is saying your name, can you see his eyes brighten, his eyebrows widen, his nostrils quiver, and his mouth begin to spread upward and outward until his face is bathed in smiles that come from deep within his heart?

We are *his* joy.

The Heart Of The Chooser.

"You did not choose me. I chose you." (John 15:15.)

A lot of times in retreats, the Friday night session will open with skits and games. In a burst of hospitality, Peg and I are often asked to be in the skits so that the people can get acquainted with us quickly. There is nothing like making a fool of yourself to break the ice.

At a recent retreat one of the games was musical chairs. It got louder and more rambunctious in uncanny proportion to the ever-decreasing number of chairs. Finally the winner was in the last chair and the rest of us were yelling.

Sometimes I talk to people who seem to think that God is playing musical chairs and that every so often, he just stops the music. There isn't any rhyme or reason or fairness to it, it's just whether you were around the corner when it stopped. And whether or not you can now beat some big guy to the last chair. And every time the music stops, somebody has to drop out. No wonder they don't like God. I wouldn't like him either if I though he was playing musical chairs with us.

But he has a chair for everybody. If you end up on the floor, it won't be because he didn't have a seat for you. It will be because you won't sit in it. And he plays the music on and on and on to give you every opportunity to find your place.

It is not always easy to believe this about yourself. It is almost easier to believe it about others. You know yourself too well to see how this could be. But the shared life can only begin to grow in you as you start to understand how very much he cares for you. It is important what you think he thinks about you.

As long as you feel that you can only hope that he isn't displeased or pouting or mad or gone. As long as you believe that he is saying or feeling about you, "Oh, no, not again?" Or, "Look at that, will he ever get that right?" Or, "She always does that." As long as your failure causes you to doubt his faithfulness, you're looking at the "choosee."

Our shared life with him begins when he chooses us. And our being chosen begins in his love for us. He is the initiator of this relationship.

In one way, the fact that he chooses us is a rejoicing kind of truth. It is like a serendipity or an extra. It is like boiled custard from the dairy, which is made only during the holidays between Thanksgiving and Christmas. You can't get it for your birthday in August. It is like a holiday or special-times-type truth, and at a retreat or a particular service, it thrills us to think that he loves us.

In a deeper way I am beginning to believe that this is really a foundation kind of truth. There is a sense in which he cannot mean all he could or should to us, until we begin to fathom to some degree how much we mean to him. All of our faith and love for him is born in our belief in his trust and love for us.

Only when you can realize he is looking at you and smiling with you and thanking the Father for you, will you begin to find the love there is in the heart of the "chooser."

I'm Not Pure, But . . .

In him you have been brought to completion. (Colossians 2:10.)

We've been studying The Beatitudes lately in our class. And looking at them for what they are, a series of statements or conditions and their corresponding rewards and promises. The sixth Beatitude has come to stand out to me above all the rest. First of all, it stands out because of its great promise.

Now, there are other promises in the Beatitudes — "the kingdom of heaven is theirs;" "consolation;" "they shall have the earth for their possession;" "they shall be satisfied;" "mercy shall be shown to them;" "God shall call them his sons." But even when you put all the promises together, it just seems to me that the richest promise of all is contained in the words, "They shall see God." I'd rather see God than possess the earth. I'd even take a chance on finding enough satisfaction and enough mercy and enough consolation, if I could just see him.

But if the sixth Beatitude holds forth the greatest promise, it also seems to have the greatest obstacle. "How blessed are those whose hearts are pure."

Now it isn't too hard to be poor or poor in spirit. Most of the time life takes care of that. Heaven knows, we will be sorrowful. Maybe from time to time, we may even develop within ourselves a gentle spirit. In quiet, pensive moments, I think we all hunger and thirst for righteousness. Now and then, we can even find mercy in our hearts, especially when we remember in the Lord's Prayer that we will find mercy in the same measure that we bestow it. I think we are even willing to be peacemakers if the cause doesn't matter to us much either way. Most of us suffer some persecution, and even though not much of it is for right, we tell everybody it is and we feel better about it.

All of these are things that we are in some measure. We might even have some chance of attaining enough merit to qualify for the reward.

But here is this monstrous door which seems to have a lock to which we have no key. Standing between us and God is the qualification "Blessed are those whose hearts are pure." Which of us is pure?

I wouldn't stand before you and say I was pure because you wouldn't believe me. It wouldn't be true. I don't meet many people who are pure, either.

It's always a little easier for me to speak away from home. You get a couple hundred miles away and you can look more pure than you do at home. It helps that you're with the people for such a short time. In three days they can't find out much about you.

I just happen to be one who cries a lot when I talk, and when you cry people think you are pure. People say, "My, my, isn't he fine?" as long as you don't get involved in the retreat and get into the volleyball games and stuff like that, where you might cheat or lose your temper. If you go to your room, they'll think you are studying and praying and that you're saintly when you are really just taking a nap. It's easy to look pure.

I would like to get to the place where I could go somewhere and talk to people and say to them, "Hey, come on, way up here where I am. The view is great. The air is clean and pure. If you could just be up here where I am." But I always seem to be puffing and sweating and blowing along the trail with everyone else and saying, "Hey, there it is, way up there. Way up there is where we ought to be."

I really think I'm getting old enough to be pure. I've been at this for thirty years. You would think that sooner or later I might turn up pure. But it really doesn't matter if I am two hundred miles from home or two thousand miles from home or at home, I'm still me. I'm still what I am. I know the gap between what I am and what I ought to be. I'm not pure. I'm always plagued by what I am. *"How blessed are those whose hearts are pure, for they shall see God."* I am a tenacious fellow. I don't give up too easily. And lately, I have a feeling about the Word. There's a lot of stuff there. If you keep looking, there must be something that will help you.

So I come back to the phrase, *In him you have been brought to completion.*

I had always taken the phrase, "How blessed are those who are pure in heart, for they shall see God," to mean that at some time in judgement some minor official would open my heart, look in and say, "You're not pure, so you can't see God."

Here I am wanting to see God. But here I am without a pure heart. And here is this verse which says, "In him I have been brought to completion." And so I went looking for a way to put these three things together.

"I want to see God."

"But you're not pure."

"I have to see God."

"But you have to be pure."

"I need to see God."

"But you need to be pure."

I wasn't getting anywhere at the front, so I went around to the back door. And one day a voice within me said, "I have seen God."

"Then you must be pure."

"I have heard his voice. I have seen his ways."

"Then you must be pure."

"In him I have been brought to completion."

There is a lady in our church and I am ashamed to confess that I only know a few things about her. First, her name is Rose and her face always seems to be tinged with just a little sadness and struggle. Second, she always sits on the right side of the middle section on the first or second pew. Third, every time there is a call for prayer or an invitation song or a concluding song, Rose goes to the altar to pray. That's all I really know about her.

Peg and I were wondering one day about how the Lamb's Book of Life would look if it depended on Rose's faith and trust. Her name would be on every page an average of three times. It would look like this: Sam, Richard, Wilhemina, *Rose,*

The Things I Believe.

Charles, Alice, John, Mary, *Rose,* Pauline, Tracey, Keith, Lucas, *Rose.*

I can just hear some minor official saying, "Who is this *Rose?*"

I'll tell you one thing I would like to see. It may be some morning at the church. I surely hope that it isn't on one of the weekends that I have retreated somewhere. It may be when Rose gets to the Gate. Wherever it is, I would like to be there to see her face break into a smile that would eclipse a sunrise on a summer morning when she finally hears for the first time, "Rose, you are all right. You are O.K. Everything is fine. You are complete."

I know about three things about Rose and I know about three things about you. First, well, I have forgotten your name, but, oh, that face. Second, I know that you have probably found your seat in life — over to the left side and four rows back. Third, I am almost certain that in your own strength you make as pathetic a figure as Rose, standing there in her frayed, grey coat that is too heavy in the spring and too light in the winter.

No, come to think of it, I know four things about Rose and you — and me. *In him you have been brought to completion.*

"It's You! It's You!"

The story begins very early on Easter Sunday at the tomb of Jesus in Jerusalem. It ends some seven miles away in Emmaus.

Mary Magdalene, Joanna, Mary, the mother of James, and some other women took spices they had prepared to the place where Jesus was buried. When they got there, the stone was rolled aside from the entrance. They went inside and found the body gone. They were standing there, utterly at a loss, when two men in bright and shining garments appeared beside them. In the women's terror, one of the men reminded them of Jesus' words about his death and resurrection.

Then the group of women began to recall what he had said and went to find the eleven and all the others and tell them what had happened. But nobody would believe them. Later that day two of the men set out on their way to the village of Emmaus. Of course, they were talking about all that had happened in Jerusalem that week. And Jesus came and walked along with them. But they didn't recognize him.

It has always interested me that they did not know who he was. More than that, though, it has always intrigued me that he did not tell them. I have always wondered why he didn't rush up to them exclaiming, "It's me! It's me! It's over! I'm back! We won! It's me! It's me!"

The thing I am beginning to see is that it seemed more important for him to wait until they said, "It's you! It's you!"

I think I can imagine a little of what Jesus must have been trying to do. It must be like encouraging your infant son to take his first steps. With open arms you wait. "Come on, come to Daddy. Let go of Mommy's hand and come to me."

You almost lean over and take his hand and pull him across the space that separates you. But that would not be walking. That would be pulling, wouldn't it? Walking is when he takes a step all by himself.

So I think Jesus is leaning as far as he can and still allowing them to come to him in faith. He reminds them of the things Moses and all the prophets had written about him. Surely, now they know. Hint after hint, clue after clue, until there was hardly anything left to say except, "It's me! It's me!"

But still nobody said, "It's you."

The sun had begun to drop in the west when they reached the village, but still they had not uttered the words of recognition. And now their roads must part. They were going home. He was going on. It was now or never. What should he do? Should he tell them now or should he wait for another time and another place?

I believe that Jesus' heart jumped within him when one of the men asked him to stay for supper and the night. Time, a little more time for them to take the first faltering steps of faith.

It was one of those evenings when father brings home an unexpected guest. The mother straightens the extra bedroom and apologizes for the supper. The kids are on their best behavior, having been reminded in the kitchen to mind their manners. They gather at the table. They ask Jesus to return thanks. They aren't sure who he is but he must be religious because he knows all that Scripture.

He takes the bread and says the blessing. And then he breaks it and passes it down the table to each of them. And they say, "It's you!"

And he is gone from them.

I think I know what happened at the supper table that night. I can imagine what made them suddenly know who had walked with them all the way and was now at the table with them.

In a family the size of ours, it is hard to get everybody to the table on time. Somebody's always hollering, "Just a minute," back down the stairs. And it always takes longer than a minute. And then somebody else gets there a little early and helps Peg put the food on the table. They put everything but the broccoli, maybe, where they can reach it from where they sit. They even corral the salt and pepper and the butter. Although it's against the rules, occasionally someone even butters his bread before the rest of us get there. I am reluctant to admit it, but I have had to call on someone to return thanks who had to pray for food of which we were about to partake as well as some that was in the process of being partaken. It's hard to pray with a hot roll in your mouth.

Finally, though, the minute is up and we are all there. We join hands and say together: "Happy is he whose help and hope is in the Lord his God. Who keeps faith forever and gives food to the hungry. Praise the Lord. Amen."

So now I'm down at the daddy's end and the food is somewhere clustered around the one who brought it to the table.

"Please pass the potatoes."

"Please pass the tomatoes."

"Please pass the meat."

"Please pass the salt." (You would think people would pass the pepper, too, when you asked for the salt, wouldn't you?)

"Please pass the butter."

And by now you are beginning to get some indication that they really wish you would stop bothering them so they could eat. You don't have any bread, but by now you decide you'll just put the butter on the potatoes and forget it. And then somebody, usually Peg, says, "Daddy doesn't have any bread. Someone pass Daddy the bread."

I'm believing that the thing that brought forth the glad recognition that night in Emmaus was just this. Jesus said, "Cleopas doesn't have any bread. Somebody pass Cleopas the bread."

And Cleopas said, "It's you! It's you!"

We can study and discuss what Jesus came to do for mankind. We can learn all the prophecies about Jesus and give our assent to them. They can even become our creeds and beliefs. But it is when we realize that he knows we do not have any bread, and that he is starting it down the table to us, that we suddenly know who he is. He has been with us in our journey. He has been there all the time.

He is with us.

Only such times of experience, only such moments can bring validity to religion. If we can hear his voice, we do not need any other proof. And if we cannot, then no other proof will do.

Of course, there are reasons for believing in God. Theologians and thinkers have gathered them up for us and distilled them into a few classical arguments. The order and purpose of the universe certainly tell us that there must have been a Designer. And both the matter and the motion of the universe point to the conclusion that there was ultimately a first cause. And the very fact that always there have been men who have believed there was a God indicates there is One. Where else would the idea have come from? And we recognize evil because we somehow perceive the good, and those perceptions bring us to an absolute good or truth.

But to understand or repeat any one of these beliefs or, indeed, all of them together, is not enough. Even if you know their "big word" names— cosmological, teleological, ontological, or whatever—they are inadequate. When life caves in, you do not need reasons, you need comfort. You do not need some answers, you need some *one*. And Jesus does not come to us with an explanation, he comes to us with his presence.

We are always seeking the reason. We want to know why. Like Job, we finally want God to tell us just what is going on. Why do the good die young and the bad seem to live on forever? If the meek inherit the earth, why do the arrogant always seem to have the mineral rights?

But God does not reveal his plan, he reveals himself. He comes to us as warmth when we are cold, fellowship when we are alone, strength when we are weak, peace when we are troubled, courage when we are afraid, songs when we are sad, and bread when we are hungry.

He is with us on our journeys. He is there when we are home. He sits with us at our table. He knows about funerals and weddings and commencements and hospitals and jails and unemployment and labor and laughter and rest and tears. He knows because he is with us. He comes to us again and again.

Waiting for us to say, "It's you! It's you!"

The Common Place Becomes A Sacrament.

Multiple Me's.

Most of the time it seems there
is just not enough of me
to go around.
At the office it is almost as
if I leave more to do than
I am ever able to get done.
And when I'm home—the yard,
the family, the woodpile,
the garage all seem to have a
rightful claim on my time.
All of the projects that I would
like to be able to begin—
the books I would like to read—
could all be done if there
were only more of me to do them.

But then there are times when
there are just
too many of me.
One of those times is when I pray.
If only Bob, the sincere, the
quiet, the desirer of holy
things could make his way
alone to the place of prayer
and make his petitions known,
and there find the
power and poise
his heart must have.
But every time he goes to pray
a whole multitude of me comes

trooping right along—
Bob the impatient,
Bob the referee heckler,
Bob the unconcerned,
and the ambitious Bob
and the unkind Bob.

And by the time they all crowd
into the closet,
there is such a din
and clamor that
I can hardly hear
the voice of God.
And then I am made to see
that what I am—
in my thoughts
at work, at play,
in traffic—
all these people
make up the person I am
when I kneel down to pray.
Oh, that I would love him so
dearly that every moment
of my life—
ease, thought, pain,
pleasure, toil, dreams—
would be but a preparation
for those times when
I shall be alone
with him.

A Baloney Sandwich.

You may come to share in the very being of God. (II Peter 1:4)

Do you remember when they had old-fashioned Sunday School picnics? I do. As I recall, it was back in the "olden days", as my kids would say, back before they had air conditioning.

They said, "We'll all meet at Sycamore Lodge in Shelby Park at 4:30 on Saturday. You bring your supper and we'll furnish the iced tea."

But if you were like me, you came home at the last minute. When you got ready to pack your picnic, all you could find in the refrigerator was one dried up piece of baloney and just enough mustard in the bottom of the jar so that you got it all over your knuckles trying to get to it. And just two slices of stale bread to go with it. So you made your baloney sandwich and wrapped it in an old brown bag and went to the picnic.

When it came time to eat, you sat at the end of a table and spread out your sandwich. But the folks who sat next to you brought a feast. The lady was a good cook and she had worked hard all day to get ready for the picnic. And she had fried chicken and baked beans and potato salad and homemade rolls and sliced tomatoes and pickles and olives and celery. And two big homemade chocolate pies to top it off. That's what they spread out there next to you while you sat with your baloney sandwich.

But they said to you, "Why don't we just put it all together?"

"No, I couldn't do that. I couldn't even think of it," you murmured in embarassment, with one eye on the chicken.

"Oh, come on, there's plenty of chicken and plenty of pie and plenty of everything. And we just love baloney sandwiches. Let's just put it all together."

And so you did and there you sat, eating like a king when you came like a pauper.

One day, it dawned on me that God had been saying just that sort of thing to me. "Why don't you take what you have and what you are, and I will take what I have and what I am, and we'll share it together." I began to see that when I put what I had and was and am and hope to be with what he is, I had stumbled upon the bargain of a lifetime.

I get to thinking sometimes, thinking of me sharing with God. When I think of how little I bring, and how much he brings and invites me to share, I know that I should be shouting to the housetops, but I am so filled with awe and wonder that I can hardly speak. I know that I don't have enough love or faith or grace or mercy or wisdom, but he does. He has all of those things in abundance and he says, "Let's just put it all together."

Consecration, denial, sacrifice, commitment, crosses were all kind of hard words to me, until I saw them in the light of sharing. It isn't just a case of me kicking in what I have because God is the biggest kid in the neighborhood and he wants it all for himself. He is saying, "Everything that I possess is available to you. Everything that I am and can be to a person, I will be to you."

When I think about it like that, it really amuses me to see somebody running along through life hanging on to their dumb bag with that stale baloney sandwich in it saying, "God's not going to get my sandwich! No, sirree, this is mine!" Did you ever see anybody like that—so needy—just about half-starved to death yet hanging on for dear life. It's not that God needs your sandwich. The fact is, you need his chicken.

Well, go ahead—eat your baloney sandwich, as long as you can. But when you can't stand its tastelessness or drabness any longer; when you get so tired of running your own life by yourself and doing it your way and figuring out all the answers with no one to help; when trying to accumulate, hold, grasp, and keep everything together in your own strength gets to be too big a load; when you begin to realize that by yourself you're never going to be able to fulfill your dreams, I hope you'll remember that it doesn't have to be that way.

You have been invited to something better, you know. You have been invited to share in the very being of God.

Fields Or Farms?

Jesus loved to tell us about the Father, about his will and purpose and about his love and compassion for us. He tried to tell us what the Father and the kingdom were really like. So again and again he tells us they are: Like a man who..., like a mustard seed, like yeast, like ten virgins, like a king. When we listen to him, we can always find a peg on which to hang the truth he comes to share.

One afternoon he was standing on the prow of a boat that had been tied to the shore. He was telling the people who had gathered at the water's edge about the Father. Over in the distance, perhaps, they could all see a field and, in it, a man sowing seed. But even if there hadn't been a sower in the afternoon sunlight, they could still picture one slowly going back and forth across the field, scattering the seed with the motion of his arm and digging into the bag slung beneath his arm for another handful.

And Jesus continued with his planting:

> A sower went out to sow his seed.
> And as he sowed some of the seed fell on the path,
> where it was trampled on and where
> the birds could come and eat it.
> Some of the seed fell on the rock and when
> it came up it withered and died
> for it had no moisture.
> Some of the seed fell in among thistles
> and the thistles grew up with it
> and choked it.
> Some of the seed fell into good soil and grew
> and yielded a hundredfold.

This simple story must have been readily understood by all of those who were listening to him that day. I know that I have always understood its rather transparent truth and knew just who he was talking about, haven't you?

Well, I didn't know just exactly who he meant by path and rock and thistles, but at least I knew who he was talking about when he spoke of good, rich, deep soil that produced as much as a hundredfold. It is very obvious, to me at least, that he was talking about me. Or was he?

Lately I have been thinking that this is a story about a foursome that consists of me and me and me and me. I'm old Mr. Goodsoil himself, of course, but I also answer to Pathway, Rocky, or Thistles. The parable is all about me. And it is coming to me that I am not a field, I am a farm.

I have some fields that I have cultivated with his help and they have, and do, bring forth an increase. But across some of the land there are pathways that have been trampled and hardened because I always went the easiest and shortest way.

I took those paths over and over. And the commerce of life has gradually worn them down.

And it is not hard for me to remember my dreams and plans at the beginning of many a planting season. I have watched, with excitement and enthusiasm, the tender young shoots springing up out of the ground. But I also recall the tears and frustration that were mine as they wilted and died because there was no depth to my preparation and commitment.

Down across the creek from the field behind the barn, there is a patch of rich ground. It is already plowed and planted. But I suppose it is also filled with the seeds and roots of thorns and thistles and weeds that I have either invited to come or allowed to stay. And in time they will choke out the life that he wants to bring me in increase. I am not a field, I am a farm.

Let me show you a new way to read this story.

A sower goes out to sow
and some seed falls on the path
some falls on rocks
some falls among thorns
and some into good soil.
And the sower goes out to sow.
and some seed falls on the path
some falls on rocks
some falls among thorns
and some into good soil.
And the sower goes out to sow
and some seed falls on the path
some falls on the rocks
some falls among thorns
and some into good soil.
And the sower goes out to sow...

You should read it about ten times this way until you begin to realize two things.

One is that the more one becomes, the more he sees his need of becoming. The deeper the roots of one's life go, the more he is impressed with their shallowness. The more conscious one is of closeness to God, the more he is aware of the distance that separates him from God. And we realize that we are not fields, we are farms.

The second is that always the Sower goes out to sow. Always he comes to you, never tiring, never discouraged that you have far more poor soil than you do good. Always he comes, never despairing of seeds that perish.

Confession.

Confession is kind of a one-time word with us Nazarenes. We just use it once, and once we get by that, we don't use it anymore. If we are visiting in services and somebody prays, "forgive us for our sins," we just kind of shudder. Probably for various reasons.

I did a Bible study group a few months ago and the discussion was on confession. The young pastor almost said that it would be all right if we confessed. Some of the saints in the church took him to task. They were so adamant about the fact that we were not supposed to confess that before it was over I almost had something to confess about.

I know that in fairness to them and what they were talking about was that they were defining sin as a willful transgression of a known law of God. And they believed that you could live each day without willfully going against what you knew God wanted you to do. And to them that was what confession was for. But it seems to me, too, that we have lost all the goodness that this great word can bring to us by making it a one-time word in our midst.

Confession comes from a couple of Greek words which I can't pronounce. One word means, "to say," and the other word means, "the same." So the word "confession," simply means "to say the same."

It's not like saying, "Yeah, I did it, but they made me do it." Or, "If you knew what I had to put up with at home you would understand." That's not saying the same. Saying the same is saying "Whatever that was, that was me."

Now I know I am not deeply theological enough to get into the determination of the definition of sin, but I want to suggest we leave the word "sin" over here for a while, for a moment at least. And let's talk about the failures and the lapses and the hurts and the guilts and all of the other things that we load on to our backs from time to time and try to make it through life with.

When I think about our need for confession, for some reason I think of an uncle of mine and an old car he had. He had this old Cadillac, a two-door Coupe DeVille. I think at one time it had been blue and white, but because of the accumulated dust and soot you could not really tell what color it was. I don't know what all was in the trunk of that car, but if it was anything like the back seat, it was an amazing car.

He used to drive his car down to the Benson Printing Co. Other people parked their car. Not Uncle W. A., he just got close enough to where he thought he wanted to be and abandoned his car. I guess he figured it was going to be too heavy for a wrecker to pull away anyway.

Let me tell you about the stuff in his car. He was a very thorough man and started out to build himself a new house. He bought a lot in Belle Meade, a very exclusive neighborhood in Nashville, and started to build the house.

One day he asked if I would like to go see his house. We rode out Belle Meade Boulevard and turned there at the gate to Percy Warner Park and turned back to the right and there was a lovely home that was beautifully landscaped. We drove into this fine driveway and pulled around the back and walked up the patio and he opened the door and I looked in. Inside there was nothing but stud walls and electric wires and plumbing pipes. It turned out it had taken him about seven years to get this far in his house building. The neighbors had gotten an injunction and said, "You can do what you want to on the inside of the house, but you have to finish the outside."

I think if you went down through his old car layer by layer, you would have known the story of the construction, for he was an investigator. There were concrete blocks and bricks and pieces of wood and plans and paint chips and drapery samples and catalogs of plumbing and light fixtures. The carpenters would no more than get one wall up when he would come out and say, "Well, that's a beautiful wall, let's move it over here." And his car was just a strata of his seven years of home-building.

I think I was thinking about the word "confession" in this connection. What we do when we throw away the word confession is we do away with our way to clean out the back seat. And so we go around with the righteousness that is our own.

Even though the whole world can look in the back window and see that our righteousness is not too righteous.

"Is He Garbage-Can Mad?"

Therefore, live your lives in union with him. (Colossians 2:6)

I know that I could be more holy if it wasn't for certain things that keep going on around my house. All of our bedrooms are on the second floor with the exception of the guest room and half-bath downstairs. Peg and I sleep in one corner and we have a child at present in each of the other corners.

When you go up the steps you enter a small hall. The first thing you're likely to hear is Patrick playing an album by John Denver. That's not too bad because I happen to like John. Though I don't think his voice will last if he continues to sing that loud. Over in the opposite corner, Leigh is playing Janis Ian. I like Janis, too, and I also understand that she has to sing at the top of her lungs to be heard over John. The thing that makes it hard to adjust to is that son Tom is playing the local headache station over the top of the other two. My kids do not have any hearing defects but I suspect that with our three phonograph/radios going full blast they soon will.

I just know I could be more saintly if I could have a little more peace and a little less music. I'm convinced that I could move up closer if KDA-FM were not a 24-hour station. Sometimes I think that if I could just ride over the hill on my Honda I could sure be more noble and pure. If I could just get away from it all, I could write poetry and dream dreams and pray prayers. I could make my own music if I needed any. My life would be in union with the great sources of creativity and inspiration. I would be pious and holy. And I would probably be bored and lonely, too.

I don't think God especially wants me to be pious and saintly 'way over on the back of Comer's farm by myself. I think what he would probably really like for me to do most is treat each one of the roomers on my floor with kindness and love mixed with a liberal dose of holiness—even when the music is four decibels above the threshold of pain.

Paul's injunction is to live our lives in the present context of "noise." Fortunately, he did not counsel us to go find a situation where things will be more conducive to being mild-mannered and pious. He doesn't say that when you reach another age and part of your present struggle is over, you can then come around and talk to God. Right now, right where you are—that's where he wants to share your life.

Frankly, there are some places in my life in which it is difficult to believe that he would like to participate. As I am sure you have discovered in my writing (especially since I have tried to tell you), I am a very kind, quiet, mild-mannered, interested, compassionate, loving individual. *Except when I'm mad.*

There is a scale at my house for registering temper. To my shame, I hold the dubious honor of posting the highest reading ever. All outbursts of anger are measured against my record.

Until the boys got old enough to carry the garbage out, I had to do it. I grew up in a time when the two chief duties of a husband were to bring the money in and carry the garbage out. It was a good day for me when the boys were finally old enough to to begin to carry it out and scatter it around on the ground near the cans. They got just enough in the can to entice the neighborhood dogs to turn it over and aid in the distribution process. Such things as pushing the trash down and putting the lid on securely seemed to be taking unfair advantage of the dogs.

I really got tired of picking that stuff up. I was out early one Saturday morning and I don't remember exactly what happened. Something just got all over me. I don't even remember how the lid got on the roof. I really do think that the can already had that huge dent in it.

But now at my house they say, "Is he mad?"

"Yeah."

"But is he garbage can mad?"

To this day I wish I hadn't done that. It is difficult to see how God would like to be a participant in the life of anybody who acts like that. But he didn't say to me, "Son, when you can get your act together and stop behaving that way and start treating the ones you love the most as if you do and when you can pick up a little garbage without feeling like a first-century martyr and when you can stop raising your voice and throwing garbage can lids on the roof, I might be willing to visit you sometime."

No, it's always the same. I know he would like for me to quit acting like that. I certainly hope he is succeeding in the process of remaking me. (A trash compactor has helped some.) But he still desires to come and have union with me. The starting place is in *my life*.

If the Scripture means what it seems to, he is softly saying, "I want to be a part of your life. I want to be included in the retreats and the good services and the times of honor and accomplishment. And when the garbage is on the ground and the supper is late and the cake fell and the washing machine broke and you took it out on your kids or some other innocent bystander, I want to be there, too. "When you are pushed and shoved and crowded and you end up striking back. When they call and say it's not working out like you hoped and you're about as frustrated as you can be. When you are just having a good laugh about something and something else comes along and makes you cry and weep. That is where I want to be.

"It is in the failure, success, joy, sorrow and shame that I want to bring graces and power to you. Your life may be wonderfully good or painfully bad or terribly mediocre. More probably, it's some curious mixture of the three but *"let me in."*

Sorrow Into Joy.

Sometimes in retreat prayertimes, I will ask people to envision a blank sheet of paper with a horizontal line across the middle. Then, giving them time for reflection, I ask them to remember the good things that have happened to them across the years, to think about them and rejoice over them. And I have them "write" those things one by one on the paper above the line. (I confess that I often "watch and pray" so that I may enjoy the looks of peace and pleasure on the faces in front of me.)

Then, to help them get a truer perspective of how God works in their lives, I also suggest they recall the evil things that have come to them as well, the deep troublesome times that threaten to engulf their souls. I ask them to "list" those below the line. And I watch the expressions of pain move across their faces as they recall things that have swept in on them with devastating suddenness and fury. I try to close these prayertimes by reminding the audience that the whole paper can be committed to him. He is the God of the list on the top and the God of the list on the bottom.

A very interesting thing always happens afterwards. Sometimes just one person and sometimes several people will find me afterwards just to talk. The places may vary, but the conversation is always the same,"You know, when we were listing those things on the paper in prayer, and we put that stuff above and below the line? There were some things that, for the life of me, I didn't know where to put. Even now I am not sure. Some of those things are so evil it would seem their place would be a foregone conclusion. The day they happened, I knew all right. The bottom of the bottom wasn't low enough. I did not know whether I would make it or not. But now, looking back, I'm not so sure. Some of them seem to be creeping over the line."

In their eyes there usually is a depth that reveals a mixture of both joy and sorrow, both peace and pain. Their brows are often furrowed and many times their hair is gray. But they say to me, "I guess I have to write it above the line." Even out of the darkest circumstances his call to us can be heard.

More and more it seems that those of us who make up retreats are a microcosm of society in general. One has only to show a little bit of openness and willingness to listen, to be allowed into the worlds of hurt reflecting all of the ills of society. For we are, or carry the burdens of , the sick, the deranged, the illegitimate, the elderly, the divorced, the poor, the unloved, and the unwanted. We are all there. Almost anything that has happened anywhere has happened at sometime to one of us.

I listen to people and my heart breaks for them. Sometimes I think I would like to put my arms around them and promise them that I will personally see that nothing else bad ever happens to them again. But I cannot even protect my own from the hurts of life. There are only about three things I know to say to them. The first is that I will pray for them.

Sometimes I think we just say that we will pray for someone because there doesn't seem to be anything which we consider practical or helpful we can do, something like sit with the children or cook supper or run some errands. So we say, "I'll pray for you." I am coming to believe that there is nothing more important that we can do for anyone than to pray for them. I confess to them that I am not so good at it, but I do have time, and I will pray for them and for their son, or daughter, or estranged husband, or diseased body, or perplexing situation.

I have found that offering to pray for someone often leads me to ask if there is anything else I can do. For we cannot let them into our hearts alone. Prayer is not an escape from the pain and reality of the world; rather it is a clearer, more compelling awareness of it. And we are led to some other way in which we may be of help.

The other thing that I always want to do is impart this truth — God is able to work in the darkest, direst set of circumstances. Many times, in light of the story just told me, it seems impertinent or even irreverent to suggest it. Still, on the basis of the gospel, and on the basis of my own experiences, I want to tell those people that I believe God will turn their sorrows into joy.

I know there are terrible and tragic things which befall people. There are wrongs that can never be righted again, events and misfortunes that are still as unfair and as bewildering years later as they were the dark night that they occurred. And even though it seems almost a sacrilege to say it to the broken, wounded person who stands weeping before me, I always find myself telling them, "Someday you will sing about this very sorrow."

We may lay claim to the promises of God in a moment of profession. We may rest on them. We may trust them implicitly. We may live in accordance with the precepts and admonitions. We may read and memorize the words of Jesus and be certain that they are true. We may have no doubt that God will be with us always because he has promised us that he would. But somewhere on the journey, pain or sickness or sorrow will overwhelm us like a flood. And we will realize that we are not alone. Then the promise will be ours. Our faith will belong to us.

Knowing his presence, knowing that he is indeed who he says he is, and knowing that he can do what he claims he can do become the truths that form his message to us. That message tells us "in all things" he is working for our good. And the joy of "knowing him" is the joy that transforms our sorrows.

I was in the music business for twenty years. In all that time I did not write one song. Only a time or two did I even help with one. Phil Johnson, talented young songwriter, producer, and friend at the company, came into my office one morning and wanted me to listen to a new song he had written. It was to be recorded that very afternoon. It was such a lovely idea for a song that I suggested that he hold it for awhile to give it time to grow and come to full blossom in his heart and mind. He was gracious enough to accept my suggestion and even asked if I would like to work on it with him. As I recall I wrote a verse and helped some on the chorus. I still believe the things we wrote are true.

He never said you'd only see sunshine,
He never said there'd be no rain,
He only promised a heart full of singing
About the very things that once brought pain.
Give them all, give them all,
give them all to Jesus,
Shattered dreams, wounded hearts,
and broken toys;
Give them all, give them all,
give them all to Jesus,
And he will turn your sorrows into joys.

The Commonplace Becomes A Sacrament.

Of Discipline And Desire.

A couple of winters ago, I was in a motel in South Carolina trying to write a short essay on the Beatitude about hungering and thirsting after righteousness. When I arrived at the motel, there was a basket of fruit, crackers, and candy in the room. Down the balcony there were drink, snack, and ice machines. There was a Shoney's next door, a McDonald's nearby, and a Bojangles across the street.

My schedule on the road that week was about the same as usual. I would try to get up around seven to study and work an hour or so before eating breakfast. Then there was a small prayer and study group at the church at eleven, and then some friendly members were taking turns feeding the "evangelist" and his wife. There must have been some kind of "cookoff" because it seemed that each day the meals got bigger and better. In the afternoons, I studied and read before supper and the service. Someone took me out for a snack afterwards and I just ate something light with them—like a hot fudge sundae.

Needless to say, I was having a bit of difficulty in coming to a way of understanding and expressing the deep meanings Jesus must have had when he spoke of our quest for righteousness in terms of hunger and thirst. I think he was trying to ask us how much we really want goodness.

I guess the part discipline must play in our spiritual development is understood well enough, for it figures into every other area of our lives. No skill, it seems, comes to us without a price.

But the other word that occurs just as often in discussions about life in the spirit is not as easily understood. We do not fathom its meanings as readily because it is too often not a word in our experience. But it is a term that the saints often use. Strangely enough, once they begin to use it they speak less and less of having to discipline themselves into patterns of prayer and devotion. The word is *desire.*

As a word, desire probably doesn't carry as strong a set of meanings to us as the word discipline. Discipline is a kind of tough, unbending word. It resists attempts to round off the edges. And it doesn't want to hang around with qualifiers like nearly or partly or half. It either wants to be used like it is or left alone. Desire, though, comes in such a variety of shapes and strengths that one has to study it some each time to understand its meaning.

Desire would bring about a quiet, almost unnoticed change in the very sources out of which our prayer springs. It would be the beginning of a difference in our prayers. No longer would we pray because we feel the necessity to pray—but we would be praying because the thought of spending the day without the companionship of the Father has become unthinkable.

The light on the faces of those who pray out of desire, the very radiance of their words, written or spoken, is unmistakably bright. It is not so much what they claimed to have attained. Often, they lament the weakness of their desire. Rather, it is in the adoration and praise with which they speak of what they have seen and heard.

Sometimes when I am working upstairs in my study I will hear Peg down in the kitchen with measuring cups and the mixing bowls. Then there will be the sounds of the mixer in the house. And I hear the oven door opening and a pan sliding on the shelf. After a while, there comes wafting up the backsteps the sweet aroma of a lemon pound cake with apricot nectar baking in the oven. (For my money, it is hard to do anything wrong with a lemon or an apricot.) There is the faint sound of the confectioners sugar icing bubbling in a pan on top of the stove. I hear the oven door open and shut for the last time. I hear her tapping the pan until the cake comes out on the antique stand. Then I know she will be pouring that hot, sugary icing over the cake. I can almost see it running down the sides and piling up in little puddles on the stand.

I am listening very attentively now as she washes the pans and bowls and puts them on the drainer to dry. And she leaves the kitchen. Suddenly, I need a drink of water. In the kitchen, I look carefully in all directions. Then I reach around on the back side and pinch off some of that warm, moist cake. And the icing gets all over my fingers. Usually I find that I have pinched off some cake about the same place where Peg had already taken a pinch before she left the kitchen.

Obviously, I don't have any rules for this ritual, nor do I need any. I don't make myself listen to her progress. And I don't have to force myself to show up when she is gone from the kitchen. There isn't any discipline involved at all. (Lack of discipline, maybe.) The explanation is clear enough. I just love cake — especially warm lemon pound cake made with apricot nectar with sugary icing still oozing down the sides.

I have known a few people, and I have read of others, who talk about God with the same excitement and delight that I use to describe warm cake. They will tell you of their struggles and strivings to maintain spiritual discipline. But they also will tell you of mornings when they were waiting on the porch for the sun to come up because they could not wait to meet him.

These truly devout people speak of coming to a place where turning to him is the finest thing that happens in their day. Not because they should, although they should. Not because it is necessary, although it is necessary. Not because they feel they have to, although one really has to. But because they want to. They truly desire him.

They have come to a place in their lives where they have learned that going somewhere without him is like not going anywhere at all.

Can You Sing Without Billy?

We were in Sunday school class recently, visiting before time for the lesson to start. In the informal setting, we mingled with coffee, spiced tea and doughnuts, occasionally letting one eye drift down to read the name badge on the lapel. As we seated ourselves, greetings were extended to the visitors. Someone made announcements about upcoming activities including a Valentine banquet, and where and when to turn in the money. Up to this point we could have been almost anybody—the PTA, the Kiwanis, the Rotary, Volunteer Firemen, or any one of a thousand groups or organizations. Coffee, name badges, comments on the weather, announcements, and small talk catch just about everybody.

Then a young singer, Billy Crockett, was introduced and he stood before us with his guitar. He asked us if we would sing with him before he sang for us, and he softly led us: "On a hill far away stood an old rugged cross . . ." and then, "He leadeth me, oh blessed thought, O words with heavenly comfort fraught," and next, "This is my Father's world and to my listening ears . . ." and last "Christ the Lord is risen today, A-le-lu-jah . . ."

Suddenly we were not the PTA or the Rotary or Volunteer Firemen. We were worshippers. In our acknowledgment of him in a few verses of song, each of us, in a way that was uniquely private and corporate, had heard the speaking voice of God.

One night recently we were coming to the end of a dinner party at our house. Peg had cooked a delicious meal and we had visited in the living room afterward for a long time. We were all close friends and it seemed so good to have a quiet, unhurried time to be together. We laughed and talked and commiserated about our kids. Finally one couple said that they would have to be going and everybody else got up and put on their coats too. We were standing in the hall by the front door visiting for a final moment or two. Someone suggested we pray together before we parted. With bowed heads we lifted our hearts together to him and as we did the bonds of friendship slipped tighter around us as we all recognized the calling voice of him who makes us one.

I know it sounds better to sing when Billy Crockett plays his guitar. But you can hum a chorus or two of an old hymn to yourself in the car on the way to work. And I know it's easier to pray when you are in a circle of old friends with locked arms. But you can breathe a prayer in the elevator on the way to the dentist's office.

If you will acknowledge, recognize, hum, pray, if you will commit yourself to this process of listening, you will begin to realize that the voice you have heard so often across the days of your life has been his voice.

Branches Are For Bearing Fruit.

"My Father is the Gardener, I am the Trunk, you are the branches and branches bear fruit." (John 15)

I think of a car I happened to be driving behind in a recent election year in our state. We had a gubernatorial candidate whose name was Jake Butcher. It is not easy to build a campaign slogan around the name "Jake Butcher." It sounds like an announcement for a meat-cutters' convention. The slogan was "Jake in '78." which, incidentally, turned out to be erroneous. On the left side of the bumper was this campaign message, "Jake in '78." In the middle of the bumper was a sticker that read, "Jesus is Lord." And on the right side was this startling revelation: "Sailors have more fun." It made one wonder who was driving the car and where on earth he was going!

It isn't that most of us don't have any direction at all. Usually, we have so many directions we are trying to go that no one is the least bit surprised that we aren't sure where we are going, either. I have always felt a little more comfortable with the car whose bumper sticker stated honestly, "Don't Follow Me—I'm Lost."

Sometimes, it is hard to remember, if indeed we ever really knew, even *why* we are. Most of us could be filed under Miscellaneous.

Two of the things I believe are always present in the words of Christ are high privilege and deep responsibility. And I think they are both here, too.

There is a very satisfying privilege to those of us he is calling branches. What he is really saying presents itself to me in a way that is so simple that I don't know why I often overlooked it.

If I were part of a tree, I don't think I'd want to be the trunk. In the first place, a great part of the trunk is buried in the dirt and mud. The bigger the tree, the more there is way down there where it is dark and dirty. Always, it has to keep spreading out down in the earth in search of moisture and nourishment. And then the branches are not usually very thoughtful and they reach out in every direction as far as they can and they love to swing in the wind. And the more fun they have, the bigger the problems of weight and balance for the poor old trunk. Then there are the obvious hazards of sign hangers with hammers, and romantics with knives, not to mention woodpeckers and lumberjacks.

I think I'd rather be a branch. In the spring, branches burst into delicate buds. They furnish shade for summer picnics. They are ladders for little boys to climb to the skies. Branches blossom and flower to tell us all that there will be more trees. And branches bear fruit—like big, juicy red apples that you can shine on your sleeve and bite into while the juices dribble down your chin. I'd rather be a branch than a trunk.

And Jesus is saying to us all that he will be the trunk and we can be the branches. Can you hear him saying to you that he will bear you up in the summer's sun, in winter's storm? That he will nourish and water you, that you will only be barren for a season? That you will soon burst forth in leafy foliage, in radiant blossom, and in life-giving fruit? He is saying something very good to us when he says, "My Father is the Gardener, I am the Trunk and you are the branches."

I know I am an inveterate privilege-looker, but one can hardly fail to see there is also a lot of responsibility here as well. It seems that it goes without saying but just let me remind you of some things of which his words remind me.

One is that gardeners do not bear fruit. You never saw a gardener with tomatoes hanging down from his arms, did you? Gardeners select the field and prepare the soil and plant the seed and chop the weeds and prune the plants. But they don't bear fruit.

And trunks don't bear fruit. They support the weight and seek out the moisture. They hold the branches up to the sunlight. They bear branches but they don't bear fruit.

Branches bear fruit and we are the branches. Suddenly, he seems to be saying to us that if there is any fruit borne in the places we are, we will be the bearers. And if we are not fruitful, there won't be any fruit at all. At least, not until he grows some new branches.

In this simple way, he is telling us that we are to be doing what branches are supposed to do. He is talking about our purpose and our place in life.

If you have the feeling that you are the one who is supposed to keep the saints free of weeds, lay down the hoe. That is the gardener's job. The Father is the Gardener. If it seems to you the weight of the whole church is resting on you, set it down. The trunk will take care of that, and Jesus is the Trunk. You are a branch and branches bear fruit, much fruit—fruit that will last.

"I am the vine, my Father is the Gardener, and you are the branches." And the branches that live in the Vine will be cultivated and tended by the Gardener and they will be nourished and supported by the Vine.

And they will bear much fruit.

You *Should* Lay Down Your Life.

"There is no greater love than this, that a man should lay down his life for his friends." (John 15:13)

Some people love rules. Generally, I suspect it is because they are the rule makers. Maybe it is because I never seem to get to make the rules, but I like the word *should* better than the word *ought*. And I like *ought* better than *must*. Usually it is the rule makers who use ought and must. But I like *should* best.

The rule makers love to post the rules. Once on a trip, I saw a sign in a village in England that read: "Parking Restricted Between 1st April and 30th September Each Year to Two Consecutive Hours At Any One Time Between The Hours 8:30 a.m. and 6:30 p.m. on Any Day."

I was glad I was on a bus.

Then a couple of years ago I was speaking at a retreat at a conference ground in southern California. Out in front of the dining hall was a large paved area. It was guarded by a sing which read: "No Parking—Ever."

I wanted to rent a car. Something within me wanted to see if there really wasn't some time, even if it was in the wee hours of the morning, when you could just park there a minute or two. But the sign said ever. Not now, not during the millenium, not during eternity, not during lunch, not ever.

So you can see why I am intrigued by this use of the word *should* in this great statement of Jesus', "A man should lay down his life."

He could have said *ought* and it would be a true statement. And he could have said *must* and, of course, it would have been true. And he could have said *will* and it would be just as true. Because we are all somewhere in the process of laying down our life.

Last year I stood in the early spring sunshine at the graveside service reading some scripture, making a few remarks, and praying at the burial of my aunt, Maggie Mai. My Uncle Robert had asked me to lead in these brief moments of memorial. I am his namesake and I felt honored to be invited to share in this deep time in his life. He sat quietly weeping as we buried his wife of nearly sixty-four years. As long as I can remember him, he has been a shy, dignified, self-contained man. That afternoon, in his ninety-first year, he looked so lonely and frail that my heart ached for him.

I have passed his name on to my son and he, in turn, has passed it on to his. So now there are four Robert Green Bensons. Our ages cover a span of nearly eighty-five years, but there are commonalities about us all. One, of course, is our name. Another is that it is as true of one of us as it is of the others—each of us is laying down his life. Little by little we are each in the process.

Young Rob is just losing his baby teeth. You just get two sets, you know, and here he is at age seven, losing part of the first ones already. And I am losing what most everybody loses at so-called middle age. I guess I am middle-aged but, to tell you the truth, I don't know many people who are 102. My uncle had on a hearing aid that afternoon to try to hear what I was reading. I had on bifocals to try to read what he was hearing.

But this does not seem to me to be the context in which Jesus is thinking when he said a man *should* lay down his life. He does not seem to me to be telling us that we *must* lay life down or even that we *ought* to lay it down. And he does not even seem to be suggeesting here that indeed we *are* doing so. He is reminding us that we *should*.

I am beginning to believe about the scriptures that he is always trying to say something good to me. Even when he is commanding, I think if I could understand what he meant, I would find it is always something weighted with possibilities, surrounded by joy, and rooted in peace. All for me, all from him.

And *should* is the way I hear him speaking to me. *Ought* and *must* speak with tones of enforcement, like "This is what will happen if you don't." *Should* seems to suggest more what will come to me if I do. And his voice does not ever seem to come to me in some sort of veiled threat, "If you don't..." It always seems to be coming to me as a gracious, gentle invitation, "If you do..."

So I think he is saying something very rich to us when he says, "A man should lay down his life."

One of the things I hear him saying here is that it is in laying down one's life that joy comes to us.

In this place he is using a trilogy of words. The first of the three is joy and the second is love. These two words are certainly compatible and it is not hard to think of them together. One would imagine that the third word in the trilogy would be peace or hope or grace or mercy or any of those other words we usually associate with happiness. But he is joining joy and love with death. He is saying that joy and love and laying down our lives are three ideas that just naturally belong together. They are not mutually exclusive, like somebody said about the words "military intelligence." They are friends and they travel hand-in-hand.

I am beginning to understand this a little bit. At the company I had a very good secretary. One of the things about an efficient secretary is that she keeps posted in your calendar, and hers, all the dates and appointments that are important. Each year she would mark my new calendar book with days I wanted to remember like birthdays and anniversaries. A few days before the day, Karen would begin reminding me that I should buy a gift and a card.

Sometimes, I was especially busy and each day she would remind me again, and I would tell her that I had not forgotten. But when the day came and she asked me if I had been shopping yet, I had to say no. She knew the appointments for the day and knew that I would be busy all day long with one person or meeting after another, straight through lunch. In fact, by the time I would finish, it would be past time to get home for dinner. So she would say, "Do you want me to buy the present?"

"Well, yeah," I would weakly reply.

Did you ever give your wife an anniversary present that your secretary had bought? Well, it wasn't much fun to give and I suspect it wasn't much fun to receive, either, because all of the giver that was involved were some dirty green pieces of paper. And no matter how many of them it took, it still did not represent as much as it should have, because it did not have the giver's time, his love, or his thoughts. It only took me once to see that. There isn't much joy in giving what somebody buys and wraps for you.

When Jesus says, "A man should lay down his life," I believe that what he is trying to get us to see is that this is where joy and love are found. Not just for the receiver but for the giver as well. He is reminding us to release our gifts and graces and let them flow out of us and into others, knowing that as we do, joy and love will come flowing back to us.

Over the years I have observed a change in the way we celebrate Christmas at our house. The process of opening gifts is taking longer and longer. When the kids were small, it didn't take very long at all.

At the house where we spent so many Christmases together, we couldn't see the living room from the bottom of the steps. On Christmas morning, the rule was that the kids had to wait on the third step until Peg and I gave the word. We made the coffee and arranged all the presents and things that Santa Claus had brought, although I was never one to give him much of the credit. If I bought it, I put my name on the card. And when we were ready, poised with the camera, we gave the word and it was as if some starting gun had sounded. In an instant or so, in an explosion of tissue paper, little boys were transformed into cowboys and dolls found new mothers. But the moments were soon over when someone ran outside to ride a new bike or kick a ball. It was unbelievable how quickly a time so long awaited and prepared for could be over.

It is taking longer now. And the reason seems to be that nobody wants to open what he got. He had rather see somebody else open what he was giving.

In the summer, while we were on vacation, Peg and Leigh were shopping together. Leigh finished and came out on the sidewalk where I was sitting with some other temporary shopping widowers. Peg bought something for Leigh and hid it away in her suitcase and kept it all fall. Once or twice, she thought she couldn't wait any longer to give it to Leigh, but she managed. And she had wrapped it and put it under the Christmas tree.

Now she is handing it to Leigh and kneeling in front of her, waiting for it to be opened. Leigh is like her mother, for which I am glad. All ribbons, paper, and boxes must be saved. First, she reads the card and then slowly and carefully she unwraps the gift. To Peggy, it seems like forever. But the moment finally comes and Leigh exclaims, "Oh, I saw that last summer and I wanted it but I just hated to ask."

"I saw you see that last summer," Peg smiles, "and I thought it was so much like you, I bought it for you."

And Jesus is trying to explain to us who was the happiest person that morning.

Joy and love and death are the words he is using and he gathers them up with should. *Should* because this is how joy makes it way to you.

A second thing that is occurring to me is that it is in the process of laying down one's life that God's strength restores us.

Last year I enjoyed the privilege of helping to fill the chaplaincy of my alma mater, Trevecca Nazarene College, here in Nashville. Actually, the pastor on the college church, my good friend Ed Nash, was doing most of the work. To try to maintain some continuity in the spiritual life of the students, he and I had a chapel service each week. He was nice to insist that I do the speaking. Naturally, when someone is willing to do all the work and let me do all the talking, it's a job in which I'm interested.

For the fall quarter I was using the first chapter of Ephesians as a background for my talks. Most of my previous speaking from Ephesians had been in the third chapter, so I was seeing some new things. One of these thoughts was a different way of perceiving the relationship of God's strength and our weakness. But the new and almost startling insight that came to me was the idea that our weakness also determines the manner and the measure in which God's strength comes to us.

It is not easy to describe the strength of God. You don't know what to compare it to. There aren't enough words and you can't use a yardstick. How do you say what he is and what he can be to us? Paul says that his power is "measured by the strength and might which he exerted in Christ when he raised him from the dead...."

Sometimes I think we have a notion that Christ was kind of pretending in the tomb. He was dead, in a sense maybe, but somehow he was really just waiting until Easter morning when he would get up and come on out. But it was not like that at all. He was dead-dead.

The silence of death was interrupted only by the muffled sobbing of the women who stayed and the occasional steps of the guards as they moved about to keep themselves awake.

He had said he was life but he was dead. He had said he was the way but he took the same old road that man had always traveled. He had said he was living water but there was only a puddle left in the memory of a few men and it was soon going to evaporate in the noonday sun. He had said he was bread but there were barely enough crumbs left to show what had been on the plate. He had said he was the light of the world but his tomb was as dark as every man's. He was dead.

You cannot be any weaker than dead.

And so God, the Father, who had breathed the breath of life into man, leans low and once again blows life into his Son. It throbs through is body. Decay and death are stopped. He shakes away the burial clothes. Jesus was raised from the dead but it was because he had been willing to die.

If Jesus had rather not gotten involved, if he had managed to stay aloof from the events of that momentous week in Jerusalem, if the crowds and the noise had only given him a headache and a mild rash, then a headache and a mild rash would have become the boundaries of God's power to help. Death, and only death, brings resurrection and life.

And I think Jesus is trying to tell us that the Father wants to do more for us than we can ever believe. But it is in our deaths, our defeats, our emptinesses, our discouragements, our vulnerabilities, our weaknesses, our surrenders, that he can help us. For he can only pick up what we are willing to lay down. No wonder Jesus says *should*.

We used to sing a song called, "Ten Thousand Angels." It was popular in its day and rather widely used. The thing that it says best is that, although Christ could have called ten thousand angels to his rescue, he suffered and died alone.

A friend of mine on the West Coast, Fred Bock, has an offbeat sort of humor. Once he was telling us about some songs that he had written that just missed popularity by one word. If he had just changed one word the song would have been widely used. On of his titles was, "He Could Have Called Ten Thousand Locusts." If you knew Fred, that would be as funny to you as it is to me.

But I was thinking about that later. Jesus really could have called ten thousand of anything he wanted to call — angels, armies, legions, floods, even locusts. But we are not redeemed because he could have, we are redeemed because he wouldn't.

Jesus' death on the cross was not some unfortunate act that lay in stark contrast to the way he lived. His living and his dying were lovely in their sameness. For he was always giving away parts and pieces of himself. The choices that he made were choices that led him to the cross. The conflicts came because he could not keep from laying himself down when the misfits and the needy came to him. If he could have walked on by the cripple beside the pool that morning, he would not have been accused of breaking the Sabbath and he would not have aroused the wrath of those who only knew the law. And they would not have plotted his death. But he couldn't and he didn't.

Isaac Watts wrote a phrase in what I guess is my favorite hymn, "When I Survey the Wondrous Cross." The phrase is "sorrow and love flow mingled down." Jesus is telling us and showing us that sorrow and love go together. And that it is sorrow which gives love its redemptive quality.

We should lay down our lives because that is the way we are made joyful. It is the way joy comes to us.

And then, we should lay down our lives because that is the way they become redemptive. It is the way love flows out of us.

And we should lay down our lives because that is the way we are made strong. It is the way his help comes to us.

It is not the strength of his arm that reaches out to us, it is the vulnerability of his heart.

We are not helped in our afflictions because he has the power to help. We are comforted and redeemed because his heart is broken.

The Way To Run A Business.

I read about a man who said that he never fussed at an employee in the afternoon because he liked dogs. He went on to explain that usually what happened was that the man went home frustrated and fuming and the first thing he did was to give his wife a few short answers and make her mad also. About that time the oldest son would innocently stroll through the kitchen and mom would give him a verbal blast. He would then seek out his sister and pass it on. In a little while the baby brother would come wandering in and the sister would tell him in no uncertain terms to let her things alone and stay out of the room. And the poor little brother, being low man on the totem pole, would start out into the yard and see the dog is asleep on the back step so he would just kick the dog. So the employer didn't bawl people out in the afternoon because he liked dogs.

And if it is true that anger and frustration can be, and is, readily passed along, then how much more is it true that love and kindness can run through a whole company.

Through my brains and intelligence and brilliance in choosing a father who was in the publishing business, I achieved, by diligence and hard work, a management position in the company. Since I was not overly trained for this position except through experience, I made a sincere effort to belong to enough management book clubs and take enough magazines like *Fortune* and *Nation's Business* and *Business Week* to attempt to formulate some philosophy of management of my own. If nothing else, the books and magazines look very impressive lying around your office. But I have been trying to find out what managers are supposed to do.

This often puzzles my children, too. The young ones ask, "What is it you do? The truck drivers drive the truck, and the wrappers wrap the packages, and the key punchers punch keys, and the typists type, and the artists design and illustrate — but what is it that you do?"

Patrick was supposed to go to work with me one day last fall and I was sick and he got himself a ride and went anyway. I was told later that he tried as best he could to do what he thought it was that I did and he leaned back in my chair and put his feet on the desk and dialed the secretary to order cokes most of the day.

Somebody I would like has said about businessmen that you are "a feeling human being first and a manager second." Part of what I am supposed to do each day is to walk through the building and know as many of our people as I possibly can by their names and to be able to ask them about their wives and families and dreams as well as why they are not doing their jobs better.

I believe that openness and compassion and love are the best ways to run a business. And because we have a team of younger guys who feel this way, too, I think that our company is a redemptive place to work. We have an old building and there are times when everybody wants the one old elevator and it is a growing company and there are times when everyone wants their job out of the art department next. And there are times when tempers flare and people exchange words they should not have said. They even accuse me from time to time of getting the "tight-whites", which means that when I start through the building with my lips tight and drawn, it is time to get in your own area and get on with your job. I'm not saying that it is a perfect place to work but I am saying that the heartening sign is that when these things happen you will almost invariably find whoever had the "tight-whites" retracing his steps in a half-hour or so to apologize.

So I want to say firmly, love is the way to run a business.

"What about the bottom line, what about the ratio of the earnings to investment, what are the sales compared to last year, what is the age of the receivables, how often does the inventory turn?"

I know there are questions that must be answered but they are just effects not causes. A business is people — people who create product with other people. Product to be ordered, inventoried, wrapped, shipped, and delivered by people to people who sell to other people.

A business is people and people always respond best to love.

If you really want to lose some money on a given day, go chew somebody out in bookkeeping or shipping or somewhere in your building. Do it in front of everybody else and see how much work you get for your money the rest of the day from that person or the rest of the people who were so embarrassed for him and mad at you that the whole afternoon is spent in mumbling and grumbling about what a sorry place this is to work anyway.

I have heard people say that love is only a defense weapon or technique. No matter what it is that's going on about you, you can just fill your heart with love and sort of draw up within and keep sweet, while the world surges about you in ruin. But love is more than a defensive, protective, hide-behind fortress into which we can retreat. It is also a positive, aggressive force that can be actively and energetically used to change circumstances and situations. I do not mean that it is a way to manipulate people or to get them to do what you want them to do but that it is the finest way to bring out the very best there is within a person.

But how do you start? I've had people who said, "If I went and told my foreman that I loved him, he'd think I was crazy or I might just get slugged in the mouth." I don't know exactly where or how you can start, but somehow, in some way, whether you are the boss or the accounting department manager or a worker on the dock, you must begin. By a word, by a hand on a shoulder, by interest, by bearing burdens, by smiling, by bringing an extra piece of cake, you must let the people around you know that you care. And you can begin to transform a department or area by love, whether you are the supervisor or the newest person.

Yes, people have to be motivated, and some people will give you 110 percent and some will give you about 63 per cent and occasionally someone will have to be let go, but compassion and concern will go further in these and any other situations than fussing, ranting, and staying on somebody's back all the time or any of the other strategies that we use. Instead of the right one, that love is the way to run a business.

Bump, Bump, Bump.

We bought an old building and remodeled it for offices and warehouse space. The electrician who did the work was named Richard but he was such a talker that after awhile somebody in the building started calling him "Motormouth." He always had a smile and a ready answer to any question, serious or joking. He was a joy to have in the building. In a year or so we were making some additional changes that would require wiring and I asked if anyone had called Richard.

Somebody said, "Didn't you hear about Richard?"

"No, I didn't."

"Well, about two months ago his partner went by the trailer park to go to work with him and Richard said, 'I'll just meet you up at the job in about twenty minutes.'

"And Richard went back into the trailer. He had been arguing with his wife and went back to the bedroom and came back and touched her shoulder as she stood at the sink. She turned just in time to see him pull the trigger of the pistol he had pressed against his head."

Richard, "Motormouth," always joking, always laughing, always talking, always willing to be the butt of our jokes, was dead. I'd asked him lots of times how he was doing, but I guess I never asked him in such a way that it made him want to tell me.

Life in a way is like those electric bump cars at the amusement park. We just run at each other and smile and bump and away we go.

"How are you doing?" (Bump.)

"Hi, Motormouth." (Bump, bump.)

"Great, fantastic." (Bump, bump, bump.)

And somebody slips out and dies because there is no one to talk to. (Bump, bump, bump.)

Some Words Go Together.

I was reading the *Palm Beach Daily News*. It would take some explaining to let you know how I happened to be comfortably ensconced in Suite 4177-79 of the famous old Breakers Hotel perusing the society news of the Palm Beaches, but I was once, I really was. And let me tell you, it is a long, long way from the district campground at Sprouses Corner, Virginia, which is where I was a few days before.

The story that caught my attention was entitled "Bubbly Beginning" and it was about the dedication of the new Marjorie Meek Building for the offices of Planned Parenthood. The *Palm Beach Daily News* had covered the event in great style with ample editorial space and numerous pictures. In fact, there seemed to be room to cover all of the events of the day with aplomb. Including The Cartier International Polo Open; a guest performance of the Rochester Philharmonic; the opening of the Millie Stern, Sculptor, and Phillip Reed, Muralist, Exhibition; The Palm Beach Sailing Club Winter Finals, as well as the preview of the late Mrs. Post's Jewel Collection and numerous private parties and wedding receptions. There was a noticeable absence of any news about wars and famines and rumors of wars, but I guess a paper cannot cover everything that is important.

Gio King, a primary benefactor of Planned Parenthood of the Palm Beach Area, Incorporated, christened the new facility with a bottle of champagne and told the assembled crowd of some 250 other supporters of the organization that she was privileged to name the building in honor of the local chairperson of Planned Parenthood, Majorie Meek.

In the many pictures covering the event, several of those in attendance were wearing T-shirts with what I guess must have been the slogan or motto of the local chapter printed on them. The two words that emblazoned the shirts had a certain appropriateness about their alliance in connection with Planned Parenthood, even as they also seemed to be saying that they really did not go together at all. Although they are both good words, there is something inherent about both of them that doesn't quite go along with the other; some deep and intricate meaning that keeps them from being at home with one another. The two words were...*Love Carefully*.

The whole article brought to my mind a time some years ago when Peg and I had been riding along with the back seat of our VW filled to overflowing with our noisy children when we passed a billboard proclaiming the message of Planned Parenthood. I remember muttering above the din emanating from the rear, "Where were you when I needed you?"

Seriously, though, I have no reservations about the importance of planning for such momentous events as the bringing of another human being into the world to be nurtured and loved. Still, there was something good about the old days when kids just seemed to come along and Peg spent more time in maternity clothes than any other kind. You wondered how you were going to make it with one more mouth to feed, but you just went and and made it. And looking back at those days and events now, I wonder if we could have ever planned anything as fine as our family of five children. And I also wonder if we ever would have planned it to be so.

And I wonder if you can ever love carefully.

A cartoon in a recent New Yorker magazine showed a middle-aged couple, at least I judged them to be middle-aged, unless he was prematurely bald and she was prematurely plump, standing in the square of what appeared to be a small town. Across from them was a restaurant that offered FREE LUNCH, a library that proclaimed EASY ANSWERS, a pharmacy selling CURE-ALLS, and a repair shop that was advertising a QUICK FIX. And he said to his wife, "Hey, I like this town."

Any of those pairs of words, as difficult as they may be to find most of the time, go together much better than *careful* and *love*. The very word "love," not to mention the emotion, comes replete with risks. It always seems to take us farther than we first suspected that it would.

One cannot say, "I'll hold you, but don't rumple my clothes."

Or, "Go ahead and cry, but not in the middle of the night."

Or, "I'll take care of you when you are sick, if I can pick the time and the disease."

Or even, "Make your own decision, as long as you do what I think is best."

In fact, *but* and *if* and *so long as* are just like *careful*—they aren't to be used in the same sentence with love.

My friend, Derric Johnson, was the keynote speaker at the Church Music Publisher's Convention at The Breakers. If you are still curious as to how Peg, Leigh, Tom, and I got there, we had been invited back for old-times' sake and I was asked to serve as chaplain of sorts for the group. In his speech, Derric mentioned that we often say to each other in parting, "Take care." He thought, given the nature of life, it would be better for us to say, "Goodbye, take risks." He is probably right because well-being more often accompanies risk than it does carefulness.

I guess what I want to say is this—pick a word that will describe your way of loving. Let it be recklessly, extravagantly, profligately, lavishly, or prodigally. Let it be any word you want—except *carefully*.

The Look Of Compassion.

When I was younger and in Sunday School and youth meetings, somebody was always coming up with the idea that it would be good if everyone quoted their favorite scripture verse. This was generally followed by a loose translation of John 3:16 and a lengthy silence. Finally someone would quote that old favorite from John 11:34, "Jesus wept." I'm sure we all remembered it for its deep truth rather than for its brevity.

But what a tremendous verse, what a colossal truth! Jesus wept, he cared, he was touched, he was moved. And I like to think that weeping, caring, crying is one way to know a little bit how it feels to be like Jesus.

Once Jesus was very tired and had taken the disciples across the Sea of Galilee for a period of rest. He found that the people had seen them leaving and they had hiked around the northern edge of the sea and when the boat landed there were great crowds of people waiting for him. The scriptures said that even in tiredness and even in the press of time to be alone with the twelve, "He looked on the multitude and was moved with compassion." Have you ever thought what a beautiful look that the look of compassion really is?

The other day Peg and I were on a short trip over to Charleston, South Carolina. We were talking to the stewardess and told her we were changing planes at Washington to go down to Charleston. After a while she came back and said, "Are you talking about Charleston, South Carolina or Charleston, West Virginia?"

We told her that it was South Carolina and then she told us a story of a lady who had been on her flight a few months before. The flight was headed to Charleston, West Virginia, and the lady wanted to go to Charleston, South Carolina. The lady hadn't seen her husband in a year and he was waiting in the airport in South Carolina. She was very, very excited and mentioned South Carolina a time or two and suddenly it dawned on the stewardess what was happening and she had to tell this wife who had waited so long to see her husband that it was still going to be several hours of connecting and waiting before she could see him because somebody had just made a mistake. The stewardess was not exceptionally pretty, really just ordinary looking, but suddenly she was beautiful, for her face was covered with sympathy and caring as she remembered the young wife weeping into Charleston, West Virginia, as her husband waited for a yet to be revealed disappointment in Charleston, South Carolina.

Yesterday, my family and I were in the kitchen having a bite of breakfast before we went out into the yard to work and we heard this "Meow, meow." And we looked at the door and someone had left us a kitten. (How thoughtful!) The little kitten walked crooked. It held it's neck funny like they had left it without even stopping—just threw it out of the car.

A friend of our family said, "I'm allergic to cats. Don't bring that cat in the house. It makes my eyes water and swell up. Don't bring that cat in the house."

Some of us said, "You boys are going to the land fill with that load of stuff, why don't you take that cat for another ride. Stop this time when you let it off, but let it off somewhere."

As it always is at our house, some of our family said, "What cat."

But one of the members of our family saw a lonely, hungry kitten that needed to be picked up and hugged. A kitten that needed a bowl of milk. We looked at that kitten in different ways.

I am beginning to believe that as we live in him, when his life comes to us, we begin to see things different than we had seen them before because we are looking at them with his eyes. With his eyes we just see things in a way that we don't see when we just use our own eyes.

And when we begin to look at things with his eyes, we begin to feel different, don't we? His eyes have a way of changing us until we have his heart. The gospel always changes us. His life always changes us.

Sometimes I think that one of the reasons most of us don't like to pray is because when we pray we have to change. We have to be different that day. We have to treat people different. We have to act different. We walk different. It's just easier not to pray. It's just easier not to have his eyes and his heart.

What was it that drew men to Jesus? Yes, he spoke with authority and he did deeds of miracle and wonder, but I really think the one thing that men could not ignore was the compassion and love that drained out of his heart and on to his face and into his words and deeds.

If we abide in him as he abides in us, we begin to see things differently. We begin to look at things with his eyes.

The Case For Downward Mobility.

I had been president of the company for just a few months when I saw a book advertised by the American Management Association. The title reminded me of one of my strongest weaknesses. The book was written by Joseph Batten and was entitled *Tough-Minded Management.* Since I was not nearly as tough as I should have been, I immediately sent for the book. When it arrived and I unwrapped it, I was pleased. The title emblazoned on the dust jacket was stated three times in big, bold type: *Tough-Minded Management, Tough-Minded Management, Tough-Minded Management.*

Besides, this was the third edition and surely by now Mr. Batten was tougher than ever. Maybe by the time I finished reading and underlining, I would become a triple-tough president. And that would surely make me closer to what the company needed in the times in which we were operating.

I guess I expected too much from just one book. It was very fine and shouldn't be judged solely on its effect or lack of the same on me. Mr. Batten very lucidly explained and elaborated a basic style and philosophy of management in which I believed, and so I thought he was a very smart man. People with whom I agree seem remarkably intelligent to me. Underlying all of the management information in the book was a powerful indication of his insight into people and, moreover, into life itself. But the statement that gripped me the most from the entire book was this: "Over the long pull it is impossible to give away more than you can receive."

It seemed an unlikely place for this statement to appear. It certainly was not an expression I expected to see in regard to toughness in management. but there it was. It looked remarkably like a statement Jesus made in the fifteenth chapter of John when he said, "A man should lay down his life."

It is a radical idea to most of us that the results of our living will not be measured in terms of what we have been able to accumulate or acquire or hold tightly to. Even more startling to contemplate is that such results are important, rather, in relation to how well we have been able to let go of, to release, to lay down our lives. The society in which we live places most of its emphasis on picking up.

I think we are accustomed to phrases like:

"You've got your own life to lead."

"Business is business."

"Charity begins at home."

"Don't get involved."

"God helps those who help themselves."

"Safety first."

"Drive carefully - the life you save may be your own."

Hagar sums it up for us very well in the funny papers when he gives two rules for happiness: "Be content with what you've got," and, "Be sure you've got plenty."

For instance, at least once a year as a principal owner of the company, I was asked by the banks to submit a personal financial statement. It had a place in the left-hand column for a listing of all my assets: cash on hand, U.S. Government securities, accounts and loans receivable, notes receivable, life insurance cash surrender value, stocks and securities, real estate, automobiles, and other assets (marked itemize). On the other side was a place for a listing of all my liabilities. I always needed more room for this side. There were places to list notes to banks (secured and unsecured), loans against life insurance, accounts payable, taxes payable, mortgages against real estate, and any other liabilities (also marked itemize). At the bottom of the sheet there was a place to combine those two lines, the total assets and the total liabilities. The difference between those two numbers was called my net worth.

That number largely indicated to the bank the kind of customer I was and how I was to be treated. The larger the net worth, the more important I was to the bank. It dictated the title of the officer with whom I dealt and into which executive dining room I was occasionally invited for lunch. Generally, it seems to be true in banking that if you can prove you don't need any money, it will be very easy for you to borrow some. If you can prove that you do not need any at all, they will probably let you have as much as you want. It is only when you need it that they are a little sticky.

We all know about the process of trying to make sure that line seventeen is larger than line thirty-one, so that line thirty-three represents enough net worth to keep us afloat in the world in which we find ourselves. But deep inside, most of us have a faint suspicion that what Jesus is telling us just might be true. And we live wondering just what is real net worth.

The reconciliation of these two counter-claims on us is probably among the most difficult issues that we face. The gate to faith and freedom lies somewhere between selling all we have and giving it to the poor and obligating ourselves for far more than we need or use or can pay for. No relationship seems harder to define, or to maintain, than our relationship to our talents, strengths, weaknesses, accumulations, possessions, and energies.

And it is here that Jesus has something to tell us both with his words and his own way of living. Two questions present themselves immediately.

This life style or ethic which Jesus describes is like a road bounded on either side by a ditch. The ditches are ownership and accumulation. One is deep, but the other is deeper. The latter is almost bottomless in its subtlety. Jesus walked serenely and confidently down the road. It is quite evident that he had resolved both of these issues that beset us all.

Jesus' prayer in the seventeenth chapter of John can be looked upon as a statement of his real net worth. In a sense, it is his line thirty-three. I don't think he could have borrowed very much money against it. But it was what he owned. It was what he had accumulated. And now he is telling the Father. A few words in one of his phrases tell us those things we need to know about how he avoided the ditches, "Father, protect by the power of your name these men you have given me."

For Jesus, line thirty-three was these men. They were the sum total of his years of ministry. In nearly every sense of the word they were his. He found them, loved them, called them, taught them, led them. No one could deny that he served them. But he does not claim that they are his. He does not pray, "...my men." Rather, he says to the Father, "...these men you gave me." Jesus had long before resolved the issue of ownership.

Once the ultimate question of ownership is established, maybe our other attitudes and relationships can begin to come into proper perspective and priority. Underneath any commitment to give part of ourselves away there will be the awareness that we are releasing something that was not ours to begin with—it has been given to us. We do not have what we have and we are not what we are by the quickness of our minds and the strength of our arms—although it may have taken a liberal application of both to be where we are today.

Who made your mind quicker than those about you? Who made your arm stronger? Certainly some explanation can be found in your willingness always to do more than was required of you. Your dogged determination not to quit until you had completed more than those who were competing against you is part of the answer, too. But where did you get that will to exceed? Did you just sit down one day and decide that you would have more discipline and willpower and skill than anyone else? No. It was in you; it was there; it was a gift; it had come to you.

I do not want to make light of your blood, sweat, and tears, but others have also bled, sweat, and cried, perhaps in deeper measure than you. And it has come back to them as nothing. Your successes, your accomplishments, your ability to pile up net worth were given to you. And when you lay them down, you will not be giving away things that you skillfully put together, you will be releasing something that came to you.

The legal form for an auto title has a couple of lines marked lienholder. If you paid cash for your car, of course, there is nothing indicated on either of those lines. If, on the other hand, the money needed for the purchase was loaned to you, someone or some institution will want it indicated that they, too, have part of the rights of ownership. They hold a lien against the vehicle. If you buy a home, the term is mortgage but it means the same. This is the legal recognition that the thing described does not belong solely to you.

And the question of ownership in life will not finally be resolved for any of us until we realize that we do not hold a clear title to anything. God has a prior claim. He is a lien holder. He has the mortgage. He furnished us with the wherewithal which we used in acquisition.

And this is not always an easy admission for us to make. Probably some of the very first words we all learned were "me" and "mine." And it wasn't long afterward that we had to learn one more word, because people didn't listen to us when we said the first wo. The third word was "no."

I hadn't been in business long before I learned a basic truth. Unfortunately, it was as true about me as it was about everyone else. It had to do with signing agreements or contracts with people. The lesson was quite simple: Divide the profits before there are any. Try to make sure it is understood by everyone what is to be their share of the gains. Generally, everyone is fair and equitable over money that hasn't been made yet. But we all have a difficult time when we sit down to divide the money when it is lying on the table.

Then we begin to hear others say, and ruefully, to say ourselves, "Well, it was my idea..." "If it hadn't been for me..." "I worked longer than you did..." "I furnished the car..." "We started with my money..."

We may say any one of a dozen things but they all have a common meaning. They are said to establish our claims of ownership and they are said to minimize the rights of the other person.

One part of ownership is prudence. And one part of prudence is possessiveness. And one part of possessiveness is selfishness. And one part of selfishness is greed. And our claims to ownership find their basis somewhere in there between prudence and greed. It sounds better to call them prudent. Probably to the bystander, though, most of our prudence is hard to distinguish from greed.

We have a little dog whose name is Lady. There are times when Woman would have been a better name. She was sold to us as a French poodle but I have never seen the papers. At any rate, I don't think she is from downtown Paris. She thinks she's a hunting dog. Out where we used to live, she loved to chase squirrels and swim the lake and catch fish. At the new place, she chases the horses in the adjoining pasture. One of these days she's going to catch one and then she is going to be in real trouble.

We feed her, of all things, dog food. When our family is going to be away for a few days, we take Lady over to Peg's folks to stay. Now Peg's mother is a real dog lover. She will scramble eggs for Lady's breakfast and fry her a hamburger patty or two for lunch. At dinner she shares her roast beef or chicken with her. She treats Lady royally. When Lady comes home after such elegant dining, she is not excited about the dog food at all. In fact, she refuses to eat it.

Our neighbors have a dog they found at a service station. They felt sorry for him and brought him home to keep him from getting run over. He is not even from rural France. I think his father traveled for a living. They call him, appropriately enough, Exxon.

I learned that the best way to get Lady off her high horse and on to dog food again was to take it out on the porch and offer it to Exxon. You have never seen such looks on a lady's face as we see when she rushes out to greet poor old Exxon. No longer is it a question of whether she wants it or not. It's even deeper than need. It has become a matter of ownership and Lady is going to own it even if she has to eat it.

And one of the real probelms in ownership is the matter of holding on to what we claim to own. The process of gathering up is at the heart of our free enterprise system and as such is respected. We call it hard work, diligence, and Yankee ingenuity. Sometimes, though, our true colors are better revealed in the attitudes and actions surrounding our holding on. What seemed like prudence in possessing really becomes greed in protecting.

There is a deep correlation suggested in these words Jesus prayed, "Father, protect these men you gave me." A simple test that might help us to discern the difference in our motives between prudence and greed would be to measure our willingness to entrust what we have to the Father's watch, care, and protection.

The English word "protect" comes from a Latin word which means, "to cover in front." And we are saying something significant about ourselves in the things we cover, shield, guard, watch over, maintain, endorse, and support, because we think they are ours.

It's like the old story about the conversation between the farmer and the Lord. "If I had a million dollars I'd give it to you, Lord. If I had a thousand acres, I'd turn them over to you, Lord."

"Well, how about a pig?"

"Take it easy there, Lord. I've got a pig."

And most of us are like the farmer—we've got something and it is our got that gets us. Jesus is trying to show us and tell us where we got it. So the words, "lay down your life," are calling us to resolve the question of ownership.

I have used four words in describing the boundaries of ownership—prudence, possessiveness, selfishness, and greed. In my mind they are progressive, each one carrying a little more will or intent than the one proceeding it. You choose the one that best describes you. Whichever one you use is your description of your attitudes toward what you have. Just to make sure you know I think it is a serious matter, I did put greed in the list.

Your attic or garage or basement is probably no different from mine, stuffed to overflowing with things bought at one time or another because we thought we needed them. And probably the reason we don't need them now is because the manufacturers and advertisers of America have convinced us that we needed something else to replace all that stuff that we now have stored.

We live in a society whose chief business is creating needs for us. Its slogan is "Bigger and Better" and the name of its anthem is "Upward Mobility." Whatever it is that we need to do, somebody has thought of a better way for us to do it.

The lot on which our new house sits is just about an acre. When the amount of space covered by the house, driveway, patio, and sidewalks is taken out, I don't know exactly how much is left. But whatever there is needs mowing. There is a variety of equipment to do this job available for purchase or rental. There is a machine that you push and, as you push it, the wheels turn. They are connected to a reel and, when they turn, the reel turns and cuts the grass. You supply the power. There is also a machine that you push along, but it has a motor which turns the blade which cuts the grass. You only supply the power to turn the wheels. And there is a machine that you walk along behind, and the motor turns the wheels and the blade that cuts the grass. All you have to power is yourself. Best of all, of course, there is a machine that not only has a motor to turn the wheels and blades but a seat too — and you can ride along. All the power you have to supply is for steering. And a part of our economy is built on convincing people like me that what I really need to do the job right is the machine that I can ride on. And the advertisers work very hard to convince me that it is worth the thousand dollar difference in the machines that accomplish the task.

Then, too, if they can convince me that I need to ride while I mow, it will be much easier for the health spa, exercycle, jogging shoe, and running suit people to sell me the equipment I need to get some exercise. Not to mention the assorted medicines and tranquilizers I need to take to relieve the stress that I build up because of a lack of physical activity in my life.

And what is true about lawnmowers is true about everything we can think of from automobiles to dolls. A fearsome part of our economy over the years has been the automobile industry and its ability to persuade us to turn in our old car for a new one about every two years. And most of the time the sole reason for trading is a difference in the way the sheet metal has been crunched on the outside. Always there is a new model, something with a new feature that is given to us as the reason we should trade up.

And if we are ever to make any progress at climbing out of the ditch of Accumulation, we will have to learn to distinguish between real needs and created needs. Maybe the more proper words would be real needs and created wants.

Today we have only to ask two questions about what we want. The first is, "How much are the payments?" The other is, "How long do we have to make them?" In our credit-oriented society someone usually has a ready answer to both. And when those two questions are answered satisfactorily, we are ready to sign. If we can fit it into our financial budget, we will take it home with us or have it delivered Monday afternoon.

It may be time to see if it fits into our energy budget. For if we are going to lay down our lives, then somehow and at some place we are going to have to gain control of them so there is some left to lay down.

"Well, it is only $200 a month." But at $20 per hour you have just pledged ten hours a month, or two and a half hours a week toward a real need or a created want — chrome wheels and all. If you make half that much, you have pledged twice as much of your time and energy. If you make much less than that these days, you probably have two jobs and can't enjoy whatever it is they can't deliver until Wednesday anyway. But we have overdrawn our energy budget.

In his sermon on the mountain Jesus talked about this needless waste of our energies and emotions. His words are timely enough to have come from this morning's newspaper and speak to us where we are — "Be not anxious." Most of us have long since obligated ourselves into anxiety.

But he also suggests that there is an affection budget. In the same place he reminds us of the folly of trying to serve two masters, God and mammon. His solution is remarkably simple and direct: Seek the kingdom first. The great commandment is to love God with all of our heart. But it seems our heart is divided into a hundred pieces and scattered into all the places where we are keeping treasures.

When nearly every other voice and instinct is telling us to hold on, he is saying to let go. He is responding to our very radical need. For if our hearts do not lead us into the ditch marked Ownership & Accumulation, then it is very likely that Research & Development (along with Advertising & Marketing) will soon have us in the other. Either way we are robbed, willfully or unintentionally, of the life we need to be laying down.

The Commonplace Becomes A Sacrament.

We all are aware of how some ordinary thing can become sacramental to us. Some simple pieces of cloth, stitched together in a special way, come to represent our love of liberty and home, and are thus worthy of our bared heads and our crossed hearts. A wilted dandelion somehow forever deserves a place tucked away in our Bible because it was delivered in the grubby fist of a four-year-old. In some way, these become magnetic symbols around which our feelings gather.

One of the things I am hearing over and over again is that it is the desire and intent of Jesus to sacramentalize the commonplace — to bring the meaning and purpose that only his life can bring into the ordinary moments and places and happenings of our lives. Probably we are never far away from something which should be reminding us that we are never very far away from him.

This ability of his to make everything into a sacrament was evident from the very beginning of his life among us. Take the manger scene itself. At our house, we have a lovely set of wood carvings of the baby Jesus, Mary, Joseph, the angels, and the shepherds. It also includes some sheep, lambs, horses, cows, calves, ponies, and even a sleeping rooster. Peg and I bought the set when we were browsing through some shops in New Orleans one fall.

We had wanted a creche in our home for a long time and we were taken with the beauty of these figures. Peg is really the decorator at our house, and she has a knack for displaying things at their best and making places look special. But she agreed to let me set up the manger scene the first season. I must have done a pretty good job because I am now the official manger scene builder. She did request that I hone my skills on the sunporch the first year, but now the scene occupies the central place in our living room.

I have accumulated a box or two of materials that I use along with the carvings. There are some pieces of driftwood I picked up on our various vacations on the coast. I take them out of the box each year like old friends. I know each one of them for its special size and shape and smoothness. I wish that I could ask them questions and hear them answer back. "Where did you begin your journey? What kind of tree were you? What brought you crashing down? How did you get washed up on that lonely stretch of beach? Did you once hold up a little girl's swing or a boy's tree house? Were you part of a house or a boat or a packing box?" For I believe that everything has a story; it has been somewhere, and it is going somewhere.

I also have a collection of stones and rocks. I found them on trips, too — in fields and mountain streams and by country roads. They, too, I suspect, could tell me many things if I just knew how to listen to them. Annie Dillard wrote about a man in her neighborhood who spent all his spare time trying to teach a stone to talk. I think about him every year when I take my stones out of the box.

In early December, I get out all these manger things. With the stones, I make a rocky hillside, and with the wood, I build a barn and a stall. I carefully place the manger, the baby Jesus, Mary, Joseph, and all the rest of the figures (right down to the sleeping rooster on the roof). Then I light the candle, sit down before this scene again, and try to imagine how this holy story could ever have happened at all.

Admittedly, I have gathered up the materials for this scene from lots of places. But always I am impressed to remember that everything needed to make this sacred tableau can be found in anybody's neighborhood. Sticks and stones, straw and foliage, dogs and cats, neighbors and a virgin girl. All of them can be touched with the meaning that only Christ can bring, meaning that obliterates the lines which separate the divine and the commonplace, meaning that changes a stall into a holy place and a manger into an altar.

Men could only describe the things Jesus did as he walked among them as miracles. His mother took him to a wedding in the very first days of his ministry. She was embarrassed for her friends because the wine ran out and she turned to Jesus for help. There were six jars sitting beside the door. They were used to hold the water that Jews used to wash their feet and hands—to cleanse themselves ceremonially. They were empty, and Jesus asked the servants to fill them with water. Try to imagine their chagrin when he told them to draw out a pitcher of this bathwater and take it to the master of the feast. Try to imagine their surprise when the master tasted it and wondered why the bridegroom had saved the best wine until last. John said that this was the first of Christ's "miraculous signs."

Another day a blind man stood before him. Jesus knelt down and spit in the dust. With his finger he stirred the saliva into the dirt. Jesus took the mud, smeared in on the man's eyelids, and told him that if he would wash in the pool of Siloam, his eyes would be healed. The man did as he was told, and went back to his village seeing his home for the first time in his life.

This ability to transform the commonplace was even more evident in the events that surrounded Jesus' death. On the eve of his betrayal, Jesus and his disciples celebrated Passover in an upper room. He wanted it to be a sacramental meal, one they would always remember. So he blessed a crust of bread and a cup of wine and shared them with his disciples. From the two most common elements of every Palestinian meal he made his monument.

The reason, of course, was that he wanted symbols that were within the reach of everyone. Nobody was so poor that they did not have bread and wine. The bread might have been as hard as a stone, and the wine might have been bitter and filled with dregs, but it would serve to refresh the body in that land of sparse wells. And both would have been on the table of even the poorest of peasants.

So a supper became a sacrament, a place where the holy life of God happened. Because of that meal we should burst into song. For it is saying to us as loudly as we will let it, "There is life in the touch of Jesus."

If he can take sticks, stones, straw, bathwater, saliva, mud, and the waters of a murky pool; if he can take a crust of bread and a cup of wine; if, indeed, he can take these things and crown them with all the meaning his life can bring, why can we not see how different our lives would be if we would truly yield them to him.

Less And Less Of Us.

Let me tell you a story about being in the hospital last spring. I had been in before, but still I was impressed with the tremendous forward strides that have been made in the practice of medicine. Machines and equipment have been developed that greatly aid in the doctor's task of diagnosing the problems, prescribing the treatment, and alleviating the suffering.

But I also observed that some things still have not changed. For instance, you can get a private hospital room but you still can't get a private hospital *gown*.

I also observed that medicine, or the art of healing, is practiced (not a very reassuring term) in concentric circles that seem to be at various distances from you.

For instance, the x-ray department seemed rather far removed from me. I could always tell when I was going to be taken down there because the nurse quietly removed my water container at midnight and they left me off the breakfast list the next morning. Finally they would come and roll me down in a wheelchair and I would join a host of other people who also had not had any breakfast. We were in an assortment of robes that would have made the church drama director white with envy. And it was cold down there. You could hang meat in the x-ray department. You would think with all the other modern miracles, the x-ray table could be preheated. X-ray was always a department—never a he or she to me.

The circle came closer to me when my doctor came. We are very fortunate to have a compassionate, caring person for our family doctor. He felt my pulse and listened to my heart and talked to me. He answered my questions and Peggy's, and studied my chart and wrote the orders so that I would be as comfortable as possible while on the road to being well.

But the circle of medicine which seemed to surround me most tightly was practiced in the wee hours of the morning when, for the fourth time within an hour, I pressed the call button and someone answered, "Can I help you?"

"Yes, I need you again."

And someone came and cleaned me where I was dirty and touched me where I hurt. And she remade my bed and tucked the covers under my chin once more and said to me, "Now go back to sleep, but call me if you need me."

I mumbled some dumb apology for bothering her and making such a mess again. And the answer was, "That's okay. That's why we're here."

I think Jesus is saying to us, "You're going out to live life. Don't take too good care of yourself, find some things that count, stick your neck out, spill some blood, spread some love. The sin is not in breaking rules—it's in holding back."

A lot of sharing in our lives is on some outer circle where it doesn't cost us much at all, but I am beginning to believe that the true, meaningful experience of our lives will be in the touching and washing and smiling and lifting.

And all along there will be less and less of us because of places and hours and people where we have left part of ourselves.

Our Own True Selves.

Every now and then I find myself doing something my dad taught me when I was a kid. It's usually something I vowed I would never do when I grew up and was on my own.

I don't know why I won't go ahead and admit that I am more and more like my dad everyday. I guess it is because I would have to acknowledge that he was right about most things. For instance, he not only loved to garden, he loved to garden early in the morning. My brother, John T., and I used to argue over who was going to deliver the morning paper route and who was going to the garden with Dad to chop weeds.

Like nearly every other boy in the neighborhood, I had made up my mind that when I had my own home it was going to have a green concrete yard. But this spring I found myself planting a garden. What is worse, I found that I like to get up early in the morning to work in it. And, just like my dad, I began with a thorough research of seed catalogs. I ordered every one I could find advertised. For a while I thought just reading the catalogs would get the gardening out of my system, but it only increased my anticipation of spring. I made out the order and eagerly awaited the arrival of the package like a kid. Well, really, I was waiting on the box from Burpee like a dad. And while I waited, I read every magazine and book on how to raise vegetables I could find.

Finally, the seeds came and the weather was warm enough to turn the soil and plant my garden. I guess I should say 'gardens' because the rabbits and the cutworms quietly devoured the first one while we took a trip with the kids on their spring break. I'm watching this one like a full-time scarecrow. Peg asked if I were going to plant any onions, and I told her I didn't think so because I hate rabbits with bad breath.

But if I never bring anything into the house from the garden for the table, it will still have been worth it because I always come in filled with wonder. Something about a seed has caught my eye and my heart.

I took those tiny seeds, mailed to me in a box from Iowa, and put some of them too deep and some of them too shallow. I'm sure, now, that I planted some of them too thick and I planted some of them too thin. By all odds, I probably planted most of them upside down. They are not marked "This Side Up," you know. But the secret to their life is not written on the outside, it is within them.

External forces like rookie farmers, obese rabbits, and lumberjack cutworms may torment the roots and harass the stalk. But with whatever freedom we allow the poor seed to live its own life, its built-in energies and knowledge never give up. It knows what it is supposed to be doing and it does it. It knows the rules of life and it lives them. It goes about its business of bursting forth in root and stem and fruit. The seed knows that life is not some proper combination of external forces and factors, it springs from within.

Generally, our attempt to find remedies for life—our needs, our wants, our fulfillment—are made from the outside in. We live as if life itself was on the out-side. As if brighter paint and louder music will bring to us those meanings and joys which we so desperately long for and need.

It is probably quite significant that one of the business phenomena of our day is an industry that has come to be known by the speed and efficiency with which the product is dispensed rather than by the quality of the product itself. We do not speak of the *nourishing food* business, or the *gracious dining food* business, or the *economical food* business but we talk a lot about the the *fast food* busi-ness. Never mind the taste, much less the nutrition. It is in a pretty box and, most of all, it can be served to us in a hurry.

The society in which we live today would have us believe, or at least hope, that life will be okay if we can just get it packaged right and served to us on the run. But wrappings and to-go windows have very little to do with quality of life itself. The real processes of life take place somewhere deep within us. For within all of us there is a wish for meaning. It may only come occasionally, like a flash of sum-mer lightning, but it comes. Though we may sometimes doubt the quality of spiritual bread, we can't kid ourselves that we're not hungry.

I have an observation that I think I am ready to make about one's quest for life. It is that such a search for life and its attendant meaning is a journey on which you will come to find yourself. It is an inward journey.

One of the folk heroes at our house is John Denver. The kids have played his records and sung his songs until they are a part of many lovely memories and happy moments. My eyes still fill with tears when I hear him sing songs like "Poems and Prayers and Promises." He has captured in the words of his songs deep mean-ings that are true for all of us.

He has begun to do this with his camera as well. Not so long ago he was in New York City for the opening of an exhibition of some of his photographs of Colorado. In a television interview he was asked, "What would you like for people to say about you when you are gone?"

After a moment or two, he answered, "I think I would like for them to say, 'He became himself.'"

The task of becoming one's own self is probably more difficult than any of us imagine. A part of the problem is that we are not always so sure whether we are supposed to be radishes or tomatoes or nasturtiums or thistles. And it is further complicated by the fact that we can choose which one of those we would like to try to be. And even worse, we are all of them some of the time. But one of them is really us.

The tragedy that gradually befalls us is not that others do not know who we are, it is that we do not who we are. And that we spend our days knocking on every door we can find hoping that we will find the one that has our name on it.

When Peg and I were married, someone very close to us painted a picture for us to hang in our living room. It was, needless to say, the only original oil paint-ing that we had and, because it was done especially for us, we were very proud of it. Later on we were visiting in the home of some mutual friends and were some-what surprised to see a painting of the same scene done by our artist. It happened two other times. So now there were four of the fall forest scenes that we had seen. The painting was not quite as special as it had been before. Still, it had been done in love and it must have taken hours and hours and it was well done.

But the thing that finally kept us from putting the picture up again the next time we moved happened one afternoon in a furniture store. There, on the wall, with dozens of other "printed paintings" was our scene. Our friend had painted someone else's picture.

Many of us will never be truly happy or fulfilled because we never succeed in becoming ourselves. We never get around to being the particular person or painter that we were intended to be. We live our lives painting someone else's picture. We are not willing to take our palette and our paints and our brush and go to the mountain or the forest or the sea and labor until we have captured its beauty on our canvas. We only see their majesty through someone else's eyes and with the strokes of their brush.

Still, the quality of the seed, the life principle within us, never rests until it has made itself known and has been recognized and allowed to become that which it was supposed to be. It is true that we may ignore this call to life from time to time, but it will make itself heard again. Because, like the tiny seed, hidden somewhere within us is what we are supposed to be and what we are supposed to do.

One of the errors that we often make in this search for self is our failure to realize that the road which leads to self and the road which Jesus travels are one in the same. And the journeys that we make in directions away from him are also trips that take us away from ouselves. For some reason we think that real life is away from home and the Father and, like the prodigal son, we leave only to find that we are leaving behind the things which gave us life.

Not too long ago a couple who have been our good friends decided that they could not be a couple any longer. And so they divided their accumulated goods and the children, got a divorce, and went their separate ways. The cause, at least the one that was most visible to those of us who knew them, was an inability on the husband's part to live up to the vows of faithfulness, thus denying the marri-age its very foundations of sanctity. He readily acknowledged that probably only God could provide the strength that he was unable to find within himself. But he could not or would not ask for God's help.

Somehow, it is in his mind that in return for his help, God will want him to be somebody he does not want to be. He cannot believe that what he truly wants for himself and what God truly wants for him are one and the same. And my friend, though he might not see it now, is not just avoiding God, he is avoiding himself as well.

It is true, I believe, that when we come to ourselves, when we write our book or sing our song or fill our place, when we paint our own picture, we will have also come close to Jesus, for we will have begun to discover the life that he put within us.

It takes some real effort on our part to begin to discover who it is that we really are. We are all so conditioned by the world in which we live that we can go a lifetime and never get within a stone's throw of our own true selves.

Though it is difficult, it is necessary to try and clear away much of the debris that society places around us. Things like status, opinions of others, conformity and peer pressures which can keep us from examining the real touchstones of our lives have to be forgotten for a moment.

We have to sense our hopes and feelings about people, purposes and occupations. We have to ask ourselves some pointed, revealing questions.

"Do I like what I am doing well enough to spend a lifetime doing it? Is this the opportunity to be involved with others and life in a way that I feel good about? What would I really like to be doing? What do I really want in life? What do I see myself as in my dreams? Who do I most deeply sense that I am?"

It takes some time for us to come to ourselves. But when we do, when the deep, real part of us has spoken, we will have come to God. Because this best part of us — our finest aspirations, our highest hopes and dreams, our noblest intentions and purest desires — these are the image of God within us.

And from deep within the springs of our very beings they are calling us to become our own true selves.

A Believer In Moments.

Laughter In The Walls.

I pass a lot of houses on my way home—
some pretty,
some expensive,
some inviting—
but my heart always skips a beat
when I turn down the road
and see my house nestled against the hill.
I guess I'm especially proud
of the house and the way it looks because
I drew the plans myself.
It started out large enough for us—
I even had a study—
two teenaged boys now reside in there.
And it had a guest room—
my girl and nine dolls are now permanent guests.
It had a small room Peg
had hoped would be her sewing room—
the two boys swinging on the dutch door
have claimed this room as their own.
So it really doesn't look now
as if I am much of an architect.
But it will get larger again—
one by one they will go away
to work,
to college,
to service,
to their own houses,
and then there will be room—
a guest room,

a study,
and a sewing room
for just the two of us.
But it won't be empty—
every corner
every room
every nick
in the coffee table
will be crowded with memories.

Memories of picnics,
parties, Christmases,
bedside vigils, summers,
fires, winters, going barefoot,
leaving for vacation, cats,
conversations, black eyes,
graduations, first dates,
ball games, arguments,
washing dishes, bicycles,
dogs, boat rides,
getting home from vacation,
meals, rabbits and
a thousand other things
that fill the lives
of those who would raise five.
And Peg and I will sit
quietly by the fire
and listen to the
laughter in the walls

I'm A Believer In Moments.

In early November last year, Peg and I were taking a trip together, and while we were traveling along, we worked out our budget for Christmas. We listed all those to whom we wanted to give presents and how much we thought we could spend for them. We could have done a little better all the way around, I guess, but we also decided to spend some money on "moments."

I'm not sure that I even know how to describe a moment when it comes. Most of the time they come unexpectedly anyway. I'm not sure I know how to define it when it happens. But I know it when it does.

We put aside some money for groceries, so we could have some friends over. We set aside money to take the boys and their dates to see Dickens' great classic, "A Christmas Carol," which was going to be staged downtown at the Tennessee Performing Arts Center. For the night when Leigh came in from college, we planned a big evening out, all dressed for dinner in the Hermitage Hotel Dining Room. And there was money designated to decorate the house with candles and wreaths and angels and ribbons and bells and greenery and goodwill.

Of course, we have been around long enough to know that money won't necessarily buy a moment. You've been places, haven't you, where they said that something was going to happen and you paid your money and went and nothing did happen? But we were determined to decorate the walls, dim the lights, light the candles, ring the bells, and sing the carols so that if a moment decided it wanted to happen to us or among us, it would sure know that it was welcome.

Our family has a way of rating experiences together. One of the gauges of our pleasure was discovered when someone noticed that Peggy snorted when she was really tickled at something. Since that time the highest rating a joke can get at our house is a three-snorter. They may come when we all are laughing or teasing and they have been known to slip in along with someone's illness or struggle. The way we seem to recognize a moment at our house is that it is usually accompanied by lumps in our throats and tears in our eyes. And all of a sudden, we are standing in the midst of a moment.

On Christmas Eve the larger family gathered at our house to eat dinner and exchange gifts. Wally and Jean, Bo and Peggy's parents, Bo, Robert, Jetta and grandson Robert, Leigh, Tom, Patrick, Peg and I made up the crowd. The only empty places in the annual gathering were because Mike, Gwen, and Katie were in Colorado. It was Mike's first Christmas as a pastor and so they were not home for the holidays. (I am not as sure as I used to be that the pastor always has to be at his church for Christmas.) Sometimes a dash of sadness hastens the coming of a moment.

When the food was ready and it was time to eat we went into the living room. We stood in a circle around the *creche*. A solitary candle flickered light across the manger and the baby. With our arms around each other we sang, ". . . O come let us adore him, O come let us adore him, Christ the Lord."

A Believer In Moments.

Although I was not the ranking grandfather that night I wanted to lead the prayer. I bowed my head and, as best I could, I began to lift our thankfulness and praise for all that had come to us because he had come into the world in a manger — for family, for belonging, for grandparents and for grandchildren. And Robert added, "and for brothers and sisters." The amen was pronounced and as we started for the dining room it was easy enough to see, even through blurry eyes, that we had just experienced a moment.

There was dinner with all the trimmings — macaroni and cheese like only Grandmother Siler can make, Bo's green beans and her squash casserole, Jetta's pies and cheesecake, and Peg's turkey and dressing and rolls. When we had eaten far more than we should have, and the kitchen was clean, and the dishes were put away, we went into the den by the fire and took our places to open the piles of presents beneath the tree. There were "oohs" and "ahhs" and "thank you's" and hugs and squeals of surprise and delight as we opened the things we had bought and made for each other. I really think that those who had made gifts were the happiest of all, for they had given so much of themselves. Gwen's stuffed geese and her lacy pillows and Leigh's handpainted stationery with the paint still wet, to name a few, were gifts that drew loud praise.

Finally the gifts were all opened and the wrapping paper and ribbon had been cleaned up. Peg suggested that I read Truman Capote's *A Christmas Memory* to them all. I was happy to oblige. In fact I was just wishing someone would ask me. Fred Bock had given me the little book some weeks before and I had read it in some of the places I had spoken during the Christmas season. So I reached under my chair and pulled it out and began before the offer was withdrawn.

It is a beautiful, moving story about a Christmas when Truman was seven and living with his Aunt Sook who was in her sixties. It is a long-ago moment from his life made all the more poignant when you consider the strange directions in which he was finally taken by his fame and riches. His parents were divorced and neither wanted little Truman. So he was sent to live with some elderly relatives, and this old aunt was his best friend and companion. By the time I got to Christmas Day, when he and the old lady were flying the kites they had made for each other, our den was laden with warmth and feeling. They had made the kites because they spent all their money making and mailing fruitcakes to others. I read the things she said to him, "I've always thought a body would have to be sick and dying before they saw the Lord. And I imagined that when he came it would be like looking at the Baptist window: pretty as colored glass with the sun pouring through, such a shine you don't know it's getting dark. And it's been a comfort to think of that shine taking away all the spooky feeling. But I'll wager it never happens. I'll wager at the very end a body realizes that the Lord has already shown himself. That things as they are"— her hand circles in a gesture that gathers clouds and kites and grass and Queenie pawing earth over her bone —"just what they've always been, was seeing him. As for me, I could leave the world with today in my eyes." It was quiet enough to hear the tears gently falling from our cheeks onto our Christmas finery. Sometimes it seems like moments must travel in pairs.

Evenings like that come and go all too quickly. Too soon it was time for coats and hats and gloves and carrying-out-to-the-cars and then farewells. We were all standing in the kitchen saying our last good-byes, when Peg saw something on the counter top some friends had sent to us a few weeks before. It was an Erma Bombeck column entitled *One of These Days*. It was about some moments that had crystalized in her life. Peg began to read Erma's words: "One of these days you'll shout, 'Why don't you kids grow up and act your age?' And they will." She ends, "Only a voice crying, 'Why don't you grow up?' And the silence echoing, 'I did.' " There was enough stuff in the middle about no more nights in a vaporizer tent and no more carpools and PTA and wet-knotted shoestrings and tight boots to cause all four generations in my kitchen to stand unabashedly touched.

And we all exclaimed almost together, "What a Christmas celebration, it has been a three-sniffler." (Maybe that is not a record, but it's a good average.)

The socks will wear out and the ties will get spots on them and the sweaters will stretch out of shape. But the moments are tucked away in our memories for all time and will only improve with age. They will be brighter and happier every time we take them out to enjoy and celebrate.

I am a believer in moments.

Dedication.

Most of my writing
is dedicated to Peg, of course.

An old-fashioned girl
who said old-fashioned words with me —
to love and to cherish
and who has done so with style —
for better, for worse,
for richer and for poorer
in sickness and in health
for three decades
of our quest.

After all these years, five dear children
five grandchildren, fourteen jobs,
five pastorates, fifteen moves later...
it caught us by surprise.

We took each other's hand
and clenched them together
until our knuckles were white,
knowing full well that
we might not be able to hold on
in spite of our resolve.
So we relaxed our grip and
gently held hands in
a loving, releasing way
and suddenly, we became
more tightly bound than ever before.

By letting go...we held on.
By standing back...we drew closer.
By ceasing to clutch tomorrow...
there is nothing like today.

I'm Gonna Let It Shine.

There is always a faint sadness on wedding days because it is a day of endings as well as a day of beginnings. There are almost always two women on the second row who are weeping. Often, before the ceremony is over, there are two men sitting there helping with the sobbing. But there is also real joy as two people come to pledge their life and love to each other.

Something funny almost always happens at a wedding. Last summer my second son, Michael, married a lovely girl named Gwen. The wedding was held in her church in Colorado Springs. Just as it was time for the candlelighters to come down front, it was discovered that there were no wicks in the graceful brass rods that were to be used to light the altar candles. All of the wedding party was waiting in the vestibule. Mike and I and the best man were ready to enter the sanctuary from the front. Soon there was a frantic search in progress for two long candles which could be substituted as lighters. The lady who was in charge of the ringbearer and the flower girl joined the others in shaking down the church.

The ringbearer and the flower girl soon despaired of waiting and went ahead with the processional. Fortunately, they discovered that they were alone at the altar and returned to join the rest of the group. The incident didn't bother the bride and the groom. Mike and Gwen were well on their way to living happily ever after.

One part of the ceremony which couples often wish to include is the lighting of a candle together. This signifies their oneness. Three candles are placed on the kneeling altar. The large candle in the middle is not lighted. The smaller candles on either side of the center are burning. One symbolizes the bride; the other is for the groom. After the vows have been spoken and the couple is pronounced to be husband and wife, they kneel. When they rise, each takes their small candle and lights the large one.

I understand their reason for doing this. It is symbolic of two people becoming one. But what happens next always amuses me. When the center candle is lighted, the bride and groom blow out the small candles they are holding.

I always want to ask them if they really mean what they are doing. I don't think that I would have married Peggy twenty-five years ago if I had known that even before the echoes of the vows had faded away, she planned to snuff me out. I hardly think it would have been fair to have had the same intentions for her.

I understand the meaning of the oneness. But the deeper meaning of marriage is that two people become one so that they may each become more than they ever could have alone.

During the first years of our marriage we were struggling through graduate school and pastoring tiny churches. We had two young sons and Peg was working part of the time. It was easy to get into rather lively discussions about life in general and ours in particular. Sometimes she spoke so loudly that I even had to raise my voice to be heard.

Sometimes I had to remind her of some of her faults and failures. This, of course, was always done in order to help. She always ended such family dialogue with the phrase, "You made me what I am." The truth is, that at any point in marriage, you are in some way responsible for what the other partner is becoming. I think husbands and wives have the perfect right to say, "You are making me what I am."

Well, the years have passed and those early pressures are gone. Peg was a wonderful person then but she is super now. Bright, warm, open—she is like sunshine wherever she goes. She walks through our company and smiles and hugs and talks with everyone. In fact, I wish she would do more smiling and a little less hugging. Her visit is worth two hundred and fifty dollars for morale alone. I hope no one ever tells her that because I get her to do it for a free lunch. The thing that bugs me is that now she never says to me, "You made what I am."

But I think I helped. And I know that because I was able to get that sweet young thing to say "I do" to all those questions, I am more than I ever could have been without her. Her deep, unshaken faith in me and her love, so warmly and openly expressed have made me what I am. Her sparkling eyes have seen in me things that no one else looked deeply enough to see. In real oneness, there is an ever-growing and enriching twoness.

If you were here now I would sing you a little song we used to sing in Sunday School, called "This Little Light of Mine." The first verse was "This little light of mine, I'm gonna let it shine." We would all hold an imaginary candle real high when we sang it. The second verse was "All around the neighborhood, I'm gonna let it shine." We moved the candle around the neighborhood as we sang. Then we would hold the candle close to our faces and sing, "Won't let Satan 'whoof' it out, I'm gonna let it shine."

When we think of words like commitment and surrender, I am afraid that most of us have the idea that one of God's favorite things to do on a rainy afternoon is to figure out ways to "whoof" us out. In reality, he wants to live in union with you so that you will become far more than you ever dreamed you could be. He wants you to burn brighter and shine farther and illuminate longer than you ever thought was possible.

And our oneness with each other, and our twoness, should be the same way.

Peeking At A Miracle.

Lacey, you made us stay up all night—
And for a grandfather that is not as easy as it used to be.
Finally, at 4:10 a.m. or so, Jacquelynn Lacey Benson,
to address you properly by your full name,
your Mom headed for the room where
you would be "delivered."
So there we all were, a bedraggled bunch,
filled with cups and cups of vending machine coffee
and hours and hours of CNN News.
An assortment of maternal and paternal grandmothers,
grandfathers, aunts, uncles, and friends,
trying to look through two tiny windows
in the big doors that stood guard over the long corridor.
We watched them roll your Mom out of her room—
she disappeared around the corner past the nurses station.
We saw them dress your Dad up like a spaceman,
White crinkly overalls, green hat and mask, big blue booties—
and then the hall was empty and quiet.

Now the intensity of the waiting picked up,
I am sure the intensity of the "delivering"
was picking up for your Mom too.
"I want to see the baby."
"I think it is going to be a girl."
"I can't wait."

An eternity of almost twenty minutes went by
and then around the corner you came,
nestled in the right arm of your father
whose mask had been removed to reveal
one enormous smile of pride, awe and relief.
"It is a girl! Everybody is fine."

We crowded around for our first glimpse of you,
love at first sight I must confess.
Your Mommie's nose, your Daddy's dimple
on the miniature face instantly devasted us all
before the nurse gently led the entourage
on to the nursery door.

You and the nurse went inside.

A Believer In Moments.

The rest of us hurried around to a window
where they promised you soon would be reappearing.
I was standing with your daddy.
I guess I ought to warn you about him.
He is as quick as a flash,
never without a retort filled with humor.
He will having you laughing a hundred thousand times
before he finally has to say,
in answer to some preacher's question,
"Her mother and I."

But for this moment, his mirth was gone,
swallowed up by the deep sanctity of the miracle
that had so recently transpired before his very eyes.
"I have never seen anything like that before,"
were his quiet, reverent words.

I thought how right he was,
remembering mornings in this very hospital
when birthings of children of my own, including Tom,
had reconfirmed the miracle of life.

For better or worse, your dad has lived in the era of TV,
when the world has become, as one has described it,
a "19-inch neighborhood."
He has seen everything else,
murders, beatings, men on the moon,
rapes, robberies, men dying in battle,
fires in California, starvation in India,
riots, wrecks, and hostage taking.

Thank you, Lacey,
for reminding your Dad,
as well as the rest of us,
life is the real miracle.

Skipping Rocks.

It was a bright sunshiny morning—
the first of ten days off for me—
and I was out in the yard early—
working on a wall down by the lake.
Knee deep in pleasant, warm water
I could hardly have been happier or more at peace.

Patrick came down and began to throw rocks in the water.
You don't have to teach little boys to throw rocks
they just seem to be born both with the
skill and the desire.

He wanted me to stop and play with him.
"Teach me how to make them skip."
"In a little while," I said,
"let me get a little more of this wall built."
After a while he got tired of waiting
and started up the hill to the house.

I figured he'd be back in a few minutes,
but later in the morning when I went up for a drink
he was in the bed with a high fever.
It turned out to be a very serious illness
that was to spread through the whole family—
not to mention my vacation.
It took some of us to the hospital
and all of us to bed.
Fortunately for us it was all over
in a month or so,
having run its course with no lingering effects.
And there have been other days
and other chances to skip rocks with Patrick.

But I can still see him trudging
up that hill—
a long pull for his short legs
and I'm reminded that you never know
they're coming back—
there aren't any guarantees
and the only time you really know
you can skip rocks
is when you're saying "in a little while."

"Why Do You Kiss Me So Fast?"

A couple of years ago, we were riding along on a trip and our kids began to compile a glossary of oft-used parental expressions. It was one of those kinds of times where you were laughing to keep from crying.

"We'll see"—a term which means the same thing as "I'll think about it."

"I'll think about it"—a term which means "maybe."

"Convention"—a term which means that Mom and Dad are going to Florida and we are staying with a babysitter.

"Tomorrow"—a term used to express increments of time from a minimum of thirty days up to never.

"Ask your Dad"—a term which means "no" but it's his turn to tell you.

"Ask you Mom"—a term which means "no" but it's her turn to tell you.

Kids are smart, you know, and they know what's going on. You're not fooling them a bit. They know you're bewildered and confused and don't know all the answers and they know that the louder you say something, the less sure you are that it is right. They know that sometimes when you are shouting at them, it is because you are mad at someone else and it has nothing to do with them except that they are in the unhappy position of not being able to answer back.

But they will forgive you, if over the days and months you have made it unmistakably clear that you love them very, very much. They will accept your errors as errors of your head and of your judgement if they can only be sure that there is nothing anywhere in your heart for them except boundless, limitless love.

We have a warm, open, outgoing affection at our house. I really have to give Peggy most of the credit for this. We Bensons were "cool." We loved each other and we knew it, so we didn't have to go around drumming it into each other's ears all the time. Peg's family was a little different in that they celebrated everybody's birthday and Mother's Day and Father's Day and nearly any other day that was half reasonable for celebrating. And Peg brought this warmth to our place. You can't even mention something one of the kids did or said without this warm look with the glistening eyes covering her face.

To me our house is the finest place in the world because there is love and warmth and fellowship. Not always harmony, but always love and fellowship. We don't go to bed at night until we have all hugged and kissed and said "I love you" two or three times to each other. And nobody goes away in the morning without getting several "Have a good day's" and "I love you's." There are a lot of us and it takes a while to get it all in, but I think it is the most effective way there is for parents to raise children. Incidentally, it's a very effective way for kids to raise parents, too.

We live out a ways from town, 25 miles or so from where I work, and so it is not inconceivable on a busy day for me to leave home before the kids are up and get home after they are asleep. I have lived in my house for four or five days at a stretch and never had a meal with my kids or even seen them awake.

However, I believe so strongly in the power of love that I don't care what time I come in at night or how long they have been asleep, I don't go to bed until I have made my rounds. First I go up into Tom and Patrick's room. Tom sleeps on the top bunk and I catch his chin and turn his face toward me and look at those blond curls and his fair skin. He's a heavy sleeper and you couldn't wake him if you tried and he doesn't even know I'm there but I say, "Tom Benson, you rascal, I love you. I thought of you a lot today and every time I did, I smiled."

Then I kneel down by the bottom bunk where Patrick is asleep. Patrick is the baby of the family and he enjoys every minute of it. I don't know when he is going to grow up but the way they grow up so fast anyway, I'm not pushing him. I don't care if he takes his teddy bear to college. And he sleeps with any assortment of stuffed animals. If I can reach in and finally find the one that is Patrick, I remind him that I am so very proud to be his father and that I love him very much. He usually says groggily, "Goodnight," in a kind of "keep moving" tone of voice.

And I cross the hall to Leigh's room and she isn't quite so sound a sleeper. She is a responder, whatever expression of love you say to her will come right back. "You are so fine, Leigh, and I love you," I say and groggily the pronouns are reversed and I hear "You are fine, too, Daddy, and I love you, too." It's always hard to leave such lovely conversation as this.

Then I nearly always stop in a room downstairs where I used to have a study. It's a sad room to me because when you are the oldest and the biggest and you aren't afraid of the dark anymore, you move down there. It's almost a sort of launching pad because when they move down there you know the next move is out to college or to their own apartment or house. But I go down there and "love" across the city to where Robert lives and then across the miles to where Mike is in a crazily jumbled up dormitory room. I say, "I love you two and am praying for good days for you."

Why do you do that when they are asleep or far away, you ask? Because of two things. I think that it is part of what it means to share in the very being of God and because I think that it's the noblest and wisest thing I can do as a parent.

And it is doubly effective at our house because Peggy has already made the rounds before me. Between us we want to stuff into the "awares" and the "unawares" of our children as many smiles, songs, kisses, "I love you's," and deeds of love as we possibly can.

One night I bent over and kissed Patrick on the cheek and quickly stood up and started out of the room. I was so tired I thought it was about the last "get up" I had left for the whole day, when his question stopped me cold and brought me back to his bedside. "Why do you kiss me so fast?"

Why do we let the finest, most precious moments of our lives go by without a word, thinking that tomorrow or on our vacation, there'll be time to hike and swim and love our children? Why do we withhold from them the very thing they need the most—ourselves and our love?

The time to love is now. The time to begin is right now.

Shadow.

From the time little boys are born
until they are three or so
they belong to their moms
but the next three years
belong to their dad.
I have one of those
three plus-ers at my house.
If I wear a shirt,
he wears a shirt,
if I go barefooted,
he goes barefooted,
if I read, he reads,
if I dig, he digs.
He doesn't ask to go fishing
or to the park
or swimming—
it seems enough for him
just to be with me.
I look forward to the
weekends with delight
because he will not be more
than three steps behind me.

When life beats me down a bit
and I lose the confidence
to lead, to master, to choose,
I sometimes come home
and just walk around the yard
with Tom a step or two behind.
Somehow just to feel
his trust,
his confidence,
his devotion,
gives me strength to try some more.
You can't fool a little boy
about character
and I just accept
his judgment that
there must be something
to me after all.

Tip-Toes.

We usually take our vacation as soon as school is out. I like to be long gone the morning after the last day of school. We just leave self-addressed, stamped envelopes for report cards.

This is a great plan for June, but by the last two weeks of August we wish we had waited until the last two weeks in August. We usually try to sneak in a little trip just before school starts. It's nice to be with the kids for just one more long weekend before they go their separate ways for fall months.

A couple of years ago, we were a little later than usual in taking our fall trip. Due to his deep love of education, Mike had gone back to college early. His girl-friend was also returning early. So Peg said, "We'll take Leigh, Tom and Patrick, and let's see if we can take Robert." Robert is our grandson.

She called his mother and it was decided that it would be a fun weekend for Robert. You'd be surprised how quickly a tired mother of a two-year-old and a doting grandmother can come to an agreement.

On the way to the airport Robert kept saying, "We're going to the airport to see the airplanes. But we're not going to get on 'em. We're going home in the car." But he did get on the plane with us and he loved flying.

Every afternoon in Florida, Robert and his grandfather took a nap—an event the grandfather looked forward to more than Robert did. Peg usually had to bring him over from the beach to bathe the sand off of him and talk him to sleep. I just went to sleep by myself. A little sand never bothered me at naptime.

The hotel where we stayed was an old one and we had one of those high bathtubs that stands on legs. As the water filled the tub, Peg delighted Robert by bringing out all of the toys she had brought along for just such emergencies. Peg always takes along plenty of everything when she travels. It's just better to have your stuff with you. You can never tell when your house will be burglarized.

Before she put him into the water, Robert was leaning over the side of the tub playing with the rubber duckie and all the toys. "Gran," he said. He always calls her Gran. With all due respect to the "Mee-maws" of the world, that's not what Peg wanted to be called. She chose "Gran." To tell the truth, I didn't want to be called "Pap-paw" either. We came out alright with "Gran" and "Poppa."

"Gran," he said, "see my tiptoes. I'm standing on 'em."

What makes little boys stand on their tiptoes? It's just something they all do. It is as if God had a meeting with all the little boys and gave them special instructions.

Little boys have a secret. Remember when you used to stretch and reach out for each new day? Wouldn't it be nice to just kind of lean into life again and to trust its goodness?

When was it that you began to stoop over and hold back? When did you start to play it so close to your vest?

Let Go Of Your Kids.

A couple of Christmases ago now, Robert wrote a poem for us and had it framed. It hangs in the sitting room upstairs and I often stop to read it. Peggy even stoops to suggesting that visitors go up and read it also.

> Most of the celebrations
> that I remember well at all
> took place in this house.
> If we stopped to list them
> and celebrate each one over again
> the walls would once again ring and laugh
> as they did each time before.
> Most of the people I celebrate
> still live here.
> A list of them is unnecessary
> since you celebrate them daily even now.
> Most of what I wish
> is that the celebrations would continue.
> And that I might have a hat always held for me
> and a place set even if I'm late
> and that my laughter might still
> be held within these walls
> on certain days.
> Most of what I love is you
> though not all
> and I celebrate daily
> inside other walls that surround me
> that you taught me love and celebration
> and helped me go forth to plan my own festivals.

Now, maybe that is a little much because it was Christmas. I doubt we did as good as the credit he was giving us. But even if we failed, Peggy and I wanted desperately to teach our children to laugh and celebrate and go forth to plan their own festivals.

But we also wanted them to come back to ours. Somewhere along the way we learned that we only have that which we are willing to turn loose. Those things which we have let go of are now more richly ours than ever before. Without our grasping or striving they have come back to us.

It is true for children, too. You want to hang on to them, then let go, just let go. You want to lose them for good, then hang on.

Just tell your teenagers that they'll do things your way and when they do you'll discuss it with them. In the meantime, just ignore them as much as possible. Better still, don't speak at all.

When they want to go to college one place, just say you won't help pay the bill unless they go where you want. "Over there, you're on your own. Over here, I'll pay your way." They'll go where you say but they are resentful at you for forcing them and resentful at themselves for letting themselves be forced.

When they get out of college and want to do something besides go into the wallpaper business with you, remind them of all the sacrifices you had to make to get them through. Ask them how they could be so ungracious as to want to live their own lives. Hang on. Clutch. Grasp. Whine. Pout. Don't speak. Don't show any excitement about their plans. Just hang on to your kids.

We have policemen to curb the murderous effects of hate. There is no one to deal with those who smother with love. But love can kill just as surely as hate does.

Jess Lair said a lovely thing in one of his books, "You don't raise kids. You raise carrots. You sponsor kids." They are not yours. Their lives are not a second chance for you to be head majorette, or quarterback, or student body president. You've already had your chance to botch up. (Unfortunately, your kids probably already know about that.)

Do you want to hold on to your kids?

Then let go. Laugh with them, cry with them, rejoice with them, and dream with them. But let go of them. Then when they come down the driveway to see you, you can know that the only reason they are coming is because they want to see you.

And you will begin to realize the deep joy that comes from having what you willing to turn loose.

A Secret Meeting.

"Katie, I am your paternal grandfather, Bob Benson, Sr.

"I am Michael W. Benson's dad and he is your dad. I am out here at your house for two reasons. First of all, I couldn't wait any longer to see you. You are my first grand-daughter. Then Tom Benson, Uncle Tom to you, is moving out to Colorado to work in the mountains. He just graduated from high school.

"Patrick, again uncle to you, and I are driving out with him to help him get settled and, to be very honest with you, to prolong having to say goodbye to him. For eighteen years now he has lived at home and it is difficult to see him leave. I am in your blue nursery this morning because I came in to watch you sleep. I didn't realize that you were awake. Peg and Leigh do not know that I am in here. They think I am out in the back yard weeding the garden.

"Peg is your maternal grandmother. She is my wife and your dad's mom. She is the short little lady who has been coming in at night to dry you and take you to your mother when you cry. She is the one with the big smile and the moist eyes. You see when she picks you up she feels all the joy there is in being a grand-mother. But her mind is also filled with memories of days and nights when she cradled her own in her arms.

"Your aunt Leigh is the one who will not put you down in the daytime. Her eyes are just like her Mom's—warm and moist. She is thinking about the day when she will be holding a tiny one that she has brought into the world. They both came up here a few days ago to help you and Gwen (you'd better call her Mom) when your dad brought you both home from the hospital. Anyway, I had to sneak by them to get in here with you, so I'm keeping my voice down.

"I want to tell you some things. I'll start with your dad and mom.

"Your dad is a good man. He is a good husband and I really believe he will be a good dad. He is thoughtful of others. The other night your mom was going out to dinner with Grandmother Peg and Aunt Leigh and you were staying home with him. They couldn't be gone too long because your mother was taking *your* dinner with her. While she was getting ready your daddy pressed her dress. That is like him.

"He has always had a kind heart. He was a collector of stray animals when he was little and he instantly sided with the underdog in every situation. That is not to say that he does not have his faults. He does have a stubborn streak in him. I think that it came from Peg's side of the family and she thinks that it came from mine. There really is enough of it on both sides of the tree to rub off on everyone. I am sure that in 12 or 13 years or so there will be times when you'll stop saying 'Dad' and begin to say 'Dad-dee' with much frustration and conster-nation on the last syllable. But by then you will love him so much that you will probably forgive him.

"To tell you the truth, dads are usually real dumb about a lot of stuff. I guess because they are dads, everybody, including themselves, expects them to have the answer. So they speak up and look dumber than ever. Your mother can smooth all that over. She'll help you find the right answer and show you a way to perserve your dad's dignity at the same time.

"And your dad is honest. I remember once when he was very small his mother cautioned him against riding his trike in the street. As I recall there was even a mild threat involved. The driveway went up a slight grade into a carport so it was difficult not to just coast out into the street. After he listened intently to the several warnings given he said to his mother, 'Yes ma'am, but if I do I'm sorry.'

"I think you'll like your dad.

"Naturally, I do not know as much about your mom as I do your dad. You already know some good things about her just from her holding you to herself and being so close to her while she is feeding you each time. That bond between you two will grow and grow. I didn't know her when she was a little girl. You'll have to ask Bert and Pauline about those days. They are your maternal grandparents. Bert is a teaser and you will have to check with Pauline on some of the stuff he tells you before you believe it all.

"I know you must be beginning to think that there sure are a lot of people for you to keep up with and names to remember. But you have aunts an uncles and cousins and great-grandparents. By and by, you'll get us all in our places. And I hope you will begin to be proud of your roots both in Tennessee and in Colorado.

"But I can tell you some things about your Mom, things that have happened since Mike called from college and told us about the girl from Colorado Springs that he had just met.

"For instance, see this quilt and the pads that match around the sides of the bed. See all that lace and the tiny stitching. Your Mom made them. She looked in a lot of stores and decided she could not find anything pretty enough for you. So she made these to keep you warm and protected. I suspect that you will always find your self surrounded and guarded by her love. Even when you are rocking babies of your own.

"Your mom is a little shy. But just behind that shyness, there is a competent, talented woman who makes friends, teaches school, plays the piano and organ, cooks, sews, and lives a useful life. They say that little girls are almost foreordained to grow up to be like their mothers. There will probably be a few years along in there somewhere when you will be thinking anything but that. She'll be making you wear dresses like she wanted to wear when her mother was making her wear dresses like her generation had worn when she had been a little girl. But when you get through that state, you'll probably find yourself thinking like her and doing things in the same way that she does them. I want to tell you that you have a good pattern. In this case at least, growing up to be like your mom is a worthy ambition.

"If you want to know what you are doing out here in Missouri, it is because your dad is preparing for the ministry next year and you'll be moving into a parsonage somewhere as he becomes a pastor. Probably you will move a number of times while you are growing up because that is the way it seems to be with ministers and their families. There will be some other sacrifices too, I suspect. Ministers' salaries are very often low. But there will be plenty of things that really matter—things like love, friendship, devotion, service, ideals, respect for each other and fear of God. By the time you are grown, I think you will look at yourself as being privileged rather than feeling deprived.

"I guess I ought to try to tell you a little about the world into which you have come. To tell you the truth, there are some very bad things about this world. Even in my day, I have seen some horrible things done both by nations and by the people two doors up the street. It is hard for me to imagine just what the world will have come to by the time you get to high school. It is not hard and not incorrect to see the world as more than a little inept and even decadent. And it would be easy to become discouraged at our plight. When you study some history, you will see that mankind has had its ups and downs. But the ups include some wonderful and noble things like crossing oceans and conquering wildernesses and journeying to the moon. And also on the list are deeds of courage, honor, decency, kindness and altruism.

"You will see some of all of it as you go along. There will be good and bad in nations and in the schools and in the church and in your friends and, alas, even in your relatives. You can only choose to love and foster the good and resist and forgive the wrong.

"I guess I am getting a little ahead of myself. You will come to all of this, but in the meantime there are steps to take, dresses to wear, words to learn, dolls to care for, trikes to ride, swings to swing, and, right now, a nap to take. You'll have to forgive your granddad for keeping you awake so long.

"Sleep tight."

All Them New Things.

Let me brag a little—
I have a grandson named Robert Green Benson, III.
Now, in case you're not big on family trees
that makes me Robert Green Benson, Sr.
And I have a son Robert Green Benson, Jr.
and a grandson Robert Green Benson, III.

Before he was born we were duly notified
that in the event the baby was a boy,
he would be so named
and we were to call him Robert.
Peering across the gap between the generations
I took this to mean that we were not to make the same
mistake of re-using such terms as
Bobby or little Bobby or Baby Bobby—
it was to be Robert.
It seemed like quite a handle to me
for less than ten pounds of humanity—
it seemed very awkward to say, "Goochy-goochy, Robert."

But Robert it was-
until somebody started calling him "Pookie"
or just "Pook" for short.
Now Bobby sounds better to me than Pookie
but then what do grandfathers know?

But a little while after Robert was born
Tom, my ten-year-old, said to his mom,
"Robert, sure is lucky."
And Peg wanted to know why
Robert was so lucky in Tom's mind.
"Because he gets to do all them new things."
And now she wanted to know what all
those new things were that Tom
was referring to.
"Well," Tom began.
"He's never climbed a tree
or waded in the lake
or run through a field
or felt the wind in his face
or ridden a bicycle—
ALL THEM NEW THINGS."

And later I was thinking about all of God's children
and about our life in the Spirit
and about all the wonderful surprises
and stupendous things he has for all of us to do
and see
and feel
and be
and how we just sit down where we came in
and how we have all the questions
and all the answers
and know all the things to say and sing
and how we know all the steps and plans
for everybody else and their children, too.
And about how we rigidize and dilute
and I wonder how many new joys
and insights
and ways of punching holes in the darkness
and poems
and songs and smiles
and simple pleasures we miss
because we cannot begin to conceive how lucky we are,
because in him there are "all them new things."

Two Somethings Deeper.

I have a friend whom I know casually. I had met him a time or two before and I saw him again toward the end of the summer. He was wearing a neck brace and was kind of hunched up. He didn't look like he was having much fun that day.

I took counseling in seminary, so I know how to get stuff out of people. Using one of my best counseling techniques, I said, "Did your wife hit you?" No response.

So I went to a deeper, more probing statement. "You thought they said 'Stand up' when they really said 'Shut up', didn't you?" That didn't elicit any response either, so finally I said, "Aw, come on, tell me what happened."

"Well," he said, "I'm kind of embarrassed to but I will. My son and I were up the street at the neighbors where they have a new swimming pool. They had invited us to swim and we were diving off the board. I really hate to tell you this but I hit my head on the bottom. Really, it knocked me out. If my son hadn't been there to bring me to the surface and drag me up on the wall, I probably would have drowned."

You've probably noticed that I have a quick mind—like a steel trap. Right away, I knew what had happened to him. Although I didn't share this precious truth with him, I knew the scientific principle involved. He ran out of water before he ran out of dive. He looked like it, too.

In our Sunday School class one morning, we were talking about the depth of the love of God. How deep is his love? How deep will it really go?

Someone said, "It goes as deep as you go."

I said, "Well, that's okay, except I want to add another phrase, if you don't mind."

Since I had the microphone and I was the teacher, they said I could add another phrase. "I want to say it goes as deep as you go and two somethings deeper. I don't care what. Two inches, two feet, two miles, two somethings. It is always down there just below you."

For whatever it is that plagues you, maybe some dark deed that would startle and shock us all, maybe a steady accumulation of the same thing, I want to write this very plainly. There are always two somethings deeper still. Forgiveness is not forgiveness unless it is unconditional.

One night I came in very late and the family was all in bed. In the playroom by the door on the table in a puddle of light from an overhead lamp was a note. It was like a little poster because there was some artwork on it. It said, "Dear Dad, I did something bad today. I am sorry. Please forgive me."

Tom, the writer of that note, has a little of the con man in him, too, because it also said: "P.S. I love you. Tom."

So I went upstairs to make the rounds, and to kiss my family and whisper to their sleeping forms that I love them, and I went into Tom's room. Tom doesn't ever wake up or even answer. He just sits up in the bed so quickly after you kiss him that you have to duck to keep from getting hit. It took a moment to get him back on his pillow and to put the covers up under his chin. He still didn't even know I was there. Kneeling by his bed, I whispered softly into his unhearing ear, "Tom, you are forgiven."

Some might ask how I could forgive when I didn't even know what he had done yet. It is really simple. He can't do anything for which I won't forgive him. He has "blanket" coverage.

You don't have to carry the weight of your past into your tomorrows. And you can't run out of water before you run out of dive.

Forgiveness is always two somethings deeper.

"What Are You Going To Do About It?"

The family is just about the place that I want to succeed the most. In fact, I feel that if I fail here, my life will be a failure in spite of everything else that I accomplish, and if I can succeeed here, it will somehow atone for all the other failures of my whole life. My most often and fervent prayer is that I will be successful father.

I love to sing the song that goes, "I have decided to follow Jesus, no turning back, no turning back." And I like the second verse, "Take this world but give me Jesus, no turning back, no turning back." But when they come to the last verse, I have to drop out because I cannot sing, "Though none go with me still I will follow, no turning back, no turning back."

I can't sing it. If I live my life in such a way that I must go by myself, then I think I feel like Moses must have felt when he told the Lord, "If the children don't get to go to Canaan, then blot my name out of the book, too."

I was reading somewhere of a retreat for for career men and, at the end of the weekend, the last thing each man was to do was to write a headline that he would most like to see in the newspaper about himself. One man wrote, "Henry Smith Was Elected Father Of The Year Today—His Wife And Family Were The Judges." But everyone doesn't feel this way. I have actually talked to parents who say that it never occurred to them to tell their children that they loved them. I think that some of the most effective things that I have ever done in retreats and conferences was to send people back home to express love to their kids.

I am a firm believer that the only way to even try to be a parent is with the use of the power of love. We have tried a variety of ways of disciplining our children. When they were small enough, we would give them a quick swat on the rear end. There were times when I felt that all the nerve endings that had to do with hearing, quietness, muscle control, and other vital signs were centered in that general area of the body where they sat down. And I must admit that there were times when I felt that it worked. We used to have a Volkswagen and when things weren't going right in the back seat, you could backhand everybody including Peggy with one stroke of your arm. I was the biggest and they couldn't hit me back, or if they did it was only on the kneecap and didn't hurt too much.

But then they get bigger. I used to wrestle Robert and Mike, and then Mike and I used to wrestle Robert. I try not to wrestle with any of them now. If I wanted to discipline Mike today by paddling him, I would have to say, "Mike, sir, how would you like to bend over so that I can bring you into line?" Because when he is standing up straight he is taller than I am.

When the older boys hit the teens we tried grounding them once or twice. You know, "You can't leave the yard all weekend except to go to church." I don't know who gets the worst end of that deal—the "groundee" or the "groundor." I just know it doesn't make for much of a weekend with an unhappy boy or two sitting around. And it really doesn't work because if they are old enough and mad enough, they will just leave home.

And you can cut off their allowance but who needs two dollars a week anyway. So what do you do—ignore them, just keep your head in the newspaper until they get a haircut—what do you do? I believe that the most powerful step you can take is to turn the fervor of your love up another ten degrees.

It has been my intention as a parent to believe in and respect the specialness of the calling of God in the hearts and lives of my children. I think I can accurately be described as a "nondirective" parent. I'm not sure that this is always necessarily best—and I'm not sure altogether how I came to be this way. Part of the reason is my natural readiness to avoid confrontation if I can. Part of the reason is that I want to believe everything will work out for everybody.

Then, I think, too, that I got caught in the way the generations swing back and forth in their manner of parenting. I remember one day when my dad and I were walking along on Church Street in front of Harvey's Department Store in Nashville. I noticed a plaque in the sidewalk which noted the paving had been done in 1927, and I asked Dad if he had walked over this same spot with his father in days gone by. He said he didn't think so. Because he had been the last child in a large family, he had always felt his dad was tired of children by the time he came along. So he didn't remember their walking many places together. Thinking that his father had not been as prominent in his life as he would have liked for him to have been, my dad decided early on that he would get involved in the lives of his children.

For instance, he was an expert at knowing things like where you were supposed to go to college. I didn't have to spend a lot of time deliberating where to pursue my education after high school. Quite simply, I went to the place where he was sending the tuition money. I graduated from high school one night at 8:00 and caught the 10:30 bus. The next morning I was 220 miles away in freshman Greek class at Asbury College. As I said, my dad got involved in the lives and decisions of his children.

Maybe this accounts in some measure for my hanging back and encouraging my five to make up their own minds. One of them will come to me and say, "What should I do about this?" And I will try to look as wise as I can. I will pause significantly, as fathers will do, indicating that I am deep in thought about the matter. Then I make a studied and weighty pronouncement. Most of the time I profoundly answer, "I dunno."

I am not at all convinced that this is a superior way of parenting. Already some of my sons are old enough to look back and point to given moments in their lives when they needed more direction than their father was able or willing to provide. But I have earnestly believed, and tried to get my children to believe, that if they listened to the quiet voice within they would know the answer, because a part of his image within them is his calling voice.

Not too terribly long ago, there were some rumors that Mike was in some trouble. First they came from school and then, of course, they grew more rampant in the fertile soil of the church. And so we called a family council for Peg and I. "What are you going to do about it?" she said.

"Well, what are you going to do about it?" was my reply. "Will we confront him and ask him about it? Will we assume he didn't and treat him like he did? Will we accuse him? Will we subtly tighten the reins of his freedom until he "cracks" and it becomes evident as to the truth of the rumors?"

Now to be sure, Peg is more of the "Let's get this all out in the open" type and I, through my natural wisdom, intelligence, and cowardice, am generally willing and able to run from all the confrontations, crises, and summit meetings that I can. Unfortunately, this time she chose to defer to me as the leader of the home and turned the matter over to me. With only a couple more questions.

"What are you going to do if it's *not* true?"

"I'm going to continue to go into his room at night and kneel by his bed and I am going to rub his back for a moment (he sleeps on his stomach) and say, 'Mike, I love you and I am proud to be your Dad. I hope you sleep well and I'll see you in the morning. Goodnight.'"

"And what are you going to do if it *is* true?"

"I'm going to continue to go into his room at night and kneel by his bed and I am going to rub his back for a moment (he sleeps on his stomach) and say, 'Mike, I love you and I am proud to be your Dad. I hope you sleep well and I'll see you in the morning. Goodnight.'"

It was a couple of months later that he came, first to his Mom, and then later to me, and said, "I was in some trouble at school but I got it worked out. I'm sorry as I can be and it won't happen again." And we were doubly proud the day that Mike wrote home from school, "Send me my Bible, I am running for freshman class chaplain." We did and he was.

I really do believe that steady, patient, unceasing, deep, expressed, *oozed* love is the only reliable option open to parents. It's better than advice, grounding, cutting the allowance, paddlings, punishments, threats, or any of the other dozens of dodges and ruses we work on our unsuspecting and waiting children. Just care, just love, just show it. *Do something.*

There have been some times when the temptation as a father has been to assume that it would be best to just go ahead and tell my children what they should do. Still, there was something that kept me from doing this. Maybe it was because I always somehow knew that I could not necessarily know what was right for a given child.

All of your children live in the same house and they ride in the same car and eat the same cereal for breakfast. They sometimes even wear the same hand-me-down tennis shoes. Your children have the same last name and the same parents. But your children are not the same. Not at all. Each one is unique. There are no "boiler plate" clauses that fit all children. They are like snowflakes with their own patterns and their own shapes and their own sizes. They have their own places to land. So their calling must come at precisely the right time and in the right way. They alone can hear the call of the One who can tell them what to be. And just because I am their parent, I cannot make them be tomatoes when they were destined to be radishes. Or scholars if they were meant to be farmers. Or accountants if what they really want is to become poets.

As a parent, I have decided that I can't do or decide or discern everything. But I can live like one who has heard the voice that called him. And I can love. And I can pray. And I can hope. And I can occasionally give advice. I can tell my children that there is a voice which will speak to them.

I can even drop hints. I can remind them (and have) that they could hear the inner voice better if they turned the stereo down, or better still, off altogether. I can say that the most important thing in life is to hear and obey the voice. And I can say that the gravest danger in all of life is to fail to hear and heed the voice.

But I cannot tell them what it will say to them. For the call that is within them is just to them.

Did They Hear My Vest?

I was invited out to a college to speak the other day—
you always want to do your best at a college.
They are such reservoirs of knowledge and erudition—
at least it seems they certainly should be
when one considers how much learning
the freshmen bring with them and
how little the seniors actually take away.
There was also the added disadvantage of
being in my own hometown—
Five hundred miles is about the distance at which I begin
to change into a downright expert on any number of
important topics and subjects.

So I had studied hard—and prayed earnestly—for seriously,
it is a deep challenge to speak to people of that age.
To try to add some direction to them
from out here where I am—
these thirty-odd years from commencement.
And to try to do so in a way that will not tarnish
the brightness of their optimism.
It is not a task that I take lightly.

And I put on my best three-piece navy pinstripped suit—
thinking maybe I would at least look like
"a wise man from the east."
And I went out to chapel and spoke.
They were courteous and they listened attentively to me.
Afterward I was talking to some students—
I wasn't mobbed or anything like that—
my safety was never endangered.
When someone looked down at my suit and said,
"Well, look at that."
And I looked down to see what it was—
only to see that my vest was buttoned wrong.

All the time I had been standing in front of those students
not to mention the faculty and administration
thinking I was looking reasonably important.
And all the time they must have been sitting there thinking
where did they get this guy
who doesn't even know how to button his clothes?

A Believer In Moments.

Since it happened—let me try to salvage
a bit of my wounded pride and honor
by philosophizing about it a minute or two.
It is not hard to button your vest wrong you know—
all you have to do is put the second button in the top hole.
Or else slip the second hole over the top button.
From then on it is easy as falling off a log.
Because the rest will follow along slick as a whistle—
all you have to do is start wrong—
ending wrong will take care of itself.

And do you know how I hear the words of Christ
coming to me these days?
Very simply.
I guess they would have to be for a
fifty-four year old who hasn't passed buttoning yet.
But I hear him saying to me
There is just one way to button your vest right.
There is just one place to begin your life.
There will always be a button left over
or an extra hole—
when you start wrong.
But if you begin right,
if you seek first the kingdom
and his righteousness—
the Father and I will guarantee that the rest will find
their rightful places.

If I could have told them anything that morning—
I mean in a way that it really stayed with them
I guess it would have been about the place to start.
I don't know if they heard my words that morning,
I just hope they heard my vest.

Tom's New Bible.

I heard a man say the other day that he believed every word in the Bible was true. I certainly am not in disagreement with him but on the other hand I am just as convinced that if and when God chooses to speak, he can and will even if somebody gets some of the words mixed up in the writing. Or in the preaching, for that matter.

My son Tom recently asked me to buy him a new Bible. I guess you can't expect the Junior Department Graduation Bible to last for a lifetime. He said he wanted one with study aids and guides so he could find things. In the mood of a happy father, I began a search for a newer translation that had adequate helps for home study. When I found a Bible I thought would be satisfactory, I called him from the store and asked him if he would rather have the hard back or a leather binding. He said he wanted a "Bible-Bible," so I took the brown leather one home and gave it to him.

In a little while he brought it back and wanted me to inscribe it for him. So in front I recorded the occasion—graduation from high school, the date, the recipient, and the givers. But over in the back where there were some blank pages for notes I wrote him a short letter. I reminded him that this was the book through which God speaks and if he would read its pages, God would surely speak to him. They might not necessarily be the exact same things that I have heard, but if he will read and listen, God would speak to him from those pages. And he will.

The temptation for me as a father, of course, is to somehow assume that it would be a lot better for me to tell Tom what God wants to say to him. That maybe if I don't explain what God is saying he will not be understood. I am slowly learning that although I deliver his message with all the earnestness I can, it is still second hand. And that it will only be life changing when it comes first hand.

The most important thing that we can tell our children is that God will speak to them. Only when they have believed this, is it time to tell them what he told us.

An Open Hand.

Children go through a stage in life when they become very possessive. It seems as if the backbone of their vocabulary is "no," "me," and "mine." Fortunately, this stage is only temporary. Most of us are out of it by the time we are 82.

When our kids were smaller, about the age of yours when they were doing the same thing, they had a closet full of toys and junk accumulated from Christmases and birthdays past. It would never occur to them to look in there on cold, rainy days when there was "nothing to do." The only time in months they ever looked at any of it was when you cleaned out the closet. On that day they brought most of it back from the garage and returned it to its place in the heap on the floor of the closet.

Some friends would come over and their little boy would go upstairs to play with yours. The first thing he did was open the closet door. Here was a veritable toy store of things he hadn't seen or played with. The following game begins.

Visiting Team: "I'm going to play with this ball."

Home Team: "Oh, no, that's my favorite ball." (He promptly grabs it away.)

Visiting Team: "I'll put on these guns and holsters and cowboy hat."

Home Team: "Just a minute, those are mine." (He lays down the ball, buckles on the guns, puts on the hat and picks up the ball again.)

Visiting Team: "Oh, well, I'll just build something with these Tinkertoys."

Home Team: "You might break those. You'd better not." (He picks up the Tinkertoys.)

Visiting Team: "Look at these cars and trucks! I'll..."

Home Team: "Uh-uh, they're mine." (He adds the cars and trucks to his ever-increasing armload.)

Visiting Team: (With a wary look on his face) "May I ride your tricycle?"

Home Team: "Come on, leave my stuff alone." (Now he is sitting on the tricycle with the hat on his head and the guns buckled on and his arms tightly clutching the ball, the Tinkertoys, the cars, and the trucks.)

Visiting Team: "I can't play with anything."

Home Team: "My arms are tired."

It is comically tragic to see that, isn't it? He was so busy holding on to everything that he didn't get to play. He can't enjoy it because he's too busy holding it for fear that someone else might get some of it. When only Tinkertoys and cars and trucks are involved, you can smile a little bit. But it is just as starkly tragic when we see adults clutching their spouses and their children, their jobs and their futures, their homes and their cars in such a jealous, protective grip. They never have time to enjoy or even have contentment because they are using all of their energy just holding on.

I know a set of brothers who operated businesses that had some overlap. Upon retirement, two of the brothers insisted that all of the money their business was worth come to them in a sale. This kept the younger men who worked for them from gaining ownership. Eventually, the business was sold to outsiders who had no pride at all in what the two brothers had done with their lives. The business became the sum total of the last two lines on the balance sheet. Before it was all over, the business was sold again and again and closed forever. The two brothers hung on and ended up empty-handed.

When it came time for him to retire, the youngest brother fixed it so the young men around him could gain control and ownership of the business in time. The business has prospered and now he has the money from the business. He also has the joy of seeing that for which he worked so hard continuing and fulfilling his dreams. He was willing to let go and now has everything he had before plus more, besides the enjoyment of it all.

Life seems to try and teach us that the more you can clutch and hold on to, the stronger you really are. That is where the power lies, in accumulating, gaining, putting together, making deals, and hanging on. Hold. Grasp. Keep. Defend. Protect. Accumulate. Gather. These are the words that indicate strength.

Here is life saying that you must hang on. Hold on tight for all your worth. Here is Jesus saying you must let go. You must hold what you have with an open hand.

We are all caught up in the problem of possessiveness. There is no way to remove it from our love. The purest love and the the the most dangerous possessiveness are bound together in a way that keeps us from completely separating them. The two are together—love, the essentially creative force, and possessiveness, the essentially destructive force.

It would have been easier if Christians were called to vows of poverty. If we knew it was God's will that none of us own cars, that all of us were allowed precisely two sets of underwear, one set of outerwear and $50 per month for rent, one pair of slippers, and one pair of shoes, we would all know where we stood.

Jesus did not make it that easy. It is in the act of surrender or commitment that the vitality of life is released for the individual. It is in release that true possession comes.

In your mind, turn the corner and ride down the street to your house. Look at your yard. The oak trees have grown, haven't they? Remember how small they were when you planted them? Go into your house and look at the things that make it your house. The way the rooms are decorated, the pictures. Remember when you bought the television? Isn't the carpet nice? Finally you bought new dining room furniture. The set you inherited when you got married has at last been moved to the playroom.

Go upstairs and look around. Look in the closets at the clothes, the ties, the shoes, the shirts, and the skirts. Look out the window at your car and maybe at your boat in the driveway. Go through your kids' rooms and see all of the junk they've put on the walls, especially the pictures in the ball outfits and camp uniforms.

Go sit down in your favorite chair now and think of all the people and relationships that mean so much to you. Think about your office and all your hopes and fears and ambitions.

Now can you put them all into your open hands? Can you imagine all that is you and yours in your hands? Then the hard question for us all comes to mind. Can you hold it all with open hands or must you grasp and hold? Is there someone or something that you feel you just at least have to keep a thumb on?

I wish for you the joy of holding life with an open hand. Just let go of all the stuff you've had to worry about and hang on to and protect and drag and fight everyone else away from. If you could just believe that you could hold them open. Hold on, clutch, grasp—and one is continually filled with fear, greed, defensiveness, struggle, and anxiety. Let go, release—and one will come to realize that he who gave you "this" will give you something better when "this" is gone away. He'll help you with your marriage. He'll help you with your kids. He'll help you with your hopes and your dreams.

The deep truth of the scripture is not, "Don't care and let go." Nor is it, "Care and hang on." It is, "Care and let go."

It isn't what you have that determines your strength now or in the future. It is what you are willing to let go of that is the ultimate test.

Cluttered.

"Do not be like them." (Matthew 6:8)

Tom has recently gone into the lawnmowing business and the garage had to be rearranged so that there was a place for his equipment to be stored at night. This happened just as Leigh was moving back home from her apartment at college and she needed part of the garage to store her furniture until she left again for graduate school.

All of this was crammed into a garage that was already filled with a workbench, a freezer, the remnants of Peg's antique business, the garden tractor and equipment and boxes and boxes and boxes of books. As Tom and I restacked and rearranged, we concluded that we certainly had plenty of stuff and that clutter was a very descriptive word for us these days.

Up the street from our house is a church with a billboard out front usually proclaiming a negative thought for the day. But the other morning, the sign cheerfully proffered some good advice, "Peace is being content with what you have."

Now I think that I am reasonably happy with what I have. At least I do not have some wish list on the back burner of my mind for a bunch of new stuff that I would like to get. "So," I asked myself as I waited for the traffic signal to change, "why do I seem to be missing what that sign is promising? Where is all the peace? Does it have to do with my fear of losing what I do have or is it my worry about my ability to pay for it all? Or am I wondering if it will all last as long as I need it, or at least until the final payment?"

In a way, I wished the sign would have just said something negative I could have ignored, instead of reminding me of the struggle in which I always seem to find myself concerning my needs.

The struggle is real to us all. Every so often, Peg will say to me, "I've got to go to the grocery store today. There is nothing in the house to eat."

Or maybe one of the boys will say to Peg, "Mom, when are you going to the store? I'm starving to death."

Sometimes I ask her to wait until later in the afternoon so that I can go with her. I like to go to the store with her, so we make the big trip down to Green Hills to her favorite grocery store. I watch the people and push the buggy around behind her, backtracking occasionally for an item or two that she missed as we went along. Depending on my appetite at the time, I add an unlisted item here and there to the buggy. My observation is that it probably is better to go to the grocery when you have just eaten. When you are hungry, everything looks good. Leaving Peg to check out and pay, I bring the car around to load up the five or six bags we invariably have.

When we get home, I like to help put the groceries away. I guess this is an old hold-over from my supermarket, shelf-stocking night job during seminary days or from playing store when I was a little boy. I like to restack the soup cans and add little "grocery man" touches here and there.

The strange thing about all this is that when we get back to our house in which there was "nothing to eat," there isn't much room for the goods from our latest shopping spree. The cabinets are full, the pantry is crowded, the refrigerator is crammed, and the freezer is bulging, all overflowing with "nothing to eat." It would be funny if it did not seem to be saying something deeper about us that is probably more tragic than it is comical.

And what is true about the pantry, I have also found to be true about my closet. While I was in the publishing business, I didn't spend a whole lot of time budgeting the family expenditures. Like most people, I just hoped the next raise would bring us back into line. When I returned to writing and speaking, it occurred to Peg and me that there was not going to be anybody to give me a raise next year and so maybe a budget would not be so bad after all.

So we sat down and went through a couple of years' worth of cancelled checks to see what we had done before. Going through old checks is a revealing process, to say the least. (Humiliating is another word that comes to mind.) But in due time, we came to grips with our past and made resolves and predictions for the future.

Thus it was that I found myself with a clothing budget. It was not a particularly exorbitant amount, but rather what I deemed adequate in assessing my personal needs. And the truth is that I always spend my budget, plus a little more, but I don't ever buy anything that I truly need— except socks.

I remember one morning I was up early and searching without much success for a pair of matching socks to wear to an important meeting that day. So I took all the "matchless" ones out from under the bed. Then I knelt down and begin to sing "Nearer My God to Thee" in a very reverent voice. Peg asked what in the world I was doing and I explained to her that I was having a memorial service for all the poor socks who had been widowed by the washer. And Peg, who can find things in the house that always seem to elude me, went to the drawer and produced a matching pair, thus bringing the memorial service to an end.

But on the whole I do not buy anything that I need because I already have shirts, shoes, pants, suits, coats, jackets, belts, swimming suits, underwear, handkerchiefs, ties, socks (even if Peggy does have to find them), and everything else I could possibly use both for modesty and comfort. But I spend the budget. I buy some clothes because the lapels are wider, or narrower, because there was a new color this year, because I am tired of my old jacket, because I saw a new one I liked better. It's always because of something but hardly ever because of need.

I hope that it is not a virtue to continue wearing a doubleknit leisure suit just because you cannot seem to wear a hole in it large enough to merit discarding it. Still, it does not seem to be quite acceptable to let the research & development and advertising divisions of American business define the parameters of our need for us. Especially since they make their living creating needs for the rest of us. Even now, somebody somewhere is designing a new model, something that will run faster, shred it smaller, wash it cleaner, play it more faithfully, do it in cold water, have natural shoulders, or something else that will call for trading our old one in on it.

I think we are all familiar with the problem of escalating needs. I also think that life was probably intended to be far simpler than we have allowed it to become.

In the Sermon on the Mount, Jesus acknowledges that we have needs. But he also seems to be saying that the whole process is far less complicated than we imagine. Physically, he indicates that life consists of something to eat, something to wear, and something over our heads to shelter us from the elements. Psychologically, we are rather simple as well. We need someone to love, something to do, and something to look forward to.

Most of us have ready access to food, clothing, shelter, love, purpose, and hope. So how does our life get so cluttered, and why do we spend so much of our time worrying, and so many of our weekends building new shelves in the garage? Somehow we must find some new priority or some new stick by which we measure our lives.

I don't think that I can tell you what your needs are. I am having enough difficulty in determining my own. But I do think it is fair to say that neither one of us will have much success in "not being like them" if we let society continually escalate our needs, real or imagined.

Our Daily Bread.

"Give us this day our daily bread." (Luke 11:3)

Our first son, Robert, wasn't very old and Mike was just a baby when we bought our first camera. Since then we have been through three cameras. We have enough slides to adequately defend ourselves from other people's home movies and slide shows.

I guess a camera really does two things for you. One of them is to allow you to capture the moments of your life. We have some pictures and some slides that are probably worthless to anyone else, but to us they are priceless. They are a veritable "Memory Lane" of trips, picnics, graduations, first days for first graders, dogs, houses, first dates and costumes. There are even some pictures of me. If they are a true indicator, my life has been spent largely out of focus. I don't know why they always shake the camera when I am the subject.

The other thing that cameras do is remind you that you cannot capture moments. Each picture gently and firmly reminds you that that moment is gone forever. Maybe we don't always hear its steady cadence like rows of feet on pavement, but time does have its way of marching on. One look at old hairdos, skirt lengths, and automobiles brings gales of laughter to our children. At least they are kind enough not to make direct comments about the respective ages of their parents. From time to time they do ask us to tell them how it was to live *back then*.

In our little town, a parade is always a big event. Usually by the time they get everyone enrolled who has any reason whatsoever for being a participant in the event, we are short on viewers. Fortunately, we are on a busy highway and we can trap a crowd by blocking the bridge.

One of those parade years Leigh was in the Girl Scouts. She wasn't really involved for too long because they didn't give merit badges in the area of some of her stronger interests. Such talents as giggling and telephoning are not necessarily helpful in moving ahead in scouting.

On the day of the parade she was decked out in full regalia. I was ready with the cameras. Her troop was waiting in formation to begin marching. I have one slide that shows her face. She's the fourth girl over on the third row. As soon as she saw me with the camera, she turned her head and took a half-step backward so she was hidden by the big girl in the second row. The whistle blew and the troop went forward and I have a few more slides of the back of her head.

I ran down in front of the First Baptist Church and tried again and missed. I was too out of breath to make it to the next corner. Time had moved down the main street of Hendersonville. A moment was gone forever.

Just the other day I took Tom and Patrick over in the neighborhood where I had lived when I was their age. We walked around the yard and I showed them where I had ridden a stick horse across the wilderness plains. I told them how I had slain a tribe of attacking Indians single-handedly down by the creek at the edge of the woods.

We drove around my paper route and they wanted to see which way I had walked to school. I showed them Roland Downing's house and Bill Hunt's. We went by A. D. Dumont's place. I used to admire him so much because he was an only child and he seemed to have everything by virtue of not having to share.

Tom and Patrick were really interested. They asked lots of questions about where I had gone sled riding and which trees I liked to climb. But I knew it was over when Tom, with a twinkle in his eye, asked me to show them again which house was George Washington's.

When we begin to recognize that we are to be living our life in union with Christ, we also begin to see that it is lived out in moments. While I know that this is not necessarily a profound thought, it seems to be one that we often forget.

Jesus talked about daily bread. When I read his words I always find myself looking for deeper meanings. I always have the feeling that there was more to what he said than what I have seen. Here the disciples had asked him to teach them to pray. So he gives them this prayer. It is lovely and meaningful. It has been memorized, carved into stone, and set to music from the earliest days of the church. It should be, because it came from his lips.

Still I wonder why he chose the ideas and petitions that he did for this prayer. I am sure that each phrase has rich significance. So I wonder why he mentions *daily*. We're all so busy earning our daily bread that the least he could have done was to let us condense the petition time to weekly. What is he saying? What are those words trying to reveal to us?

They suggest to me that the graces and strengths of God are imparted to us a day at a time. Like the children in the wilderness, we need to learn that the manna is daily. Life is meant to be broken down into manageable parts. We are not to live our lifetimes, or the times of our lives, in union with him, we are to live our daily bread in union with him.

Today may be our lifetime. Today is what we have. We must not waste its time or its moments in the anticipation of tomorrow.

I know there are values and necessities of preparation for the tasks and demands of a lifetime. I certainly believe in making plans for educating our children, for weddings, for retirement, and all the other issues that will confront us. But none of these are places where we will begin to live. We live now, today, and Jesus is saying, "Pray for this moment. This is the one."

I am always somewhere between amusement and another emotion, which will here remain unnamed, at announcement time in the morning worship service. I will grudgingly admit that they have to be made, but I will always question the wisdom of nearly wrecking this week's worship by telling us all the good things that are going to be happening next Sunday. In my mind I am thinking that all this good stuff next week will also be interrupted by lengthy discussions and entreaties for the week after that. I always want to say to someone, "Let's eat today's bread today."

A Believer In Moments.

It seems to me that he is using the word "daily" to remind us that life comes to us in moments. He also is saying to me that it goes in the same way.

As surely as you cannot write checks on the days that lie ahead, you cannot hoard the past. Sure, you anticipate and hope in the future and rejoice in the memories of the past. The time for doing and living is the time we call today. Life marches past us in a parade of moments.

I have had an awareness of the movement of life for a long time. What I am beginning to faintly see now is that the value of life is in the movement. If we are to find the realities that we seek, we shall find them in the passing moments of life.

Be Careful Where You Build The House.

"Anyone who hears these teachings of mine and does them is like a wise man whose house will stand the storms and tests of life." (Matthew 7:24-25)

There is a great old hymn of the church that comes to my mind. It is taken directly from the closing parable of the Sermon on the Mount. If I were before you, I would lift its matchless melody to you.

"The wise man built his house upon the rock, la la la la la la la-la la la. The rains came down and the floods came up, la la la la la la la-la la la."

Then, of course, there is the majestic, climatic second verse about how the storms came and the "house came tumbling down." Actually, this verse was the most fun because in Sunday School class we all collapsed on the floor like the foolish man's house. We don't sing it too much in our church because the pews are too close together.

In a way, it is hard to believe that a random illustration used at the end of a sermon preached on a mountainside nearly two thousand years ago by an itinerant preacher is really an absolute. That was so long ago and so far away, and in such a vastly different society, that one tends not to even give it much consideration in our complex, technological day.

But the headlines of the newspapers and the quiet tragedies and wounded lives of those you know seem to underscore its truth more than ever. Even the lives that are crashing down in your neighborhood or on your block emphasize again and again that there is just one rock and all the rest is sand.

Just recently, a fine young comedian and entertainer took his own life. He was surrounded by people who were there to help. He had already made it big. At his young age, he would just barely have been old enough to vote a few years ago. My son Tom wanted to know why he would do that. I wanted to sing to Tom that there is only one rock and all the rest is sand.

We like to invent rules and systems and feel there are newer and more practical ways of going about this business of making life work. I came across a paper the other day that I had saved. It was printed in the hand of an eight-year-old. It was a set of rules for the neighborhood club that had been formed to use the lavish facilities of a four-by-eight treehouse I had built for the boys. Complete with trapdoor entrace, the house was a perfect place for forming a new society.

The list included the colors for the structure which has yet to be painted. The roof was to be brown, the outside walls green, the inside walls orange and the ceiling purple. The color scheme alone was enough to have ended the "new order."

The rules included:
1. No visitors in the clubhouse unless a member is present.
2. Meetings are every Tuesday. (I know for a fact they didn't meet this week.)
3. Dues are 10 cents.

4. Visitor dues are 5 cents.

5. Member may forget dues only three times.

6. A fine will be a quarter.

The officers of the newly-formed association tended to follow age order strictly as indicated by: Mike — President; Jay — Vice President; Leigh — Secretary; Tom — Treasurer; Patrick — Just a person.

The minutes of that first meeting were duly signed by the secretary and they are amusing to see and read. I thought of Mike leaving his wife and schooling in Oklahoma City to return each Tuesday for club meetings for the group and of the fact that I remembered that the club never met again after the first meeting. But these future considerations did not rob the situation of a single bit of historical significance when that meeting was in progress.

The real tragedy is that grown-ups also make up little sets of rules and guidelines for life for themselves. Many times they build on premises that are set squarely on sand. They have no more chance of succeeding than a neighborhood club of six-, eight-, and ten-year-olds. There is just one rock and everything else is sand.

Consciously or unconsciously, our lives begin to polarize around some area of life. There is the job, the home, the family, the church. These areas do provide parameters for life. They have meaning that keeps us going. But somehow they must be enjoyed with the constant realization that they are sand.

Some things are, of course, thrust upon us. One such thing is work. Like all sand, it makes subtle, unnoticed changes as we go.

Sometimes I think harshly of those who set high goals of financial success and status achievement. It especially bothers me when they are willing to make any sacrifice in terms of time or principle to achieve their stated goals. I don't like the man who told his daughter she didn't know the value of a dollar. I secretly cheered when she reminded him he didn't know the value of a daughter, either.

We all know some people whose goals were right. The sand just blew in all around them. They never did say, "I'm going to work such long, hard hours that I'll never get to be with my family. I'll never have enough strength left to do something for somebody else because I intended to invest it all in my business or in getting ahead where I am." They didn't plan to and they didn't mean to, it just happened.

Almost before you know it, the company keeps you running to win a trip to San Francisco or a place in the Millionaires Club or the keys to a new car. And in the process you passed up too many of life's values. The next company banquet is for you and for forty-three years of dedicated service they give you a watch with your name on the back. Everyone says, "We'll never forget you. The old company will never be the same." Monday morning, someone new is doing a better job at your desk. Two months later, someone wonders, "What ever happened to old what's-his-name?" And you went home with a pocketful of sand. But one has to have a job.

Then, of course, there is the stuff of life. It is a common assumption that riches are some combination of cars, clothes, houses, and various other trappings of the good life. Some way though, they are all like carrots dangling on a stick in front of a rabbit. We just never seem to catch up.

A four-dollar tie ties better than a two-dollar tie. So we buy one for six dollars and finance the balance. Then we realize that the six-dollar tie makes the neatest knot and hangs the best, so we buy a ten-dollar tie and finance the rest on a three-month pay plan. I don't think God cares what kind of a necktie you wear or whether it has a special little monogram on it to tell everybody you are just a bit better dressed than the average bear. I do think that sometimes the color combination may make him squint.

I also don't think he is worried about what side of town you live on or how many square feet the house contains. The question, it seems to me, is how much of you does it take to keep juggling all the payments? Is there any of you left when it is over?

My secretary recently told me with pride that she and her husband had bought a new house. I was happy for them. I didn't have the heart to remind her that she had just promised someone that once a month until the year 2006 she would send them a given amount of money. But then we all have to have a house and a car to get to it and a mower for the grass and so on and so on.

It is a well-known and easily demonstrable fact that you can be uncomfortable in a Cadillac and cold in the best suit made. You can be lonely in a crowd. You can be doing very well and still let those down who have the highest hopes for you and your life. You can appear to be a jolly good fellow and yet make your wife and children so miserable that their only solution is to leave you. You can greet the outside with confidence, while your own heart is so poor and empty you can scarcely force the grin across your face.

And sooner or later, it becomes painfully obvious that real riches aren't always delivered by U.P.S. They are not necessarily to be found on 200-foot lots. They don't always come with white side-walled tires.

Last September Peg and I celebrated our twenty-fifth wedding anniversary. Furthermore, I signed over for another hitch. I remember when we set up housekeeping. I remember how we put everything we owned or had into a 4x8 trailer with three-foot high rail sides to move to Kansas City to go to seminary. We pulled the trailer with a borrowed car and Robert lay on a pillow in the back seat. Three years later we had filled the back half of a Bekins Van. I haven't the slightest idea what it would take to move us now. Anyone with any notion of giving me a position in another town would probably do well to purchase a truck line first. Little by little, bit by bit, grain by grain, our lives have gained momentum and we have accumulated more than our share of the relationships, joy, and stuff of life as we went.

Some people have the ability to work their way through all the clutter and stuff and select whiter, purer sand upon which to build. I like to think that I am one of them. I think so because I am a family man. I'm also a scribbler of notes and thoughts on cards, matchbook covers, old envelopes, paper napkins or whatever. I'm always jotting down a thought, whether it is my thought or a good one. My pockets have to be emptied before anything is sent to the dirty clothes basket or to the stack of stuff that Peg is going to take to the cleaners. One night I laid this profound utterance on a table somewhere: "I'm not the one who makes me happy." The next time I saw the note, Peggy had written, "Who is?" I wrote back so that she would see it, "You and them and him."

Peggy and the kids have the deepest, richest meaning to me. The warmest, most sacred places in my heart are reserved for them. Most of me and my noblest dreams kneel in worship and thanksgiving before them in the deep recesses of my heart. I think that family relationships are the purest, cleanest, whitest sand of all. It is the sand that has the least trash and is the best place of all to enjoy the sunlight of God's love. But it is sand.

Ten years or so ago, I had had a long, hard week. It was one of those first warm Saturdays of spring and I spent it in the yard. I was prostrate on the floor feeling my aches, pains, and weariness when Leigh came in. She asked me if I knew what daddys were for. I was so tired I couldn't think of a single reason. She said, "Daddys are for Saturday."

When I got upstairs I dragged out a piece of stationery and made a few notes which I came across recently. I wrote to myself then that this little five-year-old would soon begin a cycle of pupply love, boyfriends and going steady that would end with someone asking me, "Who giveth this woman?"

Today is Saturday and I'm not sure where she is in the cycle at the present. I'm casting my vote for puppy love but the boyfriend is here. I still remember the shine on her face and the twinkle in her eye when she told me what I was for. I have thought of it a lot. But this is just a temporary stop on her journey. Jesus was trying to say to me as gently as he possibly could that most of what we take for granted is really sand.

I would like to write a book and call it *Words I Didn't Used To Like*. The list would include words like confession, denial, cross, and certainly, rock and sand. For a long time, I really wished he had not chosen to call so much of my life that means so much to me "sand."

The reason the title is ...*Didn't Used To Like* instead of ...*Don't Like* is that I am beginning to see a little of what it is he was saying to me. Sooner or later I was going to be interested in doing something that mattered. He was gently reminding me of how it could be done. When I got around to it, there is a way to insure the permanence of my accomplishments, and it is by building on his teaching.

In his parable, Jesus tells us very plainly and pointedly what is the rock. The rock is his teaching. The wise man is the man who builds his house upon the rock, his teachings, his word, his principles.

It does not say directly what is the sand. But he did say that there are only two places where one may build his life. One of them is safe and the other is not. The safe place is the rock. The reasonable conclusion, then, is that if there is only one rock and it is the Word of God, the sand is anything that is not the rock.

There is just one safe place. There is only one place of permanence. There is only one sure way to make the things you accomplish last. Anything else, and everything else, is sand.

Jesus said to be careful where you build your house.

The Word That Must Be Spoken.

A Grand Old Lady.

I guess about the first place
my parents ever took me
was to see her.
She was poorer in those days—
she lived in an older house
with dark, narrow stairs,
with one room "departments."
She was always a worker though.
Her years were
filled with her service,
her house was
worn with constant use,
her heart was
extended to the needy.
She was someway tied
into most of my life—
in the greater moments—
conversion,
baptism,
marriage—
and in the daily round—
friendship,
service,
worship—

she was always right there.
She's labored long and hard,
deserves ease and contentment.
But with characteristic sacrifice
and vision she has
gone in debt again,
enlarged her house,
bought new furniture —
just to be ready to serve
my children as she served me.
What a thrill to see her
with the dignity of age,
and the energy of youth,
rolling up her sleeves to serve
a new generation's needs
in a larger, better way.
Yes, my first trip was to see her,
and someday I'll go there last —
first —
last —
and all along life's journey.
She's been my friend —
"She's a grand old lady.

"How Are You?"

There are probably more organizations in the United States per square inch than almost anywhere. Will Rogers said, "Americans will join anything in town. Why two Americans can hardly meet on the street without banging a gavel and calling the other to order."

I read the other day of 160 people who had a meeting in Staunton, Virginia, and the prize for driving the longest distance went to a couple from Stockton, California. And can you guess what drew all these people from all over the country together for a two-day convention? They all owned Edsels.

Seeking and searching for fellowship at almost any level, no matter how superficial it seems to be, is better than being alone. But it is not always easy. In fact, sharing one's real feelings must be one of the hardest things there is to do.

The other day I was riding to a retreat down in Alabama with a couple who picked me up at the airport. And we passed a theatre and Brenda said, "That was the best movie. I cried all the way through it. It was so great, the opening credits were hardly over before I was crying and I just cried all the way to the very end."

And I said to him, "John, did you cry?"

"Naw," he said.

But she said the only way he kept from crying was to laugh at her the whole time, especially when he was about to cry himself.

I go to several conventions a year and they all have at least two things in common. The first is the name badge. Generally about a week before going, I begin to train my right eye to look straight ahead at another person's face as I greet them warmly. The trick is to train the left eye to wander nonchalantly down to the lapel to find out who in the world it is I am talking to while my right eye keeps them engaged. I generally find that their left eye is doing a little homework also. All the time we are talking to each other like long lost friends and calling one another "brother" to cover up the fact that we don't even remember each other's name.

The second thing begins to evolve out of the natural question, "How are you?" If it is a group of any one kind of people, like all ministers, or ministers of music, or publishers, or bankers, or anything "elses," you begin to hear a couple of words over and over.

"How are you?"

"GR-R-EAT!"

"And how are you?"

"FAN-N-N-TAS-TIC!"

"How's the work going?"

"GR-R-EAT!"

"How about yours?"

"FAN-N-N-TAS-TIC!"

And everybody is so great and wonderful and super and colossal that you begin to wonder how anybody could possibly have taken time out for this convention. It's just great if you're doing great, and it's fantastic if you're really doing fantastic, but a lot of times they are just words that shield and hide because it's not easy to say you're doing lousy when everybody else is doing so great.

We do about the same thing when we see each other at church every Sunday. We all are quick to say, "How're you feeling?" but it bugs us when somebody thinks we mean it and they proceed to tell us how they're feeling from their left ankle all the way up.

It's really a lonely, impersonal world because we are afraid to admit or listen to true feelings. Sometimes I wonder what would begin to happen if we just began to treat each other like we all had needs and burdens and sensitivities and setbacks. And I wonder, too, how the world would be changed if we didn't think it was a mark of strength to keep from showing our feelings.

And I often wonder how our conventions and assemblies and church gatherings would turn out, and how far-reaching their results would be, if someone would just have the courage to say: "I'm not great, I'm not fantastic, I'm so discouraged, I'm about to die, and I need your prayers and love."

Especially if another one of us would have the courage to listen.

Some Christian Thoughts — Maybe.

A while back, Peg and I had dinner with some old friends. It had been a long time since we had seen each other. Our roots went back to our school days and our first pastorates in the same part of the country.

We met and greeted each other warmly and were gentle in our observations as to what the ravages of time had done to us all. We laughed at the things that had happened to us so long ago and recalled weekends and times together with them. We showed each other pictures of our children and some of us had grand-children's pictures too. We begrudgingly admitted that, for better or worse, much of what we had all expected to accomplish in our lifetimes had already occurred and we were all playing the back nine.

As usual, it ended up with the wives at one end of the table in lively conversation — they didn't even have a designated listener — and the husbands at the other having a little more difficulty keeping the conversational ball rolling. And also as usual, I tried to sit where I could participate in the men's dialogue and still monitor the women's. For I have this feeling that men don't know much after the ball scores but women know about lots of things and furthermore they are willing to talk about them. It must have been an enjoyable evening because we had soon eaten and talked from 5:30 until way past 10:00.

It was a day or so later I guess that I began to do some wondering. Was it Christian fellowship simply because we had met in seminary and because our mutual tie was that we were all engaged in some type of religious life? It occurred to me we had done just about what any group of engineers and their wives would have done who had gotten together long years after they all graduated from old State U. Or insurance salesman or hardware dealers or stockbrokers or auto dealers. It might have been a little cleaner when we met since there was no smoking, no cocktails, no questionable jokes, and no bawdy ballads, but does small talk become Christian small talk just because it is carried on by Christian small talkers?

Further stimulation for my wondering mind came the other day as I was reading a monthly paper from the presiding elder to his under-shepherds and their respective flocks. It was filled with numbers, goals, records, slogans, promotions, campaigns, and assorted propaganda about things like Christian volleyball leagues. It was not particularly unlike newsletters I used to get in the mail from Fuller Brush and Electrolux and the Better Living home freezer food plan when I was plying those various trades to finance a seminary education. Are the numbers from a church office different from numbers that a sales manager sends out from the regional office? Do they somehow become Christian numbers or do they still have just the same powers to motivate (or demotivate depending on the recipients place on the list) that numbers always have?

I know there is a difference in what they represent and that the number that represents a little boy in Sunday School is infinitely more important than the one that represents the sale of a box of tooth brushes or a deluxe sweeper or 46 pounds of ground beef. But a paper full of numbers looks a lot, and reads a lot, like a paper full of numbers.

And far be it from me to cast any disparaging remarks about the game of volleyball, even though I was totally inept the last time I was invited to play. Either I am not jumping as high or they have raised the net considerably in the past few years. There was a time when it was the one sport in which I was even remotely competitive and that was probably because they kept rotating me off the front line. But is it correct to call volleyball Christian volleyball because the ball is white and the gym is in a church and the participants are believers?

Is a denominational monthly newsletter a Christian newsletter because it is edited by a staff of Christians? Can a dinner among old friends be koinonia just because all their roots go back in the church and to church educational institutions? Or rather is there some quality of the content, of what transpires or what is written or what is discussed, which is really the thing which gives it its Christian-ness?

Now I want to let it be known that I think that Christ can and does bless volleyball games and dinner parties and even denominational newsletters. Maybe it is that precisely the point that I am wondering about is our failure to continually recognize that it is his life and his alone that has the power to make anything Christian. Maybe our assumptions that since we are Christians, and since we are doing them, then they must be Christian, too, are not correct. Maybe volleyball games are just like us, it takes him to transform them. Maybe the verse in 1 John that says "He that has the Son has life and he that doesn't doesn't" (BTV—Benson Tennessee Version) would be just as true if read, "The dinner party that has the Son has life and the one that doesn't doesn't" or "the newspaper that has the Son has life and the one that doesn't doesn't."

It seems to me there are two things we need to recognize here. The first is that we cannot make anything holy. Nothing we touch becomes sacred because of the power and authority of whoever and whatever we are. A worship service is not a worship service because it is attended by Christian people in a Christian building which is a Christian building because it was built by Christian hands and with Christian money and Christian intent. It becomes Christian worship only when he makes it so, and when he does, it can be in a cathedral or in a Greyhound bus station.

And that leads to the second thing we need to recognize, he can make everything holy. We can bring our services, our ballgames, our newspapers, and anything else to the altar and place them there. We can dedicate them, offer them, surrender them, leave them but only he can change them. Only he can make them holy. And until he does, it is just another one of whatever it was that is just like everything that everybody else is doing.

I am not suggesting that we can or should sing a verse of Amazing Grace every time the serve goes over in volleyball. And I don't think that printing a Psalm between the attendance reports from the River Zone and the Central Zone is the answer either. But I am thinking that whatever we are doing needs his blessing.

And when he comes and breathes his life into whatever it is, it will be filled with his grace, compassion, openness, awareness, fellowship, concern, forgiveness, understanding, affirmation, joy, peace, and authenticity.

I suppose my wondering has taken the wrong fork in the road when it begins to try to take the word Christian from so many things we do. Really, I think what I meant to be doing was to get it more attached to more things more often. But you can nearly always tell a fresh rose from a plastic one. And there is some subtle difference between Christians fellowshipping and having Christian fellowship.

And that difference is his life.

Bald Heads and Blue T-Shirts.

They call them "icebreakers" or "get-acquainted" games. I don't know how or where they got started or how they cover so much territory. But they show up in such diverse places as Norman Park, Georgia, and Peffelaw, Ontario, Canada. They give you a sheet of paper divided into twenty-four squares. Each one has in it a descriptive phrase such as bald head, same age, farthest distance, blue T shirt, biggest foot, unmatched socks, oldest person, or something else at least as notable. The trick is to find someone who fits the description and put their name in the appropriate square. The winner, of course, is the one who gets all the squares filled in the quickest.

I'll have to admit it does get people mixing and mingling. There are always some competitors who will race around the room filling out the sheet. But there are usually some others who aren't all that dismayed about turning in a blank sheet and so they just stand and watch. Unless, of course, they have a bald head and have to keep telling their name to the eager ones. I usually don't want to play but, even more, I don't want to look like I don't want to play. I think last time I had twelve out of twenty-four but one of them was marked "your name" so that got me started.

And I guess I will have to admit it is nice to see the shortest woman or the tallest man made into a semi-celebrity for the moment. But still I don't think that learning that Dave White happens to have on his blue T-shirt or that Jamie Brampton was a first-timer really broke much ice. It was a start but we were still a long way from community. It made us talk, we just didn't say anything.

I have observed at retreats that the measure of openness to God is usually the openness of the group to each other. And that the real beginning task in a retreat, or maybe anywhere else, is the quest for community among those present. I have often wondered what it might be like if the phrases in the squares said things like daughter ran away, just lost my job, lonely, marital problem, parent in a rest home, just learned she has cancer, praying for my son, and some of the other things that plague us all and make us one. It would probably be hard to keep from filling up all of the squares with all of the names. For whether or not we like to admit it, we really are all bound together with the bonds of our frailities and cares.

We just keep on fending each other off by asking meaningless questions and giving answers back that go with the equally meaningless ones asked us. Sometimes I wonder how much of history has actually been spent in conversation about the weather.

I read an article the other day that was about programming personal computers with enough information so that it would hold a conversation with it's owner. Speaking computers could be made to greet their users in the morning by saying, "What's the weather like out there?" or "Sleep well last night?" Reacting to key words in the user's reply, the computer would consult it's memory for the proper followup remark. If the reply is "No, couldn't sleep a wink," the computer might move to, "Really? Not feeling so good?" All this could be done in a Cyclons-type voice like the announcer on the Atlantic Airport subway train or in regular like the little man in the Datsum who tells you that your door is still open. A fact you would have discovered presently by yourself.

The writer went on to conclude that all this is not so far-fetched. "Consider, for instance, that perhaps some 90 percent of the regular communication between two people—even two close people, like husband and wife—is mundane. The bulk of daily conversation consists of simple, flat statements like 'What do you want?' 'I'm over here.' 'It's pretty good.' Moments of lyrical expression or deep emotional contact are rare even in the most intimate love affairs. If we could eavesdrop on a poet and poetess strolling through a tropical paradise, for every exclamation of lasting beauty, we would hear a hundred comments on the order of 'Hey, get a load of these coconuts.' Among people who are not emotionally involved, conversation is pure routine—'How much time do you need?' 'I'll have the fish.' 'Turn left three degrees.' All of which is to say, most of what passes between human beings could easily be programmed into a computer."

But it isn't fair to leave it here, so I'll give you the writer's final observations also. "Yet there is something they can never be, regardless of the level of technological advance...A computer's reactions aren't *real*, they are merely *realistic*...what happens when people start going straight to computers for their companionship, bypassing the danger of hurt but also the hope of transport?"

I noticed two phrases the other day in Acts 4. Both are equally unbelievable. "All the believers were one...There were no needy persons among them." Being in and around church all my life, it is hard to conceive of all being one. And being loosely attached to the human race it is impossible to imagine any group of people, however small, about which it could be said nobody had needs.

Maybe the two statements can only become true in a mysterious interaction between them. And the result is greater than the sum of the two. It is as if our need brings us together and makes us one and our very oneness drives away our neediness.

But I suspect it will start somewhere deeper than revelations about the color of our shirt or the absence of hair from our heads.

Form Without Substance.

...in him you have been enriched in every way...Therefore you do not lack any spiritual gift...He will keep you strong to the end...you will be blameless... (1 Corinthians 1:4-8)

My travels to retreats and conferences have taken me to nearly every section of the country and I am constantly amazed with the diversity of this great land. Almost every part of it has something which gives the region a distinctiveness. It seems that God has done something wonderfully different around almost every curve and just over every hill.

You cannot make the same claim for what we humans wreak on the landscape. There is an ever-expanding sameness about what has built up at the intersections and the crossroads of America.

Perhaps Exit 78 on Interstate 30 in Arkansas is as good a place as any to illustrate. Located roughly halfway between Little Rock and Texarkana, it is everything the familiar sign, "Gas, Food, and Lodging," proclaims. Everything is crowded into a half mile strip along U. S. Highway 67 and State Route 7. Standing in a row with their signs raised to the sky they beckon to the weary traveler. Anywhere, USA. Exxon, McDonalds ("50 Billion Sold"), Shell, Conoco, Gulf, Holiday Inn ("Welcome Kiwanis"), a couple of local entries — Pig Pit Barbecue, Caddos Grocery and Live Bait — and my destination, the Continental Motor Inn beckoning "Welcome Nazarenes" and "Cable TV."

As I drove down the exit ramp, it was very easy for me to feel that I had been here before. If I had any feelings of strangeness at all, they were quickly dispelled when I lugged my suitcases and boxes of books into the familiar surroundings of Room 111 here in this member of the World's Largest Lodging Chain. The use of the word "chain" seemed unfortunate to me, since I was already longing to be home.

Somewhere in the higher councils of motel management it must have been foreordained that henceforth all motel rooms contain at least one bed, one TV, one table (preferably octagonally shaped and made out of oak), two flanking chairs, one dresser with a counter smartly attached for your suitcase, two bars of soap, two bath towels, two washcloths, two plastic cups wrapped for your sanitary drinking, one splashy set of matching drapes and bedspread, and two early American prints on the wall. All of this luxury is made complete with the name of the establishment stamped on ashtrays and matches. It is hard to think of anything else one might need.

The McDonalds across the highway was not a disappointment, either, for it too had the familiar, comfortable feel of being planned at corporate headquarters. The boxes, the buns, the uniforms all made me feel like I had never left home. It's not hard to bump into the American dream these days, even at Exit 78.

Once in a while, though, it does seem to me that the dream has worn a little thin here and there. Most of the dreamers these days seem to be waiting for someone else to do, something that can be duplicated, imitated, copied, franchised, and reproduced in living plastic, preferably for a profit. If the form can be copied skillfully enough, probably no one will even notice there is a decided lack of substance. If it looks like a motel, that must be what is and if it is shaped like a hamburger, it must be one.

Some time ago in Nashville a group of enterprising investors opened a pilot model for a new chain of fast food stores, as they call them in the trade. The speciality was to be steak and biscuits. The idea was good enough, although certainly not new. A well-known personality, who for some reason was supposed to immediately remind us all of steak and biscuits, lent his name to be used for an appropriate fee. There was ample capital and the stores were bright and cheery.

There were only two minor problems. The first was that the steak was bad. The second was the the bisuits were worse. It was like the old saying, "If we had some bacon, we could have bacon and eggs, if we had some eggs." Hooray for Nashvillians. Enough of us managed to stay away to get him to go away. The rest of America owes us a heartfelt thanks for nipping this franchise in the bud.

I don't mean to seem unduly hard on the eating and lodging habits of the American public. My concern about the balance between substance and form is deeper than gas, food, and lodging. But I do think it is fair to say that we Americans have a great preoccupation with the form and only make mild protests for the substance of life itself. And my real lament is that sooner or later what is happening to us in society begins to make itself felt in the church as well.

The influence of the mass economy—standard operating procedures, checklists, symbols, signs, style, slogans, contests and other activities—begin to lead the church subtly away from being a place of substance. The danger is that it then takes its place at the intersection with all the other forms of what we call American life. And one steeple, eighty-nine pews, a six-person staff, two parking lots, and four used buses, along with fourteen special events four nights a week for every member of the family, may or may not be a church.

A couple of springs ago, I was with the teens from our church on a retreat. That Sunday morning, we met in a country church for our service. The pastor let us in at an early hour so we could have the building to ourselves. I told those young people we were going to imagine we were having church just like they were having it back home. Who, and what, did we need to have church? They began to name ushers, organist, pastors and all the other people who are to be found in and around the church. Then a member of the group took the place of each one named.

When we had finished "populating" the church, we reversed the procedure by asking who and what we could do away with and still be a church. One by one we returned to our seats as they decided you could have church without ushers, without an organist, without a choir, and finally, they even let the pastor go. When we were all sitting back down, we began to discuss who and what was really necessary to having church. Their answers finally led us to the conclusion that the church was a very simple gathering.

It takes some believers, some nonbelievers whom the believers are trying to win, and the presence of Jesus. All the rest, they concluded, was just part of the form of the church. The substance is people made alive with the presence of Christ. It is the presence of Christ that makes a group of people into a church. And all the rest of it is just form. But it seems to be commonly believed that the essence of the church is the number of activities undertaken.

I am on the mailing list of many churches from different parts of the country. And nobody can say that the church is not busy. Just reading two newsletters at random off my desk makes me glad I am on the retreat circuit. I do not think my health is good enough to be a regular attender at either of these two churches. There were three picnics, four lunches, two brunches, two canoe trips, one splash bash, one softball makeup game, one ice cream dream, one volleyball tournament, trips to the State Fair, Chattanooga, Gatlinburg, Mammoth Cave, and the International Youth Convention, two baby showers, one call for basketball, three aerobics classes, and an announcement (it seems more like a warning) that the bowling season would soon be upon us all. Needless to say, there were also board meetings, prayer meetings, committee meetings, youth meetings, senior citizens meetings, couples meetings, singles meetings, and district meetings. I am not trying to say that I think all of those activities are just form. But I do think it is fair to say this—it is going to take a whole lot of substance to make all of that form a redemptive part of the body of Christ.

The ancient prayer ending that comes down to us, "...through Jesus Christ our Lord, Amen," is more than a ritual. It is more than a formality or a formula. It is the true and significant cornerstone of our praying and our living. Life is to be found through him, in fellowship with him.

He is the place where the holy shines through. He is the point through which the life of God flows into us and into our actions. He breathes the breath of life into us and into our everydays. He is the One who puts substance into the forms of our living. He is the very substance of life itself.

But we are so often content with just the form.

No Minor Matters.

"Do not be like them (Matthew 6:8)"

I was brought up in a denomination that spent a great part of its energy and efforts in defining and avoiding wordliness. It has always seemed to me that it was easier for some of those old time preachers and evangelists to identify worldliness back in my early days. Most often it was thought of as something the women wore or didn't wear. Fortunately, as I recall it, women's clothing was not an issue that our pastor dealt with very often. He generally stated his philosophy on this particular matter by indicating he thought that if a barn needed painting it should be painted.

In our local church though, there were other matters about which the body deliberated and made pronouncements. I can remember some of these issues which seemed to be "burning" at the time. Once, one of the truly godly men of the church, who taught a class of high school boys, felt that it would be good to organize a softball team and play in the church league at Shelby Park. Someone else in the church persuaded the company where he was employed to donate some used uniforms for the team to wear. The only request made by the company, a manufacturer of candy, was that the church leave the name of various candy bars on the backs of the shirts. For this reason I played right field for a couple of years with Goo Goo on my back.

The matter was taken to the church board to see if it would be all right to put the name of the church on the front of the shirts. Much discussion ensued. It was finally decided that it would be better if the team used the class name on the uniform instead of the name of the church. Thus the team played as "Victory Class" in those early years, although I don't remember that we had very many victories in the beginning. We kept getting beat by churches that had resolved the question of softball playing many years before, churches that had decided they would use the church name and we got beat a lot by one church in particular which had also decided it would be all right if their first baseman chewed tobacco.

Finally we did begin to play with the church name on our uniforms and even won our share of championships, although the right fielder had been replaced by the time all this occurred. And chewing tobacco never was approved for the first baseman or anyone else on the team.

I remember another semi-crisis that came along in the life of the church in the mid-forties. My dad was the songleader at the time and he was very good at getting the people to sing. He was a spontaneous director who loved to change songs and tempos frequently without giving much of a warning to anyone. But with Elizabeth Pate at the piano and two or three good strong sopranos and altos on the front row of the choir watching his every move, the rest of the congregation followed whether they meant to or not.

When he had assumed his duties with the volunteer choir, he had also inherited a volunteer orchestra. He always had trouble keeping the orchestra with him as he would weave songs into medleys and moods during the song service. With his customary ingenuity, he came upon a solution to this challenge to his leadership. The church should buy an organ. But when the idea was taken to the board, some of the members were less than excited. And it was not just because of the price. Many of them had left so-called "formal" churches to come to this place where the services were warm and expressive. All those churches from which they had come had organs. In time, of course, our church joined the march of progress and today it would not seem like church without an organ.

A first reaction might be that the church had ill-spent its time in debating such minor matters as softball shirts and Hammond organs. Perhaps I thought so, too, at the time. But there was something deeper going on here, something that I came to appreciate more and more. For in the quest to be a holy people, there are no minor matters. To be taught early that nothing is neutral in the life of the spirit was to be apprised of a deep and inviolate spiritual principle.

There is hardly a paragraph in the Sermon on the Mount in which the life of the Christian is not shown to be in contrast. Sometimes it is with the Gentiles or the heathen, and sometimes with the Jews or the religious people. The Christian life is described as an ongoing choice of one way as over against another. There are two roads, two gates, two masters, two treasures, two ways of seeing, two preoccupations in life, and finally, two ways to respond to his words.

The Sermon is a system of Christian values, ethical standards, and religious practices that are to find expression in all of one's life and lifestyle. They are totally at variance with the life of those who are not attempting to base their lives on the teachings of Christ. And the thought expressed in the Sermon is the essential theme of the Bible.

In the Old Testament, God set out to call a people to himself. And the words of Jesus, "Do not be like them," are giving the same call to difference as the words God used when he told the people of Israel, "I am the Lord your God. You must not do as they do in Egypt, where you used to live, and you must not do as they do in the land of Canaan, where I am bringing you. Do not follow their practices" (Lev. 18:1-3).

The question which always must be grappled with is what the call to "difference" means. What was Jesus saying when he said that we were not to be like them? And what was God trying to get the Israelites not to do so they would not be like those in Egypt or in Canaan? It is the question that those who would follow Christ must be always asking themselves, somehow reshaped and reformulated to resist the peculiar temptations and pressures of a changing society.

I think most of us would acknowledge that we are thoroughly conditioned by the society in which we live. Our hopes, songs, actions, words and thoughts are constantly bombarded by our culture. One morning last spring I was going across a campground to speak in a retreat service. I think I like morning services best of all and, as well as I knew, my mind was ready and my heart was full. In fact, my heart was so full I was humming a song to myself as I walked along in the bright morning sunshine. You can imagine my chagrin when it dawned on me what this prayed-up, ready-to-preach-on-Christian-devotion-speaker was humming—*Welcome to Millertime*. Well, it is a catchy tune and I guess that's why they wrote it as they did. For the moment, I was caught.

Maybe the reason it seemed easier for the old-timers to define worldliness was that it was simply a question of not being like "them" or a question of abstaining from "their" practices. But with the advent of radio and televison and other mass media, no longer is it so easily done. It reaches beyond such matters as the name on a shirt or the manner of accompaniment for the singing of the congregation. Even deeper, it seems to me that worldliness is the spirit of our day. It is our being totally at home here. It is our inability to care. It is a lack of shame or indignation. Things would be so much simpler if it were only a matter of wearing black socks. But Jesus reminds us that the exterior of our lives is only the expression of the spirit within us.

Job makes an interesting commentary on his day when he writes that the "men pasture stolen flocks, they drive away the orphan's donkey and they take the widow's ox in pledge" (Job 24:2-3). Since each of these acts was a specific deed, they could be categorized and avoided. And they could be made right. But another thing was happening that must have caused even greater confusion and difficulty. Job notes that "men move boundary stones" (Job 24:2). And with the markers, or the dividers, no longer in the right place it became impossible to decide where the boundaries should be drawn. There was no reference point.

Maybe that describes our present day. The lines that once divided us from the ones whom we were not supposed to be like do not seem to be very plain any more.

The Clock.

At our dinner table the other night, Tom was telling us that one of his friends had taken his girlfriend out to dinner at the best restaurant in town. Tom was expressing amazement because it had cost the two of them $135 to eat that evening. But something else was causing Tom even more consternation. It was the fact that it took them 3 hours and 45 minutes to eat this $135 meal. Tom said, "Anything that costs that much ought to be ready when you get there."

It seems we have lost all of the concept of the working relationship that exists between quality and time. We Americans are activists and doers. It is our nature to roll up our sleeves and get the job done. And heaven help anything or anyone that gets in the way. Problems are to be solved and schedules are to be met. Time is of the essence to us.

All this is not so alien to those of us who are in body of Christ, either. It may be that one of the deepest signs of worldliness in us all is that we are watching the same clock society uses.

Last year Peg and I were up in Virginia for her Aunt Pauline's funeral. We are not any more ready for death than we are for living and it always seems to catch most of us with lots to do. We arrived at the motel late that night, bleary-eyed and exhaused, after a day and a half of rushing around getting ready to go. Almost too tired to sleep, we turned on the TV and were greeted on the religious network by an old acquaintance from my gospel music business days who had slipped into a new role as TV host and also into a new hairdo. So we stayed with him until he waved good-by an hour or so later.

One of his guests reminded me about this business of the clock. He was a very handsome and impressive young minister of the gospel. And he had a powerful story to tell. Even as a boy he had held preaching services in his own backyard. From that modest beginning a large congregation had been born. But the reason for his being on the program on this particular evening was to tell of an occasion of healing in his own life.

Some time before, he had been holding a revival in his own church. During this meeting he had begun to have problems with his throat and with his speaking voice. From listening to him on the program it was apparent that he had preached with power and enthusiasm. We could imagine his use of his deep, pleasant voice as he expounded the gospel, exhorted the believers, and confronted the unrighteous. When he went to see a physician, he was told that he should not even carry on a conversation for three months. Ninety days of silence was not something that he thought would be worthwhile for him to be doing. So he went immediately to his study where he began to pray, "Help me, God, I do not have three months." And he was healed and went on with the meeting.

I think maybe I had better let you know just here that I am not writing about his healing. I believe it occurred as he told it. And I can rejoice with him for his trust in God and for the miracle of healing itself. Since I am quite sure I would not be around to be writing a book if it were not for the healing power of God, I want to say that I believe in healing. But I do want to comment about his clock, and about what I think it is saying about patience and trust. Both his and ours.

Can you imagine telling God — the God in whom there is no beginning and no ending, the eternal, always was and always will be God, the God who buries tulip bulbs in the darkness of the soil, the God who hides oak trees in acorns, this God — that you don't have three months? It seems bold to me, to say the very least, to say this to God who knew you long before you ever came to be. To suggest to this God — who has promised to gather up all of your life and transform it into the goodness of his purpose — that he should get on with it because you don't have time to dilly-dally around is pretty daring!

I can almost hear God saying, "I think I'll just heal him. It will be easier than explaining it him." But I would like to have suggested to this preacher that God could probably teach him more in ninety days of "hush" than he could learn in thirty years of listening to himself.

But waiting is not easy for us nine-to-fivers. Last fall I was up in the mountains of New Mexico for a week. Early in the week, I addressed a group of pastors. When they departed to go back to their respective labors, I stayed on to meet with a group of their parishioners who came in a day and a half later. My life that week took on a very relaxed, orderly, quiet posture. There was time to read and to write, to walk and to pray. I went on walks in the woods and to concerts played by mountain streams splashing across grassy meadows. I saw art shows put on by wild flowers in glorious whites and pinks and purples. There were no telephones, televisions, or radios. Silence and solitude became welcome companions.

Having secured a little bit of serenity with even so tenuous a grasp, I found myself wondering why the rest of these retreaters drove their cars back and forth between the lodge and the dining hall and why they rushed off to play golf or tennis or go shopping back in town. It seemed to me, as the self-proclaimed guru of the week, that they attacked every hour of the retreat as if their coming could only be justified by thoroughly filling every moment. They gave trophies for golf and horseshoes and volleyball and for the skits and the games. But there were no prizes or premiums for naps or for walks in the woods or for stillness. From my new-found place of quietness, I pondered all their ant-like scurrying.

Then I remembered how I had come to this place in the mountains. I had spent three exhausting and frantic days prior to arriving here. I had spoken three times the first day, driven almost all of the second, and flown across the country on the third to be here to talk to these people about slowing down the pace of their lives. On the last Sunday, I was planning to close the sermon and a car door at about the same time and hurry to the airport in Albuquerque some three hours away to catch the first plane I could to get home.

I am beginning to get a sneaking suspicion that some things will only come to us by waiting and that some things will never happen for us because we are in too big a hurry to let the time go by in which they can come true. We are not very patient people.

I often talk with people who firmly believe that God has some rich and deep purpose for their lives. It is evident they are sincere in their willingness and desire to find and fulfill that plan. But they experience difficulty because they cannot seem to trust the God who has ordained such purposes to also bring it about in his good and providential timing. They can't believe that when something finally does occur, it will be with such obvious rightness that they will almost blush to ever have doubted it would be. They will wonder why it was so difficult to continue the present path with dedication and joy until some new word came to them.

To be able to do so, we must become aware that there is some other way of accounting for time. We must begin to hear, however faintly at first, the rhythm and movement of the One who set it all in motion when the world began.

"Come Just As We Are."

We seem to have a variety of ways of explaining what Jesus meant by "love one another." Even though he threw some additional light on the subject when he said everybody loves their loved ones but, "I'm talking about loving your enemies also."

Our story has a tendency to sound more like this: "I love you but I don't like you. I love your soul but your big old body and your personality just drive me up the wall." Unfortunately, all the souls I ever saw were housed in bodies and amplified through personalities.

Or you'll hear somebody say, "I love you in the Lord." Like if you ever fall from grace or fellowship, then you're the very first guy I mean to drop from my list.

Somebody will say, "I love you enough to get to heaven," as if to say as soon as we get there I'm gonna bust you in the mouth or bend your halo or at least stomp one of your wings.

Some time ago on the radio I heard a song that I liked. The lyrics were talking about a place where "everybody knows your name, and they're always glad you came." Somebody told me that it was the theme song for a television program about a saloon. I still wish they'd been singing it about the church.

In the *Reader's Digest* some time ago, there was a little paragraph about a Sunday school class that was searching for a name. It was a class of people who had been drawn together mostly because they were all filled with same kind of hurts and needs and dreams. There were lots of suggestions for a name but one was chosen because it seemed to say what everybody wanted it to say about them. It was "The Come Just As You Are Class." I think I would have voted for it, too.

There is some keen insight into the gospel in that name. Those people were looking for a name which best described what was unique to them as a class. They must have decided that the strongest bond holding them together was not one that tried to describe their strengths. It was their weaknesses that made them one.

If the word gets around that they are really living up to their name it may create a problem, because somebody is going to "come just as they are." And some time in the future the name might have to be discreetly changed to something like "Come Just As *We* Are."

The Word That Must Be Spoken.

Bill Gaither and I were sitting on the edge of the darkened stage as the second Praise Gathering for Believers was about to begin. Over six thousand people were in the audience. Even with the lights from the exit signs, the auditorium was almost totally black.

From the back of the auditorium, Doug Oldham began to sing. The people quieted down to hear Doug's warm voice as he slowly sang his way toward the front. About halfway down the aisle the spotlights caught him. He stopped and, in the midst of that expectant throng, he continued to sing.

When Doug finished singing he was going to introduce Bill and me. We were to welcome everyone to Indianapolis for what we hoped and prayed would be three days of life-changing worship and praise. Neither of us was too certain about what he was going to say and each of us was graciously deferring to the other.

Doug finished and gave us the microphone and the spotlights were on us. We began to try to welcome the people. We were just having some fun with the audience when I remembered something I had seen Chico Holliday do at a great evening of music in California a few months earlier.

I asked the people to identify themselves. "All the Methodists, say 'Methodist' together." Then I called, in turn, for Baptists, Presbyterians, Lutherans, Nazarenes, Church of God-ers, Pentecostals, and on down through a list of all the groups that I could call to mind.

Then I asked everyone to call out the name of his group at the same time. On a signal everyone identified his church. It came out something like *Baptodistyri-anazalutheranevepenschurchofgod.*

Some groups are a little more active in their worship and they sounded out the strongest. But apparently some people from the more reserved groups had gotten some practice at basketball games or somewhere. They were not to be out-done. It was one more confusing sound of Babel.

After the confusion died down, I asked the audience to say "Jesus." When we spoke his name together there was such a unity that you could hardly believe the beauty. Bill said, "Let's whisper it together." That was the prettiest sound I think that I've ever heard. "Jesus."

Jesus is the name which unites us and makes us one. When we all speak at once the names of the doctrines which divide us, it comes out in a word that nobody understands. We create a sort of religious shouting and shoving match. Hardly anyone other than the shouters and shovers is interested in the contest.

When we say his name together we make a beautiful sound which becomes "music in our ears, the sweetest name on earth."

Now, we don't all say the name of Jesus the same way. On almost back-to-back programs on the radio, you hear various preachers say "Jesus." They each say his name in such a different way that you wonder if they are all saying the same word. Some have perfected a pronunciation that comes out smoothly like "Je-suzz." Isn't that lovely? Just hang on the "suzzz." "Je-suzzz." It makes him sound so warm and sweet.

The next program is hosted by some good old-time preacher who is proclaiming the gospel as if he were fighting bees. He makes the name of Jesus a three-syllable word as he shouts, "Je-sus-aahh!" with great, moist emphasis on the "aahh!"

But regardless of how we speak the name of Jesus, it is the word which must be spoken. It is the one name which, when lifted up, draws all men in the same direction.

A Basket Full Of Weakness.

There was a deep spirit of forgiveness and acceptance among the people who were up at this year's Homecoming, a retreat we have put on with our friends for the last couple of years. I think it began with something which was done at registration—under some mild protests and questioning I might add. "Do I have to?" and "What are these for?" were the two most often asked questions. There was a reason for making an instant photo of everyone as they signed in at the lodge. But we didn't tell anyone what it was. "Just bring it along to the opening session," was the only instruction given as we were handed our picture mounted on a card.

There was one thing we wanted to try to begin the very first time we met. Retreats are alike in many ways. The first day and a half or so seems to be spent in trying to become a group. Usually this really begins to happen about midway through the final service and then everybody suddenly wonders why we had wasted all that time walking around like strangers. So we had planned to open up the retreat trying to get the "Sunday and good-by" feeling on a "Friday and hello" after-noon. And the ability of a group to become a community—or better still, "the body"—always seeems to come in some direct proportion to the willingness that they have to give themselves to each other.

In many ways, it would seem that this sense of belonging would be just what everybody is seeking and it would come about very naturally and very quickly. But the truth is that more of us go along through life with enough masks in our luggage to keep ourselves cleverly disguised in almost any situation, including retreats. And it is difficult to share ourselves with a new circle of people.

Certainly we don't want people to know the worst about us. But, paradoxically, it is only those who know the worst about us, and still believe in us anyway, that we really trust. And it is not just the worst that we hide either, we are afraid to reveal our best as well. We are very careful with our "I really do like you's" and our "I care about you's." So carefully hiding our worst and cautiously guarding our best, we try to build some new community on the safe middle ground of anonymity.

It was our hope that the picture on the card could become both a symbol and a way of our giving ourselves to each other. During the first session, there were admonitions made about openness being the key to community and community being the key to any kind of life-changing process. Nearly always what happens to us from above is conditioned by what is going on between us.

So there was a time during the first session for each of us to write about our-selves on the card under the picture. Things like who we were, what we were hop-ing for, our defeats, our successes, what it was that made us sing and what it was that made us sad. We were to write as much as we were willing to let the others know about us. It was a quiet, solemn time when the only sounds you could hear were pen and pencil points scratching across the cards in our laps as we reduced the whole of our experiences to a series of marks, slashes, dots, and scribblings that would let other people into our hearts.

When we finished writing, and if we were willing to trust the rest of the group with the person we described on the card, we placed it in a basket at the front of the room. The basket was going to be put at the entrance to the prayer chapel. Then, as the people went in to pray they would take a card with them to the altar and make that person a matter of special prayer and concern. On the last day, we all took a card from the basket to take home with us and made a covenant to continue to remember the person pictured and described for the coming year.

The picture cards came to give us all a sense of belonging to each other. Each time we went to the chapel we felt we were meeting someone in a new way. We also realized that we, too, were being picked out of the basket and someone was looking at our faces and reading our scribblings and praying for us and for the things we had been willing to confide to the community. We began to be bound up together as we saw, and were seen, in the light of our hopes and dreams, and our heartaches and struggles.

One afternoon, my son Robert was standing in the back of the chapel and he noticed more than one person digging through the pictures in the basket. He later said he thought to himself that it was not quite fair for a person to read through all the cards if they were not going to take them inside to pray over them. Then he realized the people were looking for their own cards. Evidently there were some things they wished to add, some things they would like for the "body" to know and care about. They had come to believe they could trust the rest of us. There did indeed seem to be a reservoir of acceptance and love turned loose among us that weekend.

But it only happened because we were willing to be bound together by our weakness. And because out of our weakness, there came strength.

Burying The Wounded.

Upon his retirement, my father undertook to compile a family history of the Bensons. Like everything he decides to do, he did it methodically and well. He has always been very proud of his father and mother and wanted to know more about his ancestors. His own father and his paternal grandfather were both good businessmen and devout churchmen. But working his way along the trunk and out on some of the limbs of his family tree, my dad made some interesting discoveries.

He traced us back up into east Tennessee, into Smith County around Carthage. Such a search takes you to the courthouse for deeds and titles of properties bought and sold. Unfortunately, the first Benson up there that my father could tie us all to must have been very poor. At least, according to the courthouse records, he never owned any land. Furthermore, there was a ferry up at Carthage that ran back and forth across the Cumberland River which cost a nickel to ride and you had to sign the register when you rode it. Evidently old John R. didn't have a nickel because he doesn't show up in the records as ever having made the trip. Fortunately for our family pride, things have been more impressive since we moved to town.

For a long time Dad didn't think too much about Mom's side of the tree. She was from Alabama and I'm not sure he thought they had family trees down there. But he decided that his children would also be interested in their mother's people and he persuaded Mom to do some research on her ancestors. She keeps finding all kind of landowners right on back to William Penn. It discouraged my father a little, I think.

If you keep poking around in family trees, you will eventually have to do what someone has called having to "deal with direness." One of my uncles was rather famous and once was greeted with a parade upon his return from New York. Unfortunately, the records show he was returning from an extended stay in prison at Sing Sing.

In a lot of places I go, I find that people love singing songs that say, "I'm so glad I'm a part of the family of God," and "We're part of the family that's been born again." You can start one of these songs and everybody will just join right in with great joy and conviction. But it is not very much different in the "family of God" than it is the "family of Benson." The body of Christ is always having to learn to deal with something that one of us has gone out and done. Maybe it was even one of our children or one of our children's children.

Even though the church is a body of people who are called to great things, a body that is given diverse and wonderful gifts, it is still true, sooner or later (and too many times it is sooner), one of us goes out and does something that is just really dumb. We knew it was dumb when we were doing it and that just made it all the dumber. And all of the sudden the community which hopefully had been going about loving one another is called on to do some bearing up and some forgiving.

One summer Sunday morning, our family decided to visit the services of a church about which we had heard a lot of good things. The pastor happened to be preaching that day on the matter of disciplining errant members of the congregation. He was contending for the right of the elders to deal with such matters as might arise. He was also reminding the elders of the sacred responsibillities and duties involved even in potentially painful situations. Although we were only visitors, he was contending and reminding so earnestly that we could not help but suspect there were some matters that had already come up.

He offered as evidence for his sermon some paragraphs from the constitution of his particular denomination. The official rules stated that in any such circumstances there were three factors to be considered. The three points themselves were not necessarily surprising. But the order of importance which they were given was mildly disturbing to me, to say the least.

First, in all matters, God was to be glorified. Certainly it seemed this should be the first priority of the church. It was the order of the next two propositions which disturbed me. Secondly, the pastor went on to say, the body was to protect its own purity. Finally, the errant member was to be ministered to. I wasn't sure that point numbers two and three were in the proper order. I'm still not.

Forgiveness isn't much of a trick if everybody is glorifying God. And it isn't too difficult if nobody is doing anything to embarrass or discredit the rest of us. Where it really gets to be a chore is when someone goes and does something dumb. In fact, that's the problem with the whole matter of forgiveness. There is always this relationship between the senselessness of the deed itself and the depth of the need for forgiveness. The darker the deed, the deeper the necessity for the healing balm of mercy.

More and more I am coming to believe that the body is bound together by its weaknesses. That part of being " a part of the family" often demands dealing with direness. And that we are not always so good at dealing with it, either. Before we can begin to affirm others in their gifts, we will have to accept them and forgive them because they are weak as we are weak.

Burying the wounded so the rest of us will be healthy doesn't seem like much of a way to build an army.

Why Don't We See Him?

A friend of mine was pastoring in a small town in West Virginia. The town was squeezed in between the riverbank and the hills. As it grew, it had to climb its way up the hillsides.

The church where my friend pastored called me to preach at a revival meeting. I stayed in the guest room at the parsonage. Every morning I would take a walk up into the hills behind the church. I liked to sit on a wall high above the little business district and watch the people below.

I would ask my friend to go with me but he never did. I sometimes could see him down below as he walked three blocks to the post office and then back again. I kidded him because he never "looked up into the hills." He just plodded along, looking at the pavement. One day while I was there, he found a quarter in the gutter.

He was really proud of that quarter but it reminded me of the story about a man who found a dime on the road when he was a little boy. He was so impressed with getting something for nothing that for the rest of his life he walked with his eyes on the road. After forty years he had picked up nearly thirty-five thousand buttons, more than fifty thousand pins, four dollars in loose change, a bent back, and a terrible disposition. Perhaps the greatest tragedy was this man's lack of awareness of all that he missed along the way because he refused to look up from the pavement.

My friend in West Virginia never saw much of the majesty of life, either. As a result, his life was always hemmed in and bounded by the humdrum round of people's failures and the inequities of the system.

Why is it that we who claim to know him best often seem so unseeing and unbelieving?

We have somehow failed to follow the deep insight of St. Ignatius Loyola who taught his followers: Seek and find God in all things.

We must learn to see God in sunsets and a friend's touch on the arm. We must find him in the flames licking around a log in the fireplace, and in the snow blanketing the branches of holly trees outside the study window.

We ignore God in these and a thousand other places where he has nested his secrets. After failing to see him all week, it is no wonder that we spend our hour on Sunday in a padded pew feeling little at all. It gets pretty easy to explain why the most striking words of the sermon are "In conclusion." Our greatest response is not to God, but to the words, "In closing, we shall stand and sing Hymn 462."

It seems to me that the more I can sense God, the Creator, the more I am able to know and relate to God the Redeemer. As I begin to realize his "everywhere-ness" and his involvement in all things, I can better see his "particularness" and his intimate relationship to me. As I see his great plans and his steady dependable laws, I realize again his consistent, steady ways of hoping and planning for me. I realize again and again that he is present, and can be found, in the depths of my despair and in the heights of my joy. He is there at the brightness of noon and the blackness of midnight.

We are to see God and hear God in the smiling faces of children, in the steady hum of machinery, in the tear-stained faces of the sorrowful. He is to be found in the gliding flight of the sparrow and the gentle falling of the snowflake. When all creation becomes a reflection of God to us, when all of reality becomes a sacrament, then our hearts burst forth in joyous worship.

The life of faith is a life of searching, but it is also a life of finding. But only for those who will learn to look up and see him.

Make It Last.

I once heard a missionary tell a very moving story about an African man to whom he had given a copy of the Bible. The African was so grateful for the gift, and so profuse in his thanks, that the missionary was puzzled a few months later when they met again. For the Bible was battered and torn and it looked as though many of the pages were missing. "I thought you would have taken better care of the Bible I gave you," he remarked. "I assumed you wanted it and would treasure it."

And the African man replied, "It is the finest gift I ever received. It is such a wonderful book that I gave a page to my father and a page to my mother and then I gave a page to everyone in the village."

Some years later, I read about a book entitled *The Joys of Super Slow Reading*. In the book there is an account of a man who was imprisoned during World War II. He was only able to take a single book along with him when he was captured. Since he did not know how long it was going to be before he was rescued, he determined he would make that one book last. And he rationed out its words and pages to himself.

I certainly believe in the programs which encourage and aid us to read the Bible through in a year. My only misgivings surface through my usual flounderings in the doldrums of Deuteronomy in mid-March. But I also believe there is great value in centering oneself in a given place in the Word, and lingering there until it has had time to make an indelible impression on one's life.

It might be a good exercise for each of us to take some small portion of Scripture and, instead of approaching it with the idea of finishing it quickly, try to see how long we could make it last.

It probably would do us all good, we who have so many Bibles in so many translations, to have only a page for a while. Until we had learned it, until we had loved it, until it was ours in truth.

Shoulder To Shoulder.

For a long time now, I have felt that when I finished speaking there should be a time of guided or private prayer during which the people present could themselves speak to God. What they have to say to him may be in connection with what I have been discussing or it may be a thousand miles from my topic. But I want them to have some time to listen and to respond to the calling voice of God before we dismiss and go our separate ways.

One of the ways I sometimes get them to participate in this prayer service is to ask them to put their hand on the shoulder of the person sitting next to them. When they all cooperate, everyone is both touching someone and being touched by someone else. Then I ask them to bow their heads and close their eyes and join me in an exercise of prayer about being members of the body of Christ.

First, I ask them to feel the hand that is resting on them. I sometimes instruct everyone to give a little pat on the shoulder so that they all will be aware of the hand reaching out to touch them. I say "everyone." There are always some people who are reluctant to touch the person next to them, especially if they are strangers. And the ranks of the reluctant often swell when I get to the patting part. But most of the people will do it, even if they feel compelled to grin nervously to assure their neighbor that this was not their idea. I want each person present to sense a hand touching them. Then I want them to believe that the hand resting on their shoulder is truly the hand of God reached out to them through the body of Christ.

It is a beautiful thing to behold as people begin to realize that they are not alone. They are members of a body, the body of Christ. I ask them to take some time to give thanks for all that being members of the body has meant to them over the years. I can imagine what is going on in their hearts. For I am mindful that most of us would never have made it had it not been for the love and the prayers of those who have been the hand of God reaching out to us as the body of Christ. Nearly always the place where we are meeting is filled with the sweet sound and aroma of praise as the people meditate during this part of the prayer exercise.

There is another response that I want people to make after they have expressed their gratitude for the blessings of life in the body. I want each one to become aware of the shoulder on which their hand is laid. I want each one to consider the other thing it means to be part of the body.

Are their hands really saying to their neighbor in the pew, "This hand will paint your house, this hand will cook the meals while your husband is in the hospital, this hand will reach into its own pocket and freely share everything there is as long as there is anything at all to divide?" Are they really willing for their hand to be the open, helping, suffering hand of God stretched out as a part of the body of Christ to others?

It is true that the calling of God to us is personal. And it is true that the call comes to us in the depths of our own hearts. It is sounded into our own personality, background, and present experience. It is authentically ours.

But it is most often heard in the midst of the body. And it is lived out in the community of believers. It is understood and affirmed and believed in by the body together. It is undertaken and conserved with the mutual love and strength of the group.

I think it is because of the deep importance of body-life that so much of the teachings of the Epistles in the New Testament are given over to how we are to live with each other. Sometimes it seems that little is mentioned about winning the lost. It is as if the writers believed that if we could learn to be to each other all that we are supposed to be, the lessons we had learned in awareness and compassion would issue forth in all of the areas of our lives. And that would in turn attract and compel those who do not know the Christ whose body we form.

If we could really begin to believe this, it would change the way we look at one another. Or perhaps if we could change the way we look at each other, we ould begin to believe it. It is either one way or the other. Or both. It seems that most of the problems we have with one another begin in all the things we fail to see in each other.

We usually make our first judgments about people on the basis of what we can see with our eyes. And we are so quick to see that other persons are too fat or too thin or too ugly or too short. So on the basis of looks, size, posture, a double knit leisure suit, or something just about as essential to what a person really is, we form an opinion which we resolutely resist changing from then on. And we fail to even notice, or remember, that before us is standing a person the Father has created in his own image and into whom he has placed his kind and loving gifts.

I am convinced that marvelous things would begin to happen to each one of us in the body if we could all begin to see each other like this. I think more of us would be standing on our tiptoes reaching for the stars, if we suddenly realized that everybody else had just been waiting for us to begin.

One of the big words in the vocabulary of the church these days is "ministry." Churches are known by the number and the variety of their ministries. There are ministries to children, to singles, to youth, to senior citizens, and to any other age group sufficiently large enough to merit the interest and attention of a staff member. There are prayer ministries, cassette ministries, bus ministries, and jail ministries. Almost any activity of the church that is undertaken is listed and described as one of the ministries.

Ministry is usually thought about as something we do for someone else. That is certainly one of the ideas suggested by Jesus in his use of the metaphors "salt" and "light" in the Sermon on the Mount. His very choice of these two everyday illustrations shows his deep insight into the plight of mankind.

Jesus looked at this world and described it accurately. He hurt for this world for which he had come to die. And he prescribed a remedy for it. He said it needed salt to preserve it and light to illuminate it. And it is satisfying to think that we are the agents who are helping to keep the world from decay and darkness.

But there is something else sounding out to me from these words about salt and light. This other faintly disturbing idea is beginning to redefine the word ministry for me. Maybe it is not always some act or deed that passes virtue, goodness, and strength from those of us who are so lavishly endowed with these qualities to those less fortunate who would have had to do without if we had not come along as "ministers."

Could it have been that Jesus is calling us to be salt, so that we would be seasoning to each other? To have a kind of a quality which will release and enhance all that which had long ago been stored deep inside by God himself? We don't put salt on green beans because we like salt, you know. We do it because it makes them taste more like what green beans ought to taste like. Then we can say, "Now *those* are green beans."

And could it be that Jesus is calling us to shine light into the darkness so that whatever it is that God had placed there will be brightly illuminated? Is he asking us to bring light that is both healing and enhancing to the long-obscured works of his Father in the hearts and lives of others?

It seems very likely to me that the true essence of ministry has more to do with *being* to another than with some act or deed which we have come to believe we must be *doing* to, for, or on them. Perhaps the deepest, kindest thing we can do for anyone is to just be there for them in such a way that all that they are and all the gifts that they possess will be released and affirmed.

If this is true, it will probably begin to come about as we learn to perceive each other as Paul has suggested when he reminds us that we are all "God's chosen people, holy and dearly beloved."

Everybody needs and deserves to be surrounded with belief and affirmation that will form a pad from which their hopes and dreams and gifts can be launched. It is in the body of Christ that we are supposed to be surrounded with this seasoning, healing, enhancing love and care.

We all know how very much it means to be believed in. There was a study done by a group of researchers from Harvard. They would go to elementary school teachers at the beginning of the school year and tell them that they had designed a test which could prove most helpful to them. The results would correctly predict which students were going to grow intellectually during the coming school year. Someone called it "The Harvard Test of Intellectual Spurts" because he said it told which students were going to "spurt" that year. The educators promised it would pick out the right students and it was very, very accurate.

Given permission to give the test, they administered, unbeknownst to the teacher, an old, obsolete I.Q. test. When the students had finished the test, the papers were collected and the researchers threw them in the wastebasket. Then they picked five names at random from the rollbook and sat down with the teacher and said, "Now, these are the students in your class who are going to have a very good year. Watch these kids. One of them is Rachel Smith," they informed the teacher.

"Rachel Smith?" the teacher replied increduously, "She wouldn't 'spurt' if you shot her from a cannon. I have had two of her brothers and each one of the Smiths is dumber than the last." But the educators maintained that the test hardly ever was wrong in its findings and that Rachel's progress in the ensuing year could be readily observed.

You can imagine what happened that semester, can't you? Yes, you can. Rachel never had a chance to be her same old self. Under a barrage of "Rachel, would you write this on the board this morning," "Rachel will lead the line to the lunch room today," "Is that a new dress, Rachel? It sure is pretty," "Thank you, Rachel, that was very good," Rachel 'spurted' all over the place. And so did every name they put on that list.

According to Paul, every one of our names belongs on a list like that. We are all "God's chosen people, holy and dearly loved." I think one of my all-time favorite quotes is from a little boy in elementary school who said, "My teacher thought I was smarter than I wuz. So I wuz!" And all of us need to be in a body that believes we are smarter and better and more gifted than we have ever dared to think we were. For this is one of the ways that each of us will begin to hear the calling voice of God.

We need to see that we are to be giving life even as we are receiving it, that we are to be nurturing even as we are being nurtured, that we are to be healing even as we are being healed.

One of things that the hand on our shoulder in the prayer exercise is saying to each of us is a deep, affirmative, "I believe in you." And our hand should be saying to the one whose shoulder we are touching, "I believe in who you are, and what you can become, because of the gifts that God has put within you."

The Simple Fruits Of The Spirit.

"My Father is the Gardener, I am the Trunk, you are the branches and branches bear fruit." (John 15)

I once saw a sign on the front of a church that announced, "Our Soul Goal for September is 200." The phrase "soul goal" makes me think of something like scalps or notches on a gun. It does not adequately describe what I believe Jesus was trying to accomplish through us.

Jesus was always aware that souls are packaged in bodies, and they are people. People get cold and hungry and thirsty and lonely. Sometimes they get sick and sometimes they are thrown into prison. And he tells us that they are very important to him, so important that whatever is done or left undone in their behalf was just the same as doing or not doing for him. His life is interwoven with people.

So closely does he identify himself with people everywhere that he tells his disciples, "When they are hungry, I am hungry; when they are cold, I am cold; and wherever you find them, remember that when they bleed, I bleed; when they cry, I cry; when they are thrown into prison, I am thrown into prison. And whatever you do for them, you are doing for me. And whenever you pass them by, you are passing me by."

In the strictest sense, I believe that when we think of bearing fruit we all think first of the Great Commission. We are to go, to bear witness, to baptize, and to teach. Ultimately, the things we do are done to make disciples. We understand that the task is to win souls. Still, it appears to me that even though this was the ultimate or strictest good for Jesus, he went about it in the broadest way possible.

And so I am coming to think that such a strict definition of bearing fruit just doesn't match up very well with all these things he is describing, the "whatever you do for thems," that he says are part of the work of the kingdom. They are parts of the processes of God that lead to his redemptive purposes. Anything, even down to a cup of cold water poured in his name, is properly the work of the branches, and branches bear fruit.

I want to make some simple suggestions about "cups of cold water." The first of them is *hugs.*

For a number of years Peg and I were teachers in the Sunday school. I taught the college class and she taught in the nursery. At present, we are going to class together. I think my fruitbearing still has to find its expression in some way around the church. So my unofficial post is across the hallway just outside the classroom door. We go to early service and then to Sunday school class. After class the hall is filled with people. Those of us who come to the first service are happy because we are ready to go to lunch now. The rest of the people, who are going from class to the sanctuary for the eleven o'clock service, are also happy because it is always good to be in our worship service.

Now let me tell you that I am, or at least have always wanted to be, a lover. I have never had any disposition at all to be a fighter. A couple of years ago, we were at the class Christmas party at the home of one of the three teachers. I was standing with Wilson, one of my friends, near the front door. The host and hostess were busy elsewhere in the house and, if they didn't hear the doorbell, Wilson and I let the guests in and showed them where to put their coats and how to get to the punch bowl. After a while, he said to me, "Why is it that everybody who comes in shakes my hand and hugs your neck?"

"Well, the reason is simple. When people come in, you hold out your hand. They might want to hug you, but they can't get to you with that big old hand sticking out there. If you would just open your arms, they would walk right into them." And sure enough, after about four more arrivals, he saw my point.

So I was standing at my post in the hall one Sunday after class, ready to serve, when a little old lady whom I have known for a long time came from her class toward me.

She lives alone now because her husband is dead and like the rest of us her children are too busy with their own children to come home much at all. So I opened my arms and she walked right into them. I closed them about her and told her that I loved her. I asked her how she was and she told me. And she went on to church.

Someone told me later that she had heard I had been hugging ladies at church again. When I asked her how she knew, she said, "Birchie came into the sanctuary yesterday morning and sat down beside me. With tears in her eyes, she told me that you had put your arms around her and told her you loved her."

Sometimes it is easy to recruit people for this particular ministry. I was talking about it one evening on a college campus. The next morning was High School Senior Day when kids from all over come to take a look at the school. As I came to chapel that morning, it warmed my heart to see a couple of upperclassmen already putting this good truth into practice. A college could have worse advertising.

At other times, it is a bit more difficult. Every once in a while I go to church where the pastor says to me, "I sure hope you are not one of those dudes that has us all holding hands." I hate to tell him. Sometimes, when I ask people to join hands, I tell them that Peg and I squeeze each other's hands and that means "I love you." And I ask them to squeeze hands. Not everybody get "squuz." It takes all the courage some people have just to join hands, much less squeeze. I always tell everybody that didn't get "squuz" to see me after church.

And if that is true about joining hands, you can imagine the consternation of a general call to embracing.

I'm afraid you will think I am just a sentimental, weepy-eyed, soft-hearted fool. Well, I am, but what I am saying to you is very, very true.

Now let me tell you a story about *prayers*. It, too, took place in the same hall outside the classroom where I usually "minister." This day a lady came up to me and asked me if I knew who she was. It took me a moment but as soon as she told me, I remembered. She then related this story to me.

"A few weeks ago, I was impressed to pray for you in a special way. Your face and your name were before me. And I did pray as I was directed. I started to write you a note and mention it to you, but I thought you might think I was crazy or something, so I didn't. After a while I dropped you from the list. Later, I had the same thought about you and prayed again. So when I saw you this morning, I thought I would tell you about it."

I thanked her and we visited a bit and she went on down the hall to the sanctuary.

Neither of us really had any idea why she had been led to pray for me. There didn't seem to be any special need. A few months later I came home for a week or so before going out to Oklahoma to speak. I was not feeling very well. After a few days I went to see the doctor, and he sent me across the street to the hospital. It was the beginning of a period of serious illness, emergency surgery, and slow recovery. It was eight weeks before I would finally go home again.

I do not really understand all about this. What had happened was a conversation between God and my friend that went something like this.

"Pat, I want you to be praying about Bob Benson."

"Well, all right, God, let me tell you about Bob Benson."

My first thought was, "Why should he tell her to tell him about me?" Then it began to come to me that he was telling her to tell me about him. And some two months before the reason was apparent to either of us, Pat was praying for me.

This past winter I was asked to speak in the devotional services at the Benson Choir Directors' Clinic. One morning I was standing in the lobby before the morning worship time. The pople were having coffee and doughnuts and visiting with each other before going into the conference room. I was acting like some kind of gospel hero, listening to kind remarks and autographing books. I always tell them that if I sign them, they can't return them for credit. Seriously, right then I was thinking about the next half hour and needing a moment of quiet. Someone tapped me on the shoulder and I turned to look at a young woman, who said to me, "Is there anything I can pray for you today?" It was the nicest thing that was said to me that morning.

I am learning that there isn't anything you can do for people that helps more than praying.

Let me add another to the list. It is *letter writing*. In this instance, as in prayer, its meaning is apparent to me because it happened to me.

In the hospital I received a steady stream of cards and letters from people everywhere. From Trevecca, where I had been serving as temporary college chaplain, I got a card that was twenty by forty inches. They set it in the lobby of the chapel building for several days and most of the students and faculty signed it.

Roxie Gibson, a friend of Peg's and mine, is an elementary school teacher and she had her class make cards with pictures and Scripture verses. One little girl did a lovely card with tulips and trees and butterflies. For the verse inside, she had selected Romans 10:21..."But to Israel He saith, 'All day long I have stretched forth my hands unto a disobedient and obstinate people.' ...Get well soon ...Your friend, Stacy." I sure hope she didn't know something I didn't.

The realization that so many people would open their hearts to me was a daily source of strength and help.

Just last week there was a letter from the wife of a pastor. She said that in his message that evening her husband had used something I had written. It was 1:30 in the morning when she wrote, "So thank God he is using you even today on the mission field. You are a blessing and we care about you. If you are ill, I'm sorry. If you hurt, I care. We have prayed for you every day, but felt compelled tonight to claim your healing. So out under the British sky with God's stars over-looking, we thanked God for your complete healing. God bless you today in a special way."

It was written by hand on an ordinary tablet, one of those with blue lines. It took only twenty-six pence to mail. But it is not ordinary to me. And I find myself wanting to live and write in a way that again commits to paper words that could be used by a California pastor speaking in a conference in England.

A letter, a note, a card are simple effective ways for the fruits of the branches of your life to overhang the fences of others anywhere.

So I have given three suggestions—hugs and prayers and letters. Each of them is a way for you to reach out to someone else. Each requires a bit of action on your part. Just in case even that is more initiative than you are prepared to take, I want to mention one more thing. It is the ministry of *listening*.

The amazing thing is that when one really learns to listen, much less talk is required. You do not have to have the answer, if you can truly hear the questions. I am trying to learn to look at people and listen. I am trying to be all there as they speak. I am trying not to think of what I am going to say when they finish. I am trying to listen. Sometimes I have been able to do so and when I have, it helps.

Last week I was talking to a lady in a crowded room. To tell you the truth, it was hard to keep from glancing over her shoulder at whomever I might be talking to next. Later, she wrote me a note that made me realize it was a more important meeting than I knew.

"When I talked to you yesterday, you looked at me. Right in my eyes like you really wanted to hear me, as though somehow you knew I was hurting though we didn't talk about it. I wanted you to know you ministered to me and I needed it. Sometimes people think if you're in the ministry, you don't need ministering to!"

Hugs, prayers, letters, listening. These are ordinary ways of living. But if it touches somebody, if it is done in love, and if it is done in his name, it is fruit of the Kingdom. The simplest of deeds done by the least likely of us in the humblest of circumstances can become fruit of the kingdom. When he said, "branches bear fruit," he was making a promise.

A simple thing happened to us recently which more than ever made me believe this. I was sitting in the bedroom reading when Peg came in and exclaimed, "This is why we go to that church!" I looked up and she was holding a chewing gum wrapper. And she read to me, "Dear Patrick, (that's our youngest) God loves you and so do I...Uncle Pek."

Pek Gunn is not really our uncle. But his own son died in infancy, and so he decided if he was not anyone's father, he would be everybody's uncle. Then, too, he didn't have much choice because Frances, his wife, had already decided to be everybody's aunt. She taught a Sunday school class in the children's department. She taught me and she taught Peggy. Later, she taught each of our children. She died awhile back, so she won't teach our grandson.

Peg laid the wrapper on the chest, and a day or so later, Patrick saw it and said, "Hey, that's my chewing gum wrapper." And he took it back to his room to put it among his "special" things.

Yes, I guess that's a pretty good indication of why we go to that church. If I make it, and surely I'm closer to the end than I am to the beginning, it will be because my parents got me in with the right crowd.

Do you wish you were in a crowd like that? It only takes one to start one. Someone who hugs, someone who prays, someone who writes notes, someone who listens.

Start a crowd where you are. It can be at home. It can be at church. It can be at work. It can be anywhere.

We Are Going To A Celebration.

He Said His Lines.

One of our sons, Mike,
wanted to take private speech—
he's such a talker anyway,
I recommended "hush" instead.
But it was inexpensive,
and he was interested
so we let him.

The climax of the year's labor
was a two-hour long
assortment of
clowns,
kings,
rabbits,
and forgotten lines
known as the Speech Recital
given to a devoted audience
of eager parents
and trapped friends.
Mike was a king.
He looked rather regal too,
if I do say so myself.
At least until the queen,
a head taller
and twenty pounds heavier,
stood beside him casting a pall
on his regality.
He had only three lines to say—
nine months of speech,
three short lines—
and they came very late,
in the last moment
of the last act

of the very last play.
Anyway you looked at it
he was not the star—
at least to anyone except a couple
about halfway back on the left side.

It was a long evening
and it was miserably hot
but Mike waited
and he was ready
and he said his lines
and he said them well.
Not too soon, not too late,
not too loud, not too soft
but just right
he said his lines.

I'm just a bit player too
not a star in any way—
but God gave me a line or so
in the pageant of life,
and when the curtain falls
and the drama ends—
and the stage is vacant at last—
I don't ask for a critic's raves
or fame in any amount.
I only hope he can say,
"He said his lines,
Not too soon, not too late,
not too loud, not too soft.
He said his lines
and he said them well"

A Reluctant Belief In Last Things.

I don't like good-bys.

I can't remember just how far back these feelings go, but I think they may have begun when I was seven or eight. Asthma was the culprit and the fall air was laden with football and falling leaves and asthma's accomplice, pollens. Once again breathing was so difficult for me that it was determined I needed the balmy, ocean breezes of Florida. This particular year, Mom could not get away to go with me and, I am sure with some deep misgivings on the part of my parents, I was bundled up and sent off to Miami. I was to stay with some distant friends of my folks. I had never met the lady, her mother, or her teenaged daughter, who were to be my family for some three months until Jack Frost and the winds of winter could cleanse the Tennessee air.

Some things about that fall are indelibly etched in my memory. I cannot forget the old house on N.W. 54th in Miami. It was not in very good shape because the hurricane of 1928 had severly damaged it, and since Mrs. Moore was a widow of limited means the repairs had been something less than extensive. I recall the flight down on the Eastern Airlines Silverliner with the glassine packet of airline stickers and postcards in the seat pocket in front of me. I remember Central Church of the Nazarene and Earlington Heights Elementary School and riding my bicycle over to Alapattah Center. But mostly I remember being miserably and abjectly homesick. To this day, good-bys do not come easily to me.

So as I waited for my row to be called to board Republic 393 for Chicago one morning last fall, I was engrossed in watching some rather tender and poignant farewells going on around me. And I observed more than one teary-eyed person looking forlornly at the giant bird outside the window that was in the process of gobbling up their loved one. Since I was only going to Indiana for three days, I had managed to bear up as I had kissed my family good-by before leaving the house a little while before. I wondered, though, about the reasons and the lengths and the distances of some of the separations being dramatized before me in the waiting lounge at the Nashville airport.

Finally we were all on board, watching with rapt attention the demonstration of a series of procedures to be used in "unlikely events." I noted that the plane was largely filled with business types: salesmen, executives, and presidents of Amalgamated Widget Internationals. In the seat next to me, a man armed with a handful of pencils and a calculator was already hard at work filling out expense reports and working out proposals.

In front of me, there was a man I figured was a real tycoon. I had seen him first in the terminal hard at work on the telephone up by Gate Sixteen and later in his temporary office with two brief cases and a secretary down at Gate Nineteen. He was a seasoned traveler, ignoring the row-by-row boarding sequence and coming on almost last. He had walked up the aisle as if he had come aboard to buy the plane or maybe even the airline. His secretary didn't have quite the same air of assurance as he did, but then she was carrying the two brief cases, a box, a newspaper, two coats and his cup of coffee. When they were seated in opposite aisle seats, the world of commerce resumed and a steady flow of paper went across to him for checkmarks, okays, and various other notations.

I am sure that inside I was grinning at him. For there had been a time when I was a would-be tycoon also, and thought that the world might possibly come to a screeching halt if I did not spend the hour or so in the air with an armload of something to read, write, check, or dictate. So it feels good now to check my bags, stroll on the plane in a sweater, slacks, and a pair of shoes that look like they belonged to a college professor, take the book from under my arm, and let the world run itself. In my mind I was smugly thinking, "I know what you are doing. I've done it myself and if you do it long enough, maybe you can get to the place where you won't have to do it either." It was not one of my more compassionate moments.

In Chicago, ambling off in my writer-speaker gait to the Air Wisconsin departure lounge, I saw my traveling companion from 12C striding up the corridor full steam ahead with his secretary the gear in tow. I sent him along with my hopes that he was able to buy the Loop or sell it or whatever.

In due time Air Wisoconsin delivered me to Fort Wayne and I was taken to the downtown Holiday Inn for a weekend layman's retreat. It was not exactly my idea of "woodsy," but this was to be the place.

Having arrived early in the afternoon I decided to walk around the city some. Nearby, although the neighborhood had obviously gone through many changes and was even now in the process of urban renewal, there were some lovely old churches remaining. A sign on the front of one of them interested me. In my opinion, you can gain some insight both into the pastor and the congregation by the words and nuances of church signs. This was a new one to me. At first glance, I thought it was some sort of a travesty. Walking along in the heart of the city dotted here and there with the poor and the down and the out, I wondered what I would have put on the sign in front of the church had I been the pastor. I don't think it would have been "Let the Good Times Roll."

Probably it was because after a smooth flight, a good lunch, and being checked into the complimentary Van Gogh Suite on the Concierge Floor, I wasn't as responsive as I might have been to the eschatological hope of the Christian.

I can remember when I was growing up that the word "hope" had great meaning to our congregation. They were a group of people with modest means. Many of them were factory workers making shoes in the Genesco plant, which was only a block away from the church on Main Street. Since they were not so deeply entrenched in the so-called good life, we sang a lot of songs about our hope in Jesus. Present circumstances were somehow tolerable, even with their attendant cares and sorrows, because they were viewed as only some kind of a temporary prelude to the real life we were someday going to live in his presence.

The great American dream slowly worked miracles in our midst. A generation

or two later, we are all engrossed in somehow trying to make the present permanent, thinking that with time and a little luck we can take care of our own good
times.

I am afraid I have the "this is the place" fever as bad as anyone. I walk around
my house and acre and think of all the things I would like to do to them next.
I want to extend the garden over here, move the driveway over there, build a picket
fence, add a sun porch, and finish the attic. Meanwhile, I'm planting perennials
in the flower beds. But Jesus told us that he was going away to prepare us a place—a
true, real place where we would finally really be at home. And when that place
was ready—our authentic, last, forever place—he would come back and get us
and take us there.

On two separate occasions recently I used the Lord's Supper as the background
for the services in a retreat setting. We partook of the meal at the end of each
meeting. Each time we varied the way we took the bread and the wine to try to
let a difference facet of their beauty and meaning shine through and become apparent to us.

To close the weekend, we sat in quietness and prayer and awe at what these
two sacramental things represent. One by one we came forward to take the elements. Both personally and publicly, we wanted to join Christ in the dying that
alone can lead to redemptive living.

There was one other thing that seemed to want to be said from this sacramental meal. It is the expression of Christian hope. Paul writes that we are to "proclaim
the Lord's death until he comes." In the Gospel versions, Jesus says that when this
meal is eaten together again it will be in his Father's kingdom.

In all honesty, this aspect of the communion was the hardest to define and the
most difficult one to which to relate. It seemed to have the least appeal and inspiration to us all. Maybe it is because eschatology is the study of last things, and
our first difficulty was that none of us wanted to think about end times or last
things.

For whatever the reason, whether it is preoccupation with the present, a reluc-
tance to think about the future, or both, this great claim of the gospel has lost
most of its appeal to us. And as long as most of us have reasonably good health
and prospects, it is not a provision over which we are inclined to spend much time
rejoicing.

But it is the foundation of the great eschatological hope of the Christian. It
is his promise that "the good times will roll."

Trust The Processes.

Christmas is just past. I'm in my little study over the carport. I expect Peg to come out at any time to ask me to take down the Christmas tree. We had a lovely tree this year but I think it is at least a second cousin to a porcupine. I am still nursing the scratches from setting it up. It was a good Christmas but it was the first one without Mike. He and Gwen came to see us Thanksgiving and it was only right that they went to Colorado to be with her parents for Christmas. They do have a little unfair advantage over us because of the Rockies and the ski slopes being in their back yard.

Last Christmas Mike came home from Oklahoma. We knew at the time that the wedding date was set for June and it would be the last Christmas of its kind. We were especially looking forward to his coming. He always calls from Memphis so that we will know just about when to expect him. About four hours after he called, we all drifted toward the playroom because it is close to the driveway. From there, we could see him coming down the hill. He drove around the curve by Johnson's pond and came roaring down the drive in his gray Opel for all it was worth. By the time he turned off the motor and got out of the car, we fell on him in a jumble of arms and legs and kisses and hugs. It was a fun time.

You know how Christmases are and how quickly they pass. Wrappings that took days to do are undone in moments. Before you knew it we were all standing by the car again in a jumble of hugs and kisses and prayers. Mike climbed in and started up the hill, and with a honk of the horn he was gone. Forlornly, we went back into the house.

What was it that made the "hellos" just a few short days before so meaningful? It is somehow, in some deep way, involved in the process that also includes the "goodbyes." Mike used to come down that driveway two and three times a day. We didn't go running out the door and fall all over him. If I had it to do over again, I might.

We have always hugged each other. As a family we have always expressed our love readily and openly. But it was different when you knew he was coming back by lunchtime.

I wouldn't have it any other way. It is a joy to see him going to finish his junior year in college, studying for the ministry, nailing up cedar shingles after school, saving his money to marry a lovely girl in June; I wouldn't have kept him home if I could.

But it still hurt. And in the hurt and the loneliness, there was the deep meaning of the fellowship and love between us all. The "hellos" only have their meaning in the "goodbyes." Being together takes its true perspective in being apart. The meaning is in the two taken together.

I have been aware of the movement of life for a long time. What I am beginning to faintly see now is that the *value* of life is in the movement. If we are to find the realities that we seek, we shall find them in the *passing* moments of life.

I have had some good moments. But in the context of the larger family and circle of friends, I have also stood in a dirty, crowded room waiting for someone to call the next five names. I have walked into a little cubicle and talked over a phone through wire-reinforced glass that prevented you from even touching the one you loved.

I have placed my hands on the joined hands of my sons and their chosen ones. I have earnestly asked God's favor and pronounced them "man and wife." I have also joined hearts with discouraged, beleagured people who were separated by what seemed to be irreconcilable differences.

I have been in a hospital room when the doctor came and brought the news that further surgery was necessary but it really didn't look too good. I've been there when he left us to try and adjust to the meaning of his words in our combined lives. I have been there when the phone rang and a voice from a distant place has said, "You'd probably better come."

Not all of the moments of life are good. Some of them descend upon us with blows that almost crush us. They beat us to our knees and empty our hearts of all that we know as good. We are filled anew with numbness and grief. Some of life's moments are bad.

The thing I am just beginning to catch glimpses of now is the majesty of the process. It is true that some of life's moments are good. It is just as true that some of life's moments are bad. But the simple truth I am beginning to realize is that we don't always know the difference. In a way, it seems I haven't lived long enough to write about this. In another way, it seems I have lived too long to remain silent. *We just do not always know the difference.*

Last spring one of my close friends had a heart attack. For a while it really didn't look like he would make it. But he grew better and was finally strong enough for the surgery which is supposed to give him a new lease on life. I was with him in the fall and he was still talking about the experience. We had a conversation that ran something like this:

"Well, how did you like your heart attack?"

"It scared me to death, almost."

"Would you like to do it again?"

"No!"

"Would you recommend it?"

"Definitely not."

"Does your life mean more to you now than it did before?"

"Well, yes."

"You and Nell have always had a beautiful marriage, but are you closer now than ever?"

"Yes."

"How about that new grandaughter?"

"Yes. Did I show you her picture?"

"Do you have a new compassion for people—a deeper understanding and sympathy?"

"Yes."

"Do you know the Lord in a deeper, richer fellowship than you had ever realized could be possible?"

"Yes."

"W.T., how'd you like your heart attack?"

Silence was his answer.

Now, neither he nor I would tell you to rush right out and have a heart attack. But there is a good majesty in the process. Sometimes the good shines brighter than ever when contrasted with the darkness.

I like the story of Jesus feeding the 5,000. It was late in the afternoon and they were all hungry and he found the five loaves and the two fish. It is interesting to note what he did with them.

You remember that first of all, he blessed them. He took them, lifted them to his father, and he blessed them.

We always like to be blessed, don't we? "Just bless me, Lord. It's okay. Just any time you want to, jump right in. Just break right in on anything I am doing and it'll be okay. Any time you want to, Lord, I can take it. I can handle a blessing. Send me a raise, a new house, whatever. It's okay with me."

But nobody was fed because he blessed the loaves and the fish. They were fed because after he blessed them, he broke them. It was some combination of the process between the blessing and the breaking that made them adequate to feed the multitude. I know we all ask for the blessings, and I don't think that we ought to go around asking to be broken. He might do it. Just leave that to him in his good wisdom and providence.

It is pretty easy in life for us to label the moments. This one is good and this one is bad. This is a rich blessing and this is a real setback. But the meaning is somewhere in the combination of the two. It is in the process. It is in the interworkings of the two that the deep meaning and the deep power and the deep beauty of living your life in union with him will come through.

Sometimes I have trouble talking about this. I am always afraid that someone will hear me whose heart is literally crushed in sorrow and anguish. It almost seems presumptuous for me to be telling you about your goodbyes and your griefs and to even suggest that even though it is so bad now, it will soon be okay.

But these are his promises. He has said he would turn our sorrow into joy. He told the multitudes on the mountain that those who weep are blest, for they shall laugh.

I have to believe it for you to believe it for myself.

Wherever.

I used to laugh with a friend of mine about what we were going to be when we grew up. It seemed like a funny thing to say in college, but it probably became less and less amusing as the years rolled by. My answer for a long time was that I wanted to decide by the time I was fifty years old and then I wanted to be it for five years and then promptly retire. It is becoming apparent to me that I really do not know what I am going to be when I grow up. I cannot tell you what all I believe he wants me to be or where I think he is going to lead me. I can only pray that I will have the faith and courage to say whatever, wherever.

I hope I will be like the middle-ager who hit a double while playing baseball with his kids. He was on second. His breath was on first. But his heart was roaring around third toward home.

I know *wherever* is a reckless word. There are no halfway houses on the road to *wherever.* I have to use it guardedly. Even now, I have not gone far enough for it to be a word that is really mine. But I would like to learn to live and believe so that *wherever* will hold no fears for me.

For one reason or another, I am not always a follower. Sometimes I am afraid to go. Sometimes my life is so good that I do not want to leave where I am. But when I have gone and when I have allowed it to become my word, I want to say to you unreservedly, *wherever is worth going.*

At times I have remained behind only to find myself surrounded with nothing. But sometimes I have also left all to go with him and I have known his everything. And I am convinced that if I would always go, I would always be glad.

The quest—
Wherever it takes you—go;
Whichever the task—do it.
Wherever the burden—accept it;
Whenever it calls—answer it;
Whichever the lesson—learn it;
However dark the path—follow him,
Because *wherever he takes you,*
It is worth it.

They Knew That I Knew.

One weekend I was headed west to speak to a group in retreat in the mountains of New Mexico. It was one of those marvelous weekends that only belong to September. The weather was perfect as I left home. It had rained off and on for the past few days and then very heavily the night before as Hurricane David had spent the last of its strength in a final assault on the western half of Tennessee. And now the world looked as if God had just washed it and hung it out to dry in the morning sunlight.

But the farther west we flew, the more cloudy it became. I changed planes in Dallas. If heaven is west of Nashville, I'm sure there'll be a layover in the Dallas-Fort Worth airport. As we drove across the desert, the distant mountains were almost hidden in fog. At last we climbed the mountains in dense clouds and rain. When we finally arrived at the retreat grounds, it was cold and rainy. I wouldn't have been at all surprised to find a snowstorm. And I couldn't help thinking a little bit about how nice it would have been at home going to the football game with the boys.

It was almost suppertime when we got there and the evening service followed almost immediately. There was not very much time to get my mind and heart prepared. I spent what time there was in quietness among cases of canned goods and sacks of flour in the storage room just behind the kitchen.

The lodge itself was warm and friendly and so were the people. They pulled their chairs up close to the makeshift platform alongside the fire in the huge mountain stone fireplace. It was a good room in which to sing, and the songs and hymns rang through the lodge and began to bring us together as if huddled for warmth against the chill rain ouside. There were the usual announcements and rules and greetings and then a time of prayer, and I was introduced.

With my battered NEB Version of the New Testament in my hand, I moved the few steps forward to the stand thinking to myself as I went:

Well, here you are, Mr. Speaker. You feel that you have some deep and lasting contribution to make to people like these who sit before you now. Here you are, let's hear it.

With a little humor and about the same amount of laughter in response, I began to reach out and probe for ways to establish a bond with the people gathered before me. With our heads bowed, we sang another song or two and I prayed that somehow in these times we would be bound together in ways that would be helpful and life-changing to us all.

The Book opened easily to the fifteenth chapter of John and I began to read words and phrases that were so familiar to me now.

"I am the real vine, and my Father is the Gardener."

"I am the Vine and you are the branches."

"He who dwells in me, as I dwell in him, bears much fruit."

"Apart from me...nothing...in me...and my words...in you...you shall have it."

"A man should lay down his life for his friends."

"You are my friends."

"You did not choose me: I chose you."

This was my Scripture place and my thoughts were centered around it.

Now you have to understand that I do not really have a fixed set of sermons or talks. Even though I may be speaking from the same verses over a long period of time, they are never the same talks. It is a process of growing and gathering and sifting. Some of the stories and points are the same, but they must find their shape in a given moment and at a given place for the people then and there.

Always I realize there are some people out there to whom I am speaking who have come with broken hearts and some who have come because their load was almost more than they can bear. And what I say to them must be *to them.* It cannot be something I am saying simply because I have said it before with some modicum of success. It is *to them* I want to speak.

And so I must try to have what I have gathered resting easily on my heart and mind so that I will be free to receive new thoughts about what I am to say and how I am to say it. When my spirit is really prepared and my heart is at peace, standing before people becomes both a *speaking* and a *hearing* experience for me. At times like these it seems that the Spirit is *drawing out of me* my experiences, thoughts, and hopes and *adding to me* his revelation and newness. And I feel that I am both the host and a beggar at the door. And it is these moments of inspiration, both memory and manna, that lead me out to speak and to hear.

Unfortunately for me, and even more so for the audience, this doesn't always happen. And when I am speaking and not much *comes* to me —not much comes to *me.* And I must make my way along with some stories and jokes that I have jotted down on a card and stuck a page or two over from the place from which I had hoped to be delivering a message. And at such times the card looks dustier than death and I feel like I am serving leftovers to hungry, honored guests.

It is at times like these that I wish God would give me some kind of a sign that proved to everyone that indeed he had sent me. So when I was having trouble speaking, I could at least show them the sign. But I do not seem to be equipped with a sign. One just goes in the strength of knowing. Or maybe if I had had some tremendous experience in the war but I was in the Boy Scouts during the great one, WW II. I wouldn't even mind having some fiery, pungent truth that I could zap everybody with.

But my only sign is *knowing.* The things I have to say are just simple, ordinary things that have been said before and better, as well. They do not have much meaning to others except for the quality which reveals the manner in which they came to me. I cannot always remember whether some of them are things that I have said to him or whether they are things that he has spoken to me. I only know that they are things that we have talked about together as I have followed him.

And people just know when you know.

We are prone to go forth in the supposed strengths of our name, our honors, our degrees, or whatever bits of reputation may have preceded us. But these trappings do not have any power to corroborate or authenticate the things of God. And they will not, indeed they cannot, become our credibility.

There used to be a particular name for the table on which they placed the elements of the Lord's Supper. They called it the credence table because it held the symbols of our Lord's blood and body. On it rested the things which give us validity in claiming to be the sons of God. And it is only the life of Christ through the spirit in us that can put our lives on the credence table.

And I am learning that the only thing that is really going to make a difference in the things I say and write comes when there is no discrepancy, no gap, no ground for misunderstanding between what my words and the Spirit of Life are saying. When over and above and sometimes instead of what I am actually saying, the Spirit says, "Yea verily, Amen. It's true," my life and my speaking begin to say something. When his Spirit bears witness with my spirit, the quality of my saying is bound by the quality of my following.

My dedication certificate shows that my parents dedicated me back to the Lord when I was an infant in their arms. My baptism record shows that as a teenager I was baptized in the name of the Father and the Son and the Holy Ghost as an outward symbol of the work that was done within me. I have a letter of membership which shows I am a member of the same local church that my grandparents helped to found. Over my desk on my study wall hangs an ordination certificate which indicates that I am an elder in the Church of the Nazarene with all of the rights and privileges thereto. But only the imprint of his cross on my life and my undertaking show that I am his follower.

And during that weekend in the cold rain in New Mexico, the times of meeting were warm and free. The Word moved me. It spoke to me and in me and through me.

I knew and they knew that I knew.

Camera Angle.

My dad was a photographer. It was just one of the things at which he was proficient. He was also a salesman, song leader, churchman, businessman, gardener, husband, and father in ways that generally lifted him above "run-of-the-mill" descriptions.

I think that it is fair to say that he was not a man of such wide and varied gifts that one stood in awe of him or moved aside to let him pass through. In fact, he was a rather small man. He had almost put out one of his eyes playing ball as a kid and had been prematurely bald since his early twenties. If there is a single key to his achievements it would have to be, in my opinion, diligence. He was always thoroughly prepared.

He approached photography with this typical painstaking. He came to use the skills of picture making in a roundabout way. While he was still in college he kept the books at the company where his father and his older brothers conducted a printing business. Upon graduation, he asked for a raise from the modest stipend of $15.00 he was paid for his part-time contribution to the company. The management replied, to his chagrin, that the job was only worth $15.00 a week no matter how many hours a week it took him to do it. His oldest brother, W. A., counseled him that the surest path to higher pay in the printing business lay in selling.

So the young husband loaded up a sample case and set out to sell college annuals, the specialty of the company. Since this was a seasonal business, in the summers he also began to sell yearbooks and catalogues to private camps for boys and girls in the mountains of the Southeast.

He began to realize that the use of a camera would give him a leg up on the competition. A few good photos of the campus for the division pages of an annual or a few quick snaps of the campers for the cover of a catalogue was a service that not everybody was prepared to offer. Since he was starting out in the depression years, he soon learned that one needed every legitimate advantage they could gain to make a living.

I remember going with him on some trips in the summer as his "assistant." My older brother John was probably a better helper than I and he got to go along more often than I did. The private summer camps were located in such out-of-the-way but exotic sounding places as Mentone, Alabama; Tuxedo, North Carolina; Roncevert, West Virginia; and Maryland, Tennessee. Dad took along with him great fibercases filled with cameras, film holders, flashbulbs, boxes of film, tripods, and a black rubbery-smelling cloth which he placed over his head and the camera to focus. He called his cases "plunder boxes" and you were supposed to know what was packed in which one and how to get it out for him before the kids got fidgety or the cloud overhead moved to blot out the sunshine. He thought nothing of swinging one of those "plunder boxes" on his back and starting out up a trail to get a picture of some young campers high on a mountain staring off into space. Nights were spent in some tiny town in a closet of the hotel on the square, loading film in the holders for the big 2x10 camera to be ready the next morning.

When he came home from a trip he nearly always had a few exposures left in the 4x5 Speed Graphic and he wanted to take pictures of the family at breakfast or some other seemingly inappropriate moment. He never wanted to wait until you were ready and as a result he got some rather candid shots around the house. Once he took a picture of John T. in his scout uniform. Well, John wasn't quite in the uniform and hadn't gotten around to the pants as yet. Dad assured him that it would just be a waist-up shot and banged away. John was something less than pleased when the photo came back revealing that he was not wearing under-wear with the official Boy Scout insignia. Sooner or later, Dad caught us all in some shot that we surreptitiously removed from the box of family pictures as quickly as we could.

Even in retirement, Dad was an ardent photographer as well as a student of the art, buying a complete new camera system when he was well into his seven-ties. Patrick, my youngest, found out that he was also an enthusiastic lecturer on the subject. One afternoon on a trip, Pat casually asked how a camera worked. About three hours later he managed to be dismissed from Photography 101. Dad never lost his touch with a camera, though. On one of our last family trips together before his health broke, there were three generations of us snapping away at the sights of Europe. None of us came close to the quality of the pictures he took.

He was in poor health and mostly confined to the bed for the last few years. Every once in awhile would get some new infection and they would trundle him off to the hospital for another round of tests and antibiotics. I'm sure he was think-ing each time that surely this must be the last time and that he probably wouldn't be making the trip home again. And, of course, the thought was uppermost in all our minds as well.

Once during the last trip to the hospital he was very, very low. Because of the pain and the medicine, the things that he was saying to us as we went in one by one to stand by the bed for awhile did not seem to be very lucid. We compared notes in the waiting room on his labored sentences and what it was he was trying to tell us. Mom, of course, was there the longest and she was able to put them into perspective that let us all know that maybe he was surer of the things he was talking about than we were in grasping them.

She related that he kept talking about being lifted up and away from sickness and hospital rooms and struggles. It was like he was flying free away from it all. And then he would say, "Look, Miss Jimmie." That's the way he most always addressed her. "Did you ever see anything as beautiful in your life? I wish I had my camera."

We don't usually like to admit it but we all come along to the very places we have seen our parents reach. Places, incidentally, we sometimes protested loudly that we were never going to allow ourselves to get to. I heard a thirty-year-old guy the other day say that a very frightening thing was happening to him. More and more he agreed with his dad. Both of them, he remarked, were now afraid of teenagers.

I often find myself starting into some new part of my life that is untested and untried for me. Reluctantly, I move forward, more pushed by events than by calm, certain steps of my own. Nearly always though, there is a faint pattern of my parent's footsteps to follow. Even though they were steps I may have once questioned their wisdom in taking. Or, at least, from my vantage point of youth, I certainly would have moved in a different direction. Yet, there they are, safe and true, the very way I will be going.

Now I don't know everything that I believe about heaven. It is not even easy to believe that it is *up* anymore. Now that they have rather conclusively proved that the world is round, what is up for a fellow on the other side is down for me. And watching religious television on a Sunday morning I am hard pressed to guess what heaven might be like even if I could figure out where it is and how to get there.

I guess that is why dad's words were so encouraging to me. He was a little further up the path. He has peeked "through the glass darkly."

I don't know what heaven is going to be like. I only have an old photographer's word for it. And he said, "You sure will want to bring your camera."

We Are Going To A Celebration.

Some summers ago, I was asked to perform a wedding for one of my cousins and his bride-to-be. It was to be a simple wedding in the home of the groom's mother with a feast to follow for all the guests. Sometimes, at marriages held in churches, the groom is so scared and the bride is so worried about the dresses and the mothers are so sad that the whole affair has a kind of a somber tone. It doesn't help much either when the usher asks whose side you want to sit on, as if this was some sort of a contest instead of a celebration.

The Saturday of the wedding dawned and it was a perfectly gorgeous summer day. The afternoon could not have been prettier, the home was lovely and beautifully decorated. The couple-to-be stood in the entry hall, laughing and greeting the guests. We were all friends and kinfolk, who don't get to see each other as much as we would like, and on this warm, sunny, summer afternoon, dressed in our Sunday best, we embraced each other and could hardly contain our joy. When everyone had arrived, I waited in front of the mantle in the living room as Ed and Jamie stood before me. Then all the guests, friends, and loved ones gathered in a half circle around them to be truly a part of the ceremony.

I reminded this couple that people can fall in love and do. And, unfortunately, they can fall out of love, too, and tragically, sometimes do. But I also told them marriage is a miracle that only God can perform and together we prayed that he would truly perform his miracle on this waiting couple. They said their vows and presented rings and stood with their right hands joined. The pronouncement was made and there were prayers and tears and rejoicing. I asked the groom if he would like to kiss the bride and he indicated that he would. And he did.

They turned, man and wife now, and the house was filled with congratulations and joy and hugs and kisses for everyone. There was also all about us the aroma of the feast and the sweet savor of hope and peace. It was like a phrase I had read somewhere and long ago appropriated for my wedding ceremonies, "...there were more smiles than faces and more happiness than hearts could contain."

The Bible does not deny the reality of suffering and evil. Neither of them are excluded from its pages in either the stories of the heroes and heroines or in the stories of those who seem to be only tragic victims. But in the face of all the mishaps and misfotunes that have come along to befall the human race, the Bible continues to affirm that he will get us home.

In the parable of the wedding feast, Jesus is telling us that the calling of God is an invitation to a celebration. And the prospect of that celebration is the basis of the great hope the gospel offers us all. Like the invited guests of the parable, one going to the field and another to his business, we are so preoccupied with our own affairs that we do not have the time or the inclination to remember. But we are going to a celebration.

The Bible ends with a feast.

See You At The House.

The one who calls you is faithful and he will do it. (1 Thessalonians 5: 24)

For a long time when it was halftime at football games, I wished the bands would finish and get off the field so we could get back to watching the real action. A time came, however, when I could hardly wait for the half to be over so the field would be cleared of ball players and referees. Now the main event would begin! Patrick had joined the band.

When our youngest son joined the high school band, he introduced us to a world we had not even known existed as we followed our other four through this period of their lives. We learned that "band-itry," like most everything else Americans do, was a subculture all its own. It has its own rules, regulations, contests, performances, championships, trophies, winners, losers, pageantry, intricate marching patterns, and exciting music.

At Patrick's school, the Marching Cougars would begin their season the first week in August with a six-day camp of rigorous drill and rehearsal to learn the show for the coming season. The director had already spent the first two months of the summer working on the musical arrangements and the drill itself. We always looked forward to the last day of camp, for there was an exciting (although ragged) first performance for the parents.

Every weekday afternoon for the rest of August, the band was on the practice field polishing the music and marching steps. Early in September, the performances would begin at the Friday night football games both at home and away. There were also contests and band festivals on Saturdays which were all part of the process leading up to the third Saturday in October when the Class A State Championship was held.

The climactic afternoon and evening of the state championship was a colorful panorama of bands, parents, hot dogs, music, buses, nachos, an occasional dog on the field, and the all-time All-American pastime, competition. Beginning promptly at 1:00 p..m. and every twelfth minute thereafter, there was a band of trained, excited, nervous, talented kids lined up on the far side of the field awaiting the voice of the announcer over the loudspeaker: "Field Commander, is your band ready?" This inquiry was answered by the major or majorettes in an unbelievable set of motions, gyrations and leaps that transformed the tipping of the hat and the nodding of the head into a ten-second extravaganza in itself. The announcer, over the roar of the crowd, a roar most often led by the majorette's mother and father, acknowledged this magnificent salute to readiness with the words that have been anticipated since the first moments of rehearsal camp, "You may begin."

In the next eight minutes (playing too long lowers the score), all of the hours of rehearsal and drill are put on the line. Late in the afternoon, the six finalists are announced and after a break for supper and for the spectators to get warm, the stands fill up again and the final competition begins for the trophies — First

Place and the Governor's Cup. Each of the six bands repeats its performances but this time with the excitement and confidence of being in the finals and with the hope now of being number one. The good directors, like Mr. Van Dyke, had saved a wrinkle or two for the finals. The faces in the percussion section were painted, one side blue and one side white.

When the bands have finished and the judges are finally ready to make their decisions known, the six bands are standing in a row in formation on the field. And the loudspeakers blare forth, The number six band with a score of 84.5 is...the number five band is...number four...three..." And a great roar goes up when the name of the number two band is sounded forth. A tremendous roar that drowns out the cheers for Number Two because they only band left unnamed, and its rooting section of parents and friends, has suddenly realized that there is nobody else left between them and the championship. They are Number One!

It is a moment of almost unbearable pride and excitement if your kid is one of the members of the band they are naming when they say, "And the number one band in the state with a score of 94.5 is..." Three years in a row, Patrick and the Marching Cougars were the band in which the delirious bedlam broke out. There was another year when some three-quarters of a point taught them the agonies of defeat.

The high point of a band's performance is the closer, or push, as Patrick's director called it. Usually it begins with the band close to the stands playing their final song. The intricate patterns have been marched and the percussion break has been played — and the band is in tight formation. There is a section of the music that is played softly and the band marches away, backs to the crowd. Then they wheel and march toward the stands playing full volume for the finale. It is called "blowing to the box" because the band gives the judges everything they have.

I asked Patrick if he could describe what it was like marching toward the stands filled with cheering parents and friends, playing wide open with all that paint on his face and finally coming to attention as the last echoes of the music of the concluding song of the final show are lost in the noise of the crowd. He grinned as if it were impossible to explain. I told him that if he thought it was exciting on the field he should just wait until a day somewhere, sometime when he was a dad at a state championship. And then he would see his kid turn and march toward him in perfect step with a hundred other kids, his head high and his back straight, beating fifty pounds of drums as if it were his task to set the tempo for the whole world. I told him if I was still around, I wanted to be sitting there with him. And then we can talk about what thrilling *really* is.

My thinking about this nudged me into some further thoughts about the heavenly Father. This One who is calling us. We all tend to believe (or at least fear) that the God who calls us is watching us. It makes all the difference in the world where we think he is sitting. As long as we think of him as the judge in the pressbox who is checking for smudges on our white shoes, for the misplayed notes, for marching out of step, for our hats falling off or any one of a dozen other things that can happen to us in performance, it is hard to keep from living our whole lifes in fear of a button coming off our tunics.

It was Jesus himself who reminded us that we were to call him Father — "Abba Father" — which is a lot more like calling him Dad. I think Jesus was telling us that our Father is the one in the stands who is standing on the seat, waving his coat in a circle over his head, with tears of pride and happiness running down his face.

In the last two chapters of 1 Thessalonians, Paul is writing about the second coming of Christ. In the fourth chapter, he assures the church there that "the Lord himself will come...and the dead in Christ will rise. After that, we who are still alive...will be caught up with them...to meet the Lord. And so we will be with the Lord forever. Therefore encourage each other with these words." I think he is telling us that the great foundation of our lives is to be found in the hope that these words alone can bring.

In the benediction, Paul writes that the certainty of this hope is to be found in the faithfulness of God: 'The one who calls you is faithful and he will do it."

The calling of God comes to us in the ways that I have been writing about. It can be heard deep within and it can be heard in the community of believers. It speaks to us from the providences and the purposes of God. It makes demands on us for commitments and for consecrations. It summons us to holiness and purity even as it warns us to flee evil and wickedness. To truly answer it requires of us the dedication of all of the best that we are or can be. Paul tells us, though, that the steadfastness of our hope does not rest on the strength of our arm, nor in the doggedness of our determination. Our hope rests securely in the everlasting faithfulness and goodness of the One who has called us. He is faithful and he will get us home.

See you at the house.

Publisher's Note

This book was designed by Ms. Karinne Miller (with an assist from her more than trusty sidekick, Mr. J. Mitchell Powers), typed by Ms. Debbie Simms, proofed by Ms. Bo Siler, and generally attended to by Mr. Rob Benson III.

The text was typeset by DixieGraphics/Nashville, Tennessee, using Apple Macintosh & Compugraphic equipment. The typeface is Garamond 49 (Condensed). Messrs. Larry South & James MacMurray went far beyond the call of duty to see that it happened.

All other type is ITC Typewriter or Garamond Light Condensed and was set by Graphic Composition/Menasha, Wisconsin, who performed admirably, as always.

The printing and binding was done by R. R. Donnelley with an assist from a good friend to my family, Mr. Glenn Smotherman.

Mr. Dill Beaty shot the photo that was used on the cover, Mr. Dean Dixon shot the photo of the photo so that it would work just right.

Ms. Gloria Gaither, a great friend to my father and my family, contributed the lovely poem for the back cover.

All of the above made their contributions with grace and style and a genuine concern for the quality of the work, for which the publishers are grateful.

The editor would feel the book incomplete if he did not thank Matt Steinhauer for his thoughtful reading and advice; Russ Montfort for a set of open arms on just the right Friday morning; Ron Land at Word for wanting to help be sure that the stories were heard some more; JoAnn Law for some digging and hard work; Macon Dew for his counsel; and Powers & Miller for their patience with the editor and their respect for the work.

The editor himself would feel incomplete if he did not thank Bob MacKenzie for his encouragement and wisdom since the first time that both the writer and the editor ever picked up a pen and sat down to do battle with a blank sheet of paper.

And Peggy, Mike, Leigh, Tom, & Patrick for their blessing and for their love.

And Jetta Suzanne Benson for making a home where a writer can be at home even when he has to be away, and Jetta Elizabeth Benson for the stolen time and shared apple juice that it takes to make a book come true.

R. Benson

About Generoux, Inc.

Generoux is a small Christian press formed to create platforms for uniquely gifted writers who might otherwise go unpublished. The company takes its name from the French word for "openhandedness"— a favorite theme of its founding spirit, Bob Benson.

For more information about Generoux, its writers, and its books, please contact Generoux, 172 Second Avenue South, Nashville, TN 37201. (615)726-0981.